EXPAT

INVES

WOR

AND

RETIRING

ABROAD

A FINANCIAL GUIDE

by
Robert W Maas FCA ATII
of Blackstone Franks & Co

Tolley Publishing Company Limited

A UNITED NEWSPAPERS PUBLICATION

Published by
Tolley Publishing Company Limited
Tolley House
2 Addiscombe Road
Croydon Surrey CR9 5AF England
081–686 9141

Printed and bound in Great Britain by
BPCC Wheatons Ltd, Exeter

© Copyright Tolley Publishing Company Limited

ISBN 0 85459 657–7

Preface

This book developed from an idea that Tolley had for two separate volumes, on working abroad and retiring abroad. It quickly became apparent that the expatriate worker and the foreign retiree face many of the same problems, so it seemed sensible to combine the two.

The emphasis on tax in the book partly derives from my own background as a tax specialist, and is partly because our experience with hundreds of clients who have left the UK to work or retire abroad is that tax is generally the major thing on their minds. This is not unduly surprising. Most people contemplating living abroad will have had some experience of living overseas for short periods, even if only on holiday, and will have given some thought to what this involves. Indeed, most of the problems that are likely to arise can be foreseen from chats with friends and a modicum of commonsense. However, nobody, as far as I am aware, has ever accused the UK tax system of being based on commonsense.

We have tried to be practical in this book. An inevitable result of this is that we have not gone too deeply into some of the technical issues but have tried to flag the problems, leaving the reader whose circumstances call for further enquiry to seek further advice elsewhere. I am sure that future editions can be improved by including more examples of problems that expatriates have faced in practice and would welcome a note of any difficulties — and the solutions that were evolved — that readers care to send me.

To avoid constant and potentially confusing reference to 'the husband or wife who is working', or the use of the somewhat stilted phrase 'the working spouse', it is assumed throughout that the working spouse will be the husband, but the same considerations obviously apply if it is the wife.

The book is the result of a joint effort by myself, David Franks and Bill Blevins but I must take sole responsibility for any mistakes that have slipped through.

A book always owes much to people other than the immediate authors and a preface traditionally affords an author the opportunity to acknowledge that help. In this case, special thanks are due to Brian and Vivien Markeson for reviewing the non-tax chapters and sharing with me their experiences of living and working overseas Thanks are also due to Pat Miller who helped in the research and Suzanne Monaghan who put together most of the Appendices, and both of whom shared the typing of the manuscript, and to John Higham who reviewed and commented on the manuscript. Thanks also to my many friends who have lived overseas and have recounted their experiences to me, and to the many clients whose problems have helped us to develop the experience to write this book.

R W Maas
London, EC1
1 April 1993

iii

Contents

Contents

Contents

Appendices

Index

Blackstone Franks wealth check- for peace of mind

Achieving peace of mind in their financial affairs is everybody's aim in life. Unfortunately, few achieve such a state. But the Blackstone Franks wealth check - the financial equivalent of a thorough medical check-up by your doctor - could easily be your first step to financial peace of mind. So whichever aspects of your financial security you are concerned about - investment, international tax laws or UK inheritance tax - an initial check-up with one of our qualified consultants could be just what the doctor ordered.

In the first instance contact Bill Blevins at
Blackstone Franks Financial Management Ltd
Barbican House 26-34 Old St London EC1V 9HL
or telephone him on **071-250 3300**

Members of the
Financial Intermediaries,
Managers and Brokers
Regulatory Association

Blackstone Franks

Chapter 1

Introduction

Starting a new job — or exchanging work for retirement — is never easy. Most of us thrive on familiarity. We get used to the routine, to the friends we have made in our work and to the environment in which our workplace is situated. If our employer is a large company with a strong personnel department we may have become used to turning to it to help resolve a wide range of problems, both in relation to the workplace and in our personal lives. We have even learned to live with the disappointments and the problems that inevitably accompany every job. To give up all this and start again, particularly after many years with the same employer, is always difficult. To make the break and at the same time have to cope with living in another country is especially hard.

Some readers may feel that the word 'cope' — to contend successfully with — is an unfortunate choice. After all, living in another country and getting to know its people and its culture ought to be an enjoyable experience. Indeed, most people who retire abroad will have already spent many happy holidays in the country of their choice. Most of those who work or retire abroad find the experience very enjoyable. Nevertheless, most go through an initial period where they have to adapt to a different mode of life if they are to maximise the enjoyment of their time abroad or their retirement.

Like most things in life, enjoyment of life overseas will be enhanced with proper planning. Do not wait until you arrive in the new country before identifying the likely problems and taking steps to minimise them. Some of these steps take time. For example, if the language of your chosen country is not English, life will be difficult until you can at least get along in the native language. A six-month language course before you leave England will not necessarily mean that you will land in your new country a fluent linguist. It is, however, likely to substantially shorten the time that it takes to become a part of your new community.

Many people take the attitude that English is so well known throughout the world that it is not too difficult in any country to find someone who understands sufficient English for them to be able to communicate sufficiently to get by. This may well be true insofar as you will be able to do your shopping and find your way around. However, the neighbours are unlikely to be prepared to communicate with you in English, particularly if you are in a group of which you are the only one whose native tongue is English. Furthermore, people, not unnaturally, expect a visitor to adapt to their native country, not for them to have to make an effort to accommodate the newcomer. My brother lived for a time in Montreal in Canada. There are two official languages in Canada: English and French. However, he found it very difficult to get along in English. The people at work professed not to understand him. When he dredged out of his mind the schoolboy French that he had learned ten years earlier, he was quickly accepted. Indeed, realising how difficult French was for him, in the early days people would talk to him in a mixture of French and English. The important thing as far as they were concerned was that he was trying to use their language.

Planning one's time overseas obviously depends to a large extent on why you are going. If you are retiring overseas you will probably be severing completely your connections with the UK — apart from your social ties with friends and relatives, which you are likely to plan to maintain by regular correspondence and perhaps by holidays in the UK or by their visiting you. Your planning will therefore incorporate disposing of your UK assets and buying a house in the new location. It will also need to cater for what is likely to happen over the remainder of your life.

If you are going to work overseas for an indefinite period, your planning is likely to be similar. There is not much point in keeping your UK house and letting it out until you propose to return to the UK in 20 or 30 years' time. It is unlikely still to be suitable for your needs when you eventually return. On the other hand, if you are going on a two, three or five year assignment and then intend to return to the UK you will probably want to retain your house. You will also want to maintain your savings in the UK. It is even possible that your family are not going with you, particularly if you will make frequent trips back to the UK and your work will require you to be based in a remote or inhospitable location.

The depth of planning that you can do will also vary with circumstances. A couple planning to retire overseas can — and ideally should — start planning some years ahead. They can buy or rent a property in the desired location, and stay there for their holidays or for a succession of long weekends. They can, over a period, get to know the local people and customs, so that when they eventually retire they will not be going to a strange place but will be simply spending most of their time in the future with people that they will already know on a casual basis. The move to the new country will, in practice, in many cases be irrevocable — as selling the retirement house and returning to the UK after a few months could leave them financially distressed. It is therefore extremely important to be sure that the couple really want to live in the new country.

Of course, living somewhere for five or six days at a time ten times a year is not very indicative of what it is like to live there permanently. Nevertheless, if you find that after doing this for three or four years you are not beginning to mix with the local population — or, worse, that you find attitudes locally frustrating or difficult to accept — it is improbable that living there permanently will be an altogether different experience. In such circumstances retirement to that country is unlikely to be wise. Of course, a degree of common sense is needed. The fact that, after frequent visits spread over two or three years, you enjoy staying at your holiday home in Marbella may well be a good indication that you can happily retire there. It is of very little help if the intention is to retire to Seville or Madrid, or even a little further along the Mediterranean coast. Frequent visits to your holiday home outside Marbella, bringing with you provisions from England and confining your social contact to the local English expatriate community, is unlikely to give any guidance as to what retirement there is likely to entail. Visits solely during the holiday season, particularly if this is very short, are unlikely to provide much help in deciding whether you can live there all the year round. The place may be very different in the off-season. One of my clients visited the same area for several years during the winter months and decided to buy a house overlooking the sea, only to find that on the small strip of land in front of his chosen retirement home, a huge fun fair arrived at Easter and stayed, with lights, music and all, until late August. He had wondered why he had been able to acquire his chosen property so cheaply — but then he'd never been there during that period!

We advise many clients who are retiring to Spain. When they come to us and say that they have found their dream house we generally tell them that there are lots of dream houses in Spain. It is better to rent a property for the first six months and use it as a base to really explore what is available. We have yet to meet someone who did not find something that suited him more ideally than the original idyll that he had discovered.

The person who is being sent overseas by his employer is unlikely to be given five years' notice. In many cases he is not going to be sent somewhere where it is practical to pay several preparatory visits to the new location. In any event, if he is going to work there for only two or three years he probably does not want to buy a property there, and will not learn a great deal about the people and their culture from a hotel room. It is also unlikely that he has the luxury of being able to choose whether to go to a particular place, or elsewhere, or to stay in the UK. He either puts up with the new location for the contract period, or his career, and possibly his employment, will grind to a halt. Accordingly, both the scope for detailed planning and the time available for it are likely to be very much less than for the retiree.

The long-term expatriate is again in a different position. In many cases he will know where he would like to live and will seek a job in that location rather than taking a UK job with the possibility of being relocated. Accordingly he is in a better position to plan ahead than the person who is sent overseas by his employer. In many cases he does not have to 'burn his boats'. As he will generate an income in the new location to meet his needs there, he may not need to sell his UK house and ship all his personal possessions to the new country initially. He could let the house for a year or a couple of years to retain the possibility of returning to the UK if he finds that his adopted country does not meet his expectations. He therefore does not need to plan ahead as thoroughly as the retiree. Nevertheless, he ought to plan more thoroughly than the short-term expatriate. He is unlikely to blend into the local community if he looks on the retention of his ties in the UK as providing a bolthole; the possibility of returning to the UK is a lifeline to be resorted to only when he accepts that his flirtation with the new country has failed.

A person's tax position also requires forward planning. Moving to another country can involve escaping from the UK tax net. Unless you are moving to a tax haven it will also involve coming into the tax system of the new country. It will sometimes involve being liable to tax in both the UK and the new country — although the UK will then give credit for the tax paid on the same income in the new location. Although we all moan about tax, the UK is not a high tax country in international terms. In many cases tax in the new country will be at higher rates than in the UK. If so it may help to try to retain your UK residence status for tax purposes.

Tax in the new location can often be reduced by the use of a trust to hold one's assets in a tax haven country. This depends on the tax rules in the new country. Timing is generally very important. Tax in the first year can also be reduced by timing one's emigration so as not to become resident for tax purposes until the following year. In some cases this may involve having to spend some months in a third country between leaving the UK and taking up residence in the new country.

Tax can also be reduced by simply not declaring income arising outside the new country. This is not recommended. It is fraud; and could well earn you a spell in one of the prisons maintained by your adopted country. Some people rely on the fact that non-compliance with the laws has traditionally been widespread in some countries. This is a dangerous assumption. With advances in computerisation, most tax authorities are far more efficient than in the past. This particularly applies in the European Community where countries such as Italy and Spain have made determined efforts over the last few years to deal with widespread evasion of tax and are likely to continue to tighten their systems to reduce it still further.

It also needs to be borne in mind that, in life, very little costs nothing. If you are intending to work overseas to accumulate savings, particularly if you are seeking to do this free of tax, there is probably a trade-off to be made. This may be in standards of accommodation and availability of facilities for entertainment; it may be in personal freedoms. If you are going to live in another country you must conform to its customs and respect its laws, which may clash with your own concepts of personal liberty. For example, some Moslem countries prohibit alcohol and some frown on women going out unaccompanied; some people may find it hard to adhere to such rules. If the government is unstable the price can be particularly high; it is doubtful if tax free earnings provided adequate compensation for those caught in the Gulf War!

This book does not attempt to cover the problems of living in a specific country, nor does it seek to consider the tax position in specific countries where a reader might go to live. There are two reasons for this. The first is that it is difficult to be sure that our knowledge of a large number of countries is up-to-date — and it is, in any event, likely to be too superficial to deal adequately with everything the person moving to that country needs to know. Up-to-date advice is essential; and, particularly with tax, this is best obtained on the spot. The Women's Corona Society publish a series of 'Notes for Newcomers' (at £3.50 each including postage) which contain practical and helpful information about individual countries. They cover over 100 different countries. It is well worth obtaining the Notes for the country to which you are going.

The second is that there are far too many countries in the world to cover more than a few and any selection would inevitably miss many of those to which potential readers are planning to go. Furthermore, most readers are intending to go to one specific country, so information about a number of other countries would be of little or no interest.

We have also not concerned ourselves with the basics of moving house and similar matters that are common to a move from one place to another within the UK. We have assumed that most readers are familiar with the need to have gas and electricity meters read, leave a forwarding address, etc., and have considered only those additional problems that arise where an international dimension is introduced to the move.

ExpaCare
INTERNATIONAL
HEALTH PLAN

Comprehensive medical expenses protection and 24-Hour Emergency Assistance

For international workers and their families
living anywhere in the world

Please send me the International Health Plan brochure

Name: _____

Address: _____

_____

_____

_____ Country: _____ Age: _____

Post to: Eleanor Hall, ExpaCare, Dukes Court, Duke Street, Woking,
Surrey, GU21 5XB, England. Telephone: +44 483 740090

RTA 92

Chapter 2

Residence and ordinary residence

Introduction

Anybody working or retiring overseas will almost certainly be anxious to avoid UK tax on his earnings, and, if possible, his investment income and capital gains. Indeed many expatriates go overseas with the intention of building up savings free from UK tax so that when they return to the UK they will be able to enjoy a higher standard of living than they could have hoped to achieve had they remained here. Tax planning depends on knowing how the UK taxes non-residents and what concessions it gives for overseas earnings of UK residents, and planning one's job, one's investments and one's movements to take advantage of the exemptions and concessions which the rules permit.

A person's liability to UK tax depends on a combination of three legal concepts; residence, ordinary residence and domicile. Income tax is governed mainly by residence but there are special concessions for a person who is resident in the UK but domiciled elsewhere and some concessions where he is ordinarily resident elsewhere. A person who is not UK resident will not normally be liable to capital gains tax on UK assets other than assets used in a UK trade. Liability to inheritance tax is mainly governed by domicile. A person is liable to inheritance tax on his worldwide assets if he is domiciled in the UK; if he is not, he is liable to inheritance tax on any assets that he has in the UK.

These basic rules can be overridden by double taxation agreements. These are agreements entered into by the UK government with an overseas country to try to prevent a resident of one of the countries who has income arising from the other being taxed twice. The agreement will specify which country is to tax specific types of income. It will allow some types to be taxed in both countries but will require one to give credit for the tax paid in the other country. Most such agreements contain special rules to prevent an individual being regarded as resident in both countries for the purpose of applying the treaties. These rules will determine which country will treat him as a resident.

The UK has double taxation agreements covering income tax and capital gains tax with 92 different countries. It does not, unsurprisingly, have such agreements with countries that do not have an income tax or with most that impose tax at a very low rate. It has few double tax treaties covering inheritance tax. Careful tax planning may be necessary to avoid paying tax on the same asset in two jurisdictions.

Before considering the tax rules themselves, and tax planning strategies to maximise the benefits that can be obtained, it is important to understand these three basic concepts. Unfortunately, none of them are defined in the legislation. Most depend on the application of court decisions, some of them very old. Fortunately, the Inland Revenue have set out their own interpretation of these three concepts. Whether their interpretation is correct or is open to challenge is fairly unimportant in this context. The sensible approach is to assume that their interpretation is correct and try to arrange your affairs so that under that interpretation you will be regarded as not resident, nor ordinarily resident and, if possible, not domiciled in the UK.

The meaning of residence and ordinary residence are considered below. Domicile is a far more enduring concept. Most people who go to work overseas, and some who retire overseas, will remain domiciled in the UK. Accordingly, the concept of domicile can be left to one side for the moment. It is a vital tax planning medium for the immigrant, but of little importance to the emigrant except in relation to inheritance tax. It is, accordingly, considered in Chapter 9 before dealing with inheritance tax.

It also needs to be realised that

(*a*) under UK tax law it is possible to be resident and ordinarily resident both in the UK and in another country at the same time, although it is not possible to be domiciled in more than one place simultaneously;

(*b*) the fact that the country you are going to will regard you as resident there under their own tax laws will have no effect on your UK tax status (except if you can claim the benefit of a double taxation agreement); the Inland Revenue will apply their own rules;

(*c*) having a residence permit in the UK for immigration purposes will not automatically mean that you are resident here for tax purposes; the rules are different, and

(*d*) with a few minor exceptions, nationality is irrelevant for tax purposes; retaining or renouncing British citizenship will not affect your UK tax position (except to the extent that it may influence whether you are domiciled here).

Residence

'Resident' in the UK has a very wide meaning. As a general rule, an individual will be resident in the UK in a particular tax year if:

(*a*) he lives in the UK for more than six months (182 days) in that year, or

(*b*) he lives in the UK for more than three months (90 days) on average over four consecutive tax years.

A tax year starts on 6 April and ends on the following 5 April.

There are no exceptions to the six months test. If you are present for more than 182 days you are automatically resident in the UK whatever the reason for the stay. It is therefore dangerous to come too close to the limit. It would be unfortunate to become resident in the UK for a year because your plane was delayed by fog on day 182 and could not take off until the next day or on day 178 you were taken ill and rushed into hospital for a week!

In practice, in looking at whether you have overstayed the 182 days the Revenue look only at whole days that you are in the UK. The law actually requires all of the hours spent in the UK to be aggregated to see if the total exceeds 182 x 24 hours. It is safest to count as a day in the UK every day on which you spend any part in the UK. You will then be sure of being comfortably within this limit.

The Revenue are prepared to adopt a slightly more relaxed attitude to the three month rule. They will exclude from the calculation days which (in their view) are spent in the UK 'because of exceptional circumstances beyond an individual's control'. They instance illness as an example but say that they intend to consider every individual case where this concession might be applied in the light of its own facts (Statement of Practice 2/91). Again the safest approach is to keep visits to the UK well below the 90-day level. As this is an average it does not matter if you breach it in one year (provided that the 182-day rule is not breached too) if the excess is cancelled out by a reduction in the days spent in the UK in another year.

Prior to 6 April 1993 there was a third test. A person was regarded as resident in the UK if during a tax year he had accommodation in the UK available for his use and he visited the UK, even for a single day, in that tax year. However, the abolition of this rule was announced in the March 1993 budget.

The reason for this change is of course not to make it easier for people to emigrate but to remove a deterrent for people who live elsewhere and buy a holiday home or other temporary residence in the UK for occasional visits.

The Revenue have said that where a person feels that this change will affect his residence status he can write to them at Claims Branch (International), Miss S Adey, Residence Section, St John's House, Merton Road, Bootle, Merseyside L69 9BB and the question of his residence status will then be reviewed in July after the Finance Act, which gives effect to the budget proposals, receives its Royal Assent—and thus formally becomes law. If you emigrated from the UK in the last three years and because of the availability of a UK house the Revenue were not prepared to regard you provisionally as having ceased to be UK resident, you could take advantage of this offer if you wish. However we would not advise this for most people, unless they are continuing to pay significant amounts of UK tax because of it. It is likely to prompt further enquiries into your affairs and will not head off the standard Revenue review after you have been abroad for three complete tax years, so will probably lead to extra enquiries.

If you are planning to emigrate before 31 July 1993 and will retain your UK house, or if you have previously emigrated and still have available accommodation in the UK, bear in mind that this change is to be made in the Finance Act and will not therefore necessarily happen if for any reason the relevant provision does not become law—for example the government could resign or the provision might be thrown out by the House of Commons. Both these things are improbable. Nevertheless it would be safest not to visit the UK during the period 6 April to 31 July 1993, just in case. The available accommodation rule is not currently a statutory provision but merely Revenue practice based on their interpretation of various court decisions, so it is a little odd that it is to be changed by statute rather than merely by a change of practice. Many people feel that the Revenue's interpretation is highly dubious where a person is in the UK for only a few days in the tax year. Nevertheless it has been sensible to try to work within it.

UK residence maze

To help you work out whether or not you are likely to be resident in the UK in a tax year, follow the maze below.

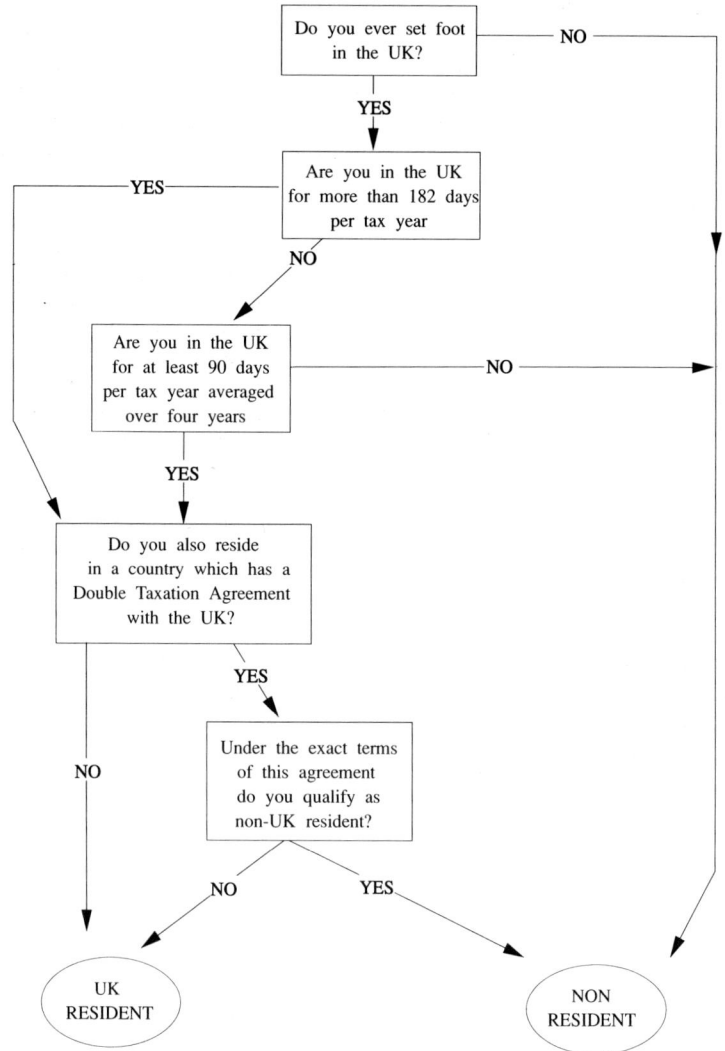

10

Ordinary residence

It will be apparent that residence is not a clear cut concept. It is almost certainly safe to rely on the tests formulated by the Revenue but there is still scope for challenging their validity.

Ordinary residence is an even more vague concept. You are ordinarily resident in the UK if this is the place where you normally live, as opposed to merely happening to be technically resident here in a year under one of the three tests of residence. Some years ago Lord Denning said that the words 'ordinarily resident' have their natural and ordinary meaning 'that the person must be habitually and normally resident here, apart from temporary or occasional absences of long or short duration'. This is not a particularly illuminating explanation. Lord Scarman explained the concept in similar terms, ' "ordinary resident" refers to a man's abode in a particular place or country which he has adopted voluntarily and for settled purposes as part of the regular order of his life for the time being, whether of short or of long duration'. The case he was hearing was not a tax case but his definition was applied in a later tax case, *Reed v Clark*.

This concerned Dave Clark, the leader of the now defunct Dave Clark Five. Dave left the UK on 3 April 1978 and moved to Los Angeles, not returning to the UK until 2 May 1979. The Revenue claimed that for the tax year 1978/79, in which he did not set foot in the UK, he was nevertheless taxable here because he was a person who 'had left the UK for the purpose only of occasional residence abroad'. Under an obscure provision in the tax legislation, first enacted in 1799 when foreign travel was a somewhat more daunting and time consuming affair than it is now, such a person is taxed as if he were resident in the UK, if he is a Commonwealth or an Irish citizen. In considering the meaning of this phrase the judge said that, to his mind, occasional residence was 'the converse' of ordinary residence. He accordingly considered whether, under Lord Denning's definition of ordinary residence, Dave Clark was ordinarily resident in Los Angeles — as, if he was, he could not have left the UK for the purpose only of occasional residence there. He felt that living in one place for an entire year was sufficient to show ordinary residence there. It is clear from the judgment that the judge attached great importance to the fact that Dave Clark had been based in Los Angeles throughout his year abroad. If he had spent a few months there, a few months in say France, a few months in Switzerland and a few months in New York, travelling around as a fiscal nomad studiously avoiding the UK, the result may well have been different. Indeed, this is the conclusion that the Inland Revenue very firmly drew virtually as soon as the judgment was published!

The Inland Revenue generally look at ordinary residence over a three year period. Once a person has been non-UK resident for three tax years they will accept, retrospectively, that when he left he ceased to be ordinarily resident here. There is a school of thought that, following the Dave Clark case, it is sufficient to leave the UK and live in one place for a complete tax year to establish non-ordinary residence in the UK. However, the Inland Revenue have given no indication of accepting this and still apply their three year rule. Accordingly, it is unwise to rely on this.

As a person can develop a lifestyle where he regularly divides his time between two or three countries, it is obviously possible to be ordinarily resident in two or more countries simultaneously. Nevertheless, if a person spends the major part of his time in, say, Spain but has a house available for his use in the UK which he visits for only a few days a year, it is doubtful whether being held to be UK resident for three consecutive years for this reason will be sufficient to also make him ordinarily resident in the UK. However, the point has never been tested in the courts.

Although the existence of accommodation in the UK available for a person's use has ceased to be a test of residence since 6 April 1993, the Revenue have said that the 'retention of a home here will continue to be a factor in considering whether he or she has left the UK permanently'. In other words, it is still relevant in considering whether a person has ceased to be ordinarily resident in the UK. This is a very important caveat, as a person who is not UK resident but is nevertheless ordinarily resident here remains liable to UK capital gains tax. It seems likely that when talking of the retention of a 'home' in the UK the Revenue in fact means the existence of available accommodation here.

If so it is important to realise that this does not require one to own a home here. Nor does it imply a legal right of occupation. Merely having a place set aside for your use (e.g. a bedroom in someone's home) could be sufficient. It is also likely to be irrelevant whether or not you use the accommodation when you visit the UK. On the other hand, a house which you own but which is commercially let is not available accommodation under the old rules and is unlikely to be such under the new.

Going overseas to work

If a person goes abroad for full time service under a contract of employment and:

(*a*) all the duties of his employment are performed abroad (or any he performs in the UK are incidental to his duties abroad); and

(*b*) his absence from the UK in the employment is for a period which includes a complete tax year; and

(*c*) interim visits to the UK do not amount to six months or more in any one tax year or three months or more on average;

he is *normally* regarded as not resident and not ordinarily resident from the day following the date of his departure until the day preceding the date of his return (Booklet IR20, para 18).

This concession is of long standing. It was introduced for income tax purposes and pre-dates the introduction of capital gains tax. Ordinary residence is not normally of significance for income tax purposes. Accordingly it may be unwise to rely on this concession to shelter a large capital gain — although the Revenue do seem to accept that it applies for capital gains tax purposes.

Going overseas for some other purpose

Usually, the Inland Revenue accept that if you are not resident in the UK for three *complete* and *consecutive* tax years, then you are not ordinarily resident from the 6 April following your departure from the UK. By concession, they generally regard the date of commencement of non-ordinary residence as the day after the date of departure. However, it may be unwise to rely on any concession, which may be revoked, where you are likely to make significant capital gains between the date of your departure and the following 5 April (see Chapter 4).

You can obtain provisional clearance that you are regarded as not ordinarily resident if you can produce evidence to show that your departure from the UK will be for at least three years. *In other words, your intention to leave the UK permanently is important.* Such evidence would include the disposal of UK accommodation and the availability of a permanent home overseas. The provisional clearance will usually have effect from the day after you leave the UK. You can lose your provisional clearance if you return to the UK before three complete tax years have elapsed.

If you cannot provide such evidence, the Revenue will wait until after the three complete tax years have passed and then make their decision based on what has happened. The clearance, if given, will normally be effective from the tax year after you left the UK.

The three-year period mentioned above is an arbitrary period deemed by the Inland Revenue to be sufficient to decide whether or not you have made a 'distinct break' from the UK.

Finally, remember that even if you obtain provisional tax clearance, if you take up residence in the UK again within the three-year period you will forfeit the exemption. It doesn't matter why you return: returning because of the illness of a loved one will not be a reason for avoiding residence status. *There is no compassionate exemption from tax.*

Retaining a UK home

If you are trying to become both non-resident and not ordinarily resident, keeping a UK home can be a major problem when it comes to UK ordinary residence. Even if you emigrate to a country with which the UK has a double taxation agreement, it will say nothing about ordinary residence, and thus cannot offer protection.

In such a case, the existence of available accommodation could lead to someone being classed as not resident but ordinarily resident in the UK, and hence liable to UK capital gains tax. So retaining a home could lead to a large tax liability.

If you have a full-time job overseas, the position is less clear, but it is often better not to have any accommodation available in the UK if there is a large UK capital gains tax liability at stake. Professional advice should be sought.

The date of non-residence

By concession, if you leave the UK to take up full-time employment abroad, you are normally regarded as becoming non-resident the day after you leave the UK, even though this may be in the middle of a tax year. A tax year starts on 6 April and ends on the following 5 April. This concession applies for both income tax and capital gains tax. If you leave to take up full-time employment abroad for a period which will exceed a complete tax year, you are regarded as leaving to take up permanent residence abroad for this purpose. By concession, so is your spouse if she goes with you. (In the past this concession did not affect the old rule that she became UK resident for any year in which she visited the UK if there was accommodation here which was available for her use. Accordingly, for the future if there is such accommodation it would be unwise to assume that she will be regarded as ceasing to be ordinarily resident in the UK if she will continue to visit this country.)

Technically, however, your UK residence extends for the entire tax year, ending on 5 April after you leave the UK. The Inland Revenue can refuse to apply the concession if they consider that you have timed your departure, or entered into a transaction, specifically to avoid tax, particularly capital gains tax. It can therefore be dangerous, for example, to realise an enormous capital gain on shares or property or on a business soon after you leave the country. It is safer to sell your assets in the tax year following your departure from the UK. A point to watch is that if you visit the UK later in the same tax year the Revenue may well contend that you remain resident here until the time that you leave for the last time in that year (and if you return shortly before 5 April and are still here on that date, that you remain resident for the whole tax year).

Similarly, if you return to the UK after having spent several years abroad and having established non-UK residence and ordinary residence, you will normally be treated as again becoming resident and ordinarily resident in the UK only from the day that you arrive back. Again, it is safer to ensure that the tax planning that you do in preparation for your return to the UK is completed by 5 April prior to your return.

Double tax treaties

Even if you are resident in the UK under UK law, if you are also resident in your new country under its domestic law you may be protected from tax by a double tax treaty. Double taxation agreements usually have a 'tie-breaker' clause to determine in which country you are to be deemed to be resident for the purpose of the agreement. This will normally provide that:

(*a*) you are deemed to be resident in the country in which you have a permanent home available to you;

(*b*) if you have permanent homes available in both countries, you are deemed to be resident in the country that is your 'centre of vital interests' i.e. the country with which your personal and economic relations are the closest;

(*c*) if this test is inconclusive you are deemed to be resident in the country in which you have an habitual abode;

(*d*) if you have one in both countries, you are deemed to be resident in the country of which you are a national. UK nationals will at this point be regarded as UK residents;

(*e*) if you have dual nationality the tax authorities of the two countries will get together and decide between them in which of the countries you should be treated as resident. If it gets to this stage you have no say in the decision.

The UK has double tax agreements covering income tax and, sometimes, capital gains tax with the following countries:

Antigua & Barbuda	India	Poland
*Australia	Indonesia	Portugal
*Austria	Isle of Man	Rumania
Bangladesh	*Israel	Sierra Leone
Barbados	Italy	Singapore
*Belgium	Ivory Coast	Solomon Islands
Belize	*Jamaica	South Africa
Botswana	Japan	Spain
Brunei	Jersey	Sri Lanka
Bulgaria	Kenya	St Christopher & Nevis
*Canada	Kiribati & Tuvalu	Sudan
China	Korea	Swaziland
Czechoslovakia	Lesotho	*Sweden
Cyprus	Luxembourg	Switzerland
Denmark	Malawi	Thailand
Egypt	Malaysia	Trinidad and Tobago
Eire (Irish Republic)	*Malta	Tunisia
Falkland Islands	Mauritius	Turkey
Faroe Islands	Montserrat	Uganda
Fiji	Morocco	*USA
*Finland	Myanmar (formerly	†USSR
France	Burma)	*Yugoslavia
Gambia	Namibia	Zambia
Germany	Netherlands	Zimbabwe
Ghana	*New Zealand	
Greece	Nigeria	
Grenada	*Norway	
Guernsey	Pakistan	
Hungary	Papua New Guinea	
Iceland	Philippines	

* *A reciprocal social security agreement also exists.*
† *The USSR agreement also applies to Armenia, Azerbaijan, Belarus, Georgia, Kazakhstan, Kyrgystan, Moldova, Russia, Tajikistan and Uzbekistan.*

If you want to use this escape route bear in mind the following points.

(*a*) You must be treated as a resident of your new country under their tax laws.

This does not mean technically resident. You must be complying with the obligation to file a tax return there. The Revenue often ask for proof that you are taxed as a resident in the new country. They could well check with the tax authorities in your new country that the source of income for which you are claiming exemption has been taxed there (if it is taxable under that country's own rules).

(*b*) A double tax treaty will not make you non-UK resident; it merely prevents the UK taxing you on those types of income that the treaty says that it cannot tax where the income arises to a resident of that other country.

(*c*) A double tax treaty is unlikely to prevent the UK taxing you on income arising in a third country, i.e. somewhere other than the UK or your new country of residence.

(*d*) Although most of the UK's double tax agreements follow a standard format, they are negotiated individually and are likely to differ in some respects. Furthermore, such agreements are not renegotiated regularly so older agreements use different versions of the standard format. Before 1963 the UK had its preferred format but there was no international standard, so this could be departed from quite significantly. In 1963 the Organisation for Economic Co-operation and Development (OECD) published a model agreement, which the UK adopted. In 1977 the OECD revised its standard and the UK adopted this as a basis for later agreements. It is, accordingly, vital to look at the individual agreement that you want to rely on, both to check the wording of the tie-breaker clause and to ascertain precisely what the agreement covers.

Notifying the Inland Revenue of your departure

There is no obligation to tell the Inland Revenue that you intend to leave the UK. This applies whether you are leaving for a few months, a few years or permanently.

The Inland Revenue do have an official form, P85, which they generally ask a person to complete before they will give a ruling on his residence status. This is not a statutory form, i.e. there is no legal obligation on you to complete it. Statutory forms can invariably be recognised because they start with 'You are required to . . .' or some similar wording. The P85 starts 'I believe you have left or are about to leave the UK. In these circumstances you may be able to claim further relief or repayment of tax.' Even in the context of Mr Major's Citizen's Charter, it is wise to assume that if the Inland Revenue offer the prospect of a tax refund to induce you to complete a form they are very anxious for you to volunteer to do so. It is also important in your eagerness to obtain your proffered refund — which in any event may well turn out to be illusory if you have UK income apart from your salary — to realise that some of the answers need very careful thought.

The first thing you need to ask yourself is should you complete the form P85 and, if so, at what stage. Before answering these questions let's take a look at the form.

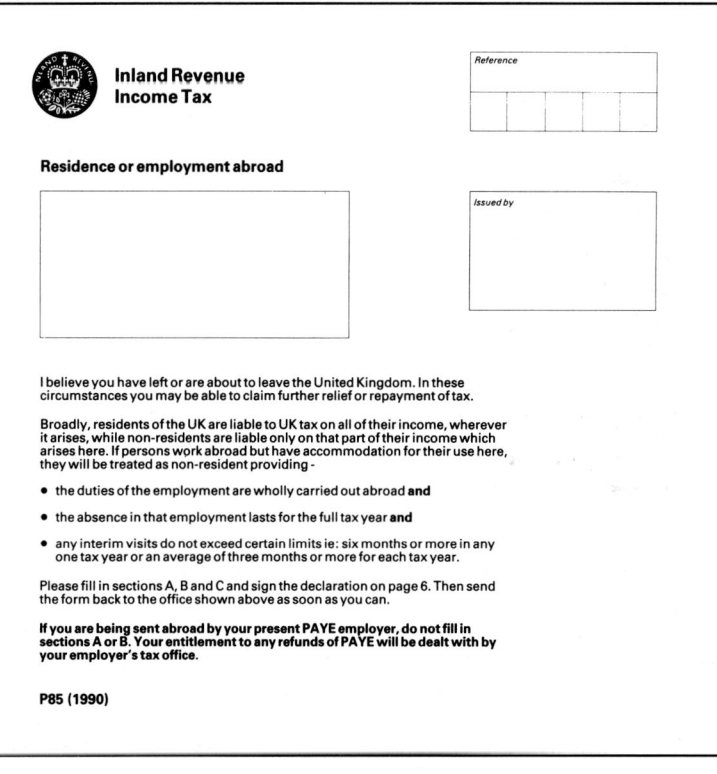

Inland Revenue
Income Tax

Reference

Residence or employment abroad

Issued by

I believe you have left or are about to leave the United Kingdom. In these circumstances you may be able to claim further relief or repayment of tax.

Broadly, residents of the UK are liable to UK tax on all of their income, wherever it arises, while non-residents are liable only on that part of their income which arises here. If persons work abroad but have accommodation for their use here, they will be treated as non-resident providing -

- the duties of the employment are wholly carried out abroad **and**

- the absence in that employment lasts for the full tax year **and**

- any interim visits do not exceed certain limits ie: six months or more in any one tax year or an average of three months or more for each tax year.

Please fill in sections A, B and C and sign the declaration on page 6. Then send the form back to the office shown above as soon as you can.

If you are being sent abroad by your present PAYE employer, do not fill in sections A or B. Your entitlement to any refunds of PAYE will be dealt with by your employer's tax office.

P85 (1990)

17

A | Repayment claim

I claim any repayment of tax I may be entitled to for the following year **and attach parts 2 and 3 of my tax certificate (form P45)**

Year to 5 April | 19

Address in the UK before your departure

Usual
signature   Date

B | Authority to pay banker, agent or other person

I authorise M

of

to receive on my behalf the amount due.

Claimant's
usual
signature   Date

C | Please answer these questions

1 What is the date you left, or intend to leave the UK?

Day	Month	Year

2 What is your nationality?

3 If you are a Commonwealth citizen (which includes a British citizen)
• on what grounds do you claim this status?

• where were you born?

4 How long have you lived in the UK before your departure?

5 To what country are you going?

6 Do you intend to stay abroad permanently?   Yes ☐ No ☐

If 'No', will you be staying abroad for at least 12 months from 5 April following your departure?   Yes ☐ No ☐

2

18

7 Please list below the periods you expect to spend in the UK during the next 3 years

Do you own the property?   Yes ☐   No ☐

If 'Yes' -
- are there any loans or mortgages on the property?   Yes ☐   No ☐

If there are, give full details in the space below. Include account/roll numbers, names of lenders and amount outstanding for each loan.

- Do you pay loan interest net after tax relief?   Yes ☐   No ☐

- Do you intend to return to the property as your sole or main residence within 4 years of the date of your departure?   Yes ☐   No ☐

8 Will either you or your husband or wife (if you are married) have any accommodation in the UK while you are away?

    Yes ☐   No ☐

If 'Yes', what is the type of accommodation and the address?

9 Will you be receiving rents, premiums or other income from property in the UK?

    Yes ☐   No ☐

If 'Yes', give the following details for each of the properties concerned -

- the type of payments (rent, etc) and whether let furnished or unfurnished

3

Residence and ordinary residence

- the approximate income each year (£)

- the address of the property

- whether you will be receiving the income direct (in the UK or elsewhere) - if so, give the name and address of the payer

- whether you will be receiving the income through an agent who manages the property for you - if so, give the name and address of the agent (or payer if the agent lives outside the UK)

10 Will you have any other source of income in the UK after you have left?   Yes ☐   No ☐

If 'Yes', please give details

If you will not be working abroad you need not answer questions 11 to 17. Go straight to question 18

11 If you are taking up employment abroad, give the name of your employer and his address. If you are employed by the UK Government, give the name of the Department and the type of job.

12 How will you be paid for your work? For example, will you be paid abroad or in the UK, by credit to your account or otherwise?

4

20

13 If any part of your pay is to be paid through an office or agent in the UK, please give the full name and address of the payer

17 What is, or will be, the type of employment abroad and will any duties be carried out in the UK (If so, give full details of these duties)?

If, your overseas work is on a days on/days off rota, please give details and say where you expect to spend the days off.

14 Will your employment be full-time?   Yes ☐   No ☐

18 If you are not going abroad to work, say why you are leaving the UK.

15 Do you hold a separate contract for your employment overseas?   Yes ☐   No ☐

16 What is the length of your contract?

19 **Life assurance**
If you move abroad, your entitlement to pay premiums net of tax relief may be affected. Please give below full details of all the premiums you will continue to pay after leaving the UK on policies taken out **before 14.3.84.**
Do not include premiums paid on your behalf by your husband or wife if he/she is staying in the UK

Name of insurance company	Policy number	Premiums payable in year to 5 April 19 £

20 Did you notify your Insurance Company of your date of departure from the UK?   Yes ☐   No ☐

Remember to sign the declaration on page 6   5

Declaration

False statements can result in prosecution

To the best of my knowledge and belief, the information I have given is correct and true.

Signature

Date

Address abroad (if known)
use CAPITALS

For use by the Tax District

Copy sent to Central Unit   Date   Init.

MIRAS 80 (if appropriate)
sent to Central Unit   Date   Init.

For use by Central Unit

Notice to PH   Date   Init.

Notice to LO   Date   Init.

6

Printed in the UK for HMSO 10/90 Dd. 0100077 C 6,750 (11037).

The form P85

Section A: How big is the tax refund likely to be? Every UK resident is entitled to a personal allowance — an amount of tax free income. For the tax year 1993/94 this is:

Age at end of tax year	Allowance £	Tax relief at 25% £
under 65	3,445	862
65 – 75	4,200	1,050
over 75	4,370	1,093

A married man can also claim an additional allowance:

Age (of either spouse) at end of tax year	£	£
under 65	1,720	430
65 – 75	2,465	617
over 75	2,505	627

The next £2,500 of income is taxed at 20%, which gives rise to a further refund of £125 (£2,500 x 5%).

The increased allowances for people over 65 and over 75 are reduced if the person's income exceeds £14,200. It (or the combined figure for a married man) is reduced by half the excess until it is back to the level for people under 65.

Most people are not given these allowances at the end of the tax year. They are given gradually over the year. If you are taxed under PAYE you get one-twelfth of the tax relief each month (or 1/52 each week). If you are not, but have untaxed income, such as a retirement pension, you effectively get it as the pension is received, as the allowance covers your tax liability on the first slice of income, e.g. the first £4,200 if you are between 65 and 75. Accordingly, if you leave the UK at the end of March you will already have had all of the tax relief to which you are entitled. If you leave at the end of December you will already have had three-quarters of it. How important is the other quarter to you?

Of course, the position is slightly more complicated than this. Some people have additional allowances. If you pay higher rate tax the PAYE system similarly spreads the benefit of your basic rate tax band. If you have untaxed income in addition to your salary this might mop up your unused allowances if you emigrate in, say, January. Remember that if you have a company car, are a member of a company private health scheme, or have other benefits in kind these untaxed benefits are in any event likely to cover your personal allowances The point is that the refund will in many, if not most, cases be small or non-existent.

Section B: If you will retain a bank account in the UK it is generally best to authorise the Revenue to pay the repayment direct into your bank account or, if you want to be able to verify when it is received, to someone in the UK who will bank it for you. If they send the repayment order (a form of cheque) to you, you either have to bank it overseas, which is likely to be much more costly, or post it back to your bank.

Section C: Before answering the list of questions, imagine that the Revenue have added the words suggested below to the end of the question. This is not to say that this necessarily explains the purpose of the question, but there is no guarantee that it is not what the information will be used for.

Questions 2–4	'These questions are not relevant to whether you are entitled to a repayment, but we would like to tuck away this form and hope that you haven't kept a copy, or if you have that you might have lost it, as we may be able to use it to trip you up at a later date if we get into an argument about your domicile or ordinary residence.'
Question 5	'because if it is a tax haven we are going to start digging to discover what you are trying to avoid, and if it isn't we might want to tip off the tax authorities in your new country.'
Question 6	'because if you answer "No" to the question you will clearly remain UK domiciled and as you will be coming back at some stage we want to make an effort to keep in touch; if you answer "No" to the second question you might as well not bother with the rest of the form because you will remain UK resident.'
Question 7	'because if these are significant we will probably defer making a decision on your ordinary residence status.'
Question 8	'because, in the past, if so you will be resident here in any year that you visit the UK unless the exemption for overseas work applied, and in the future, because this may make you ordinarily resident here. We would like to know if you own the property because it makes it easier to collect tax from you if we know you have assets here. We want to know about the mortgage so that we can make sure that the lender stops giving you tax relief for the interest under MIRAS if you answer "No" to the last part of the question.'
Question 9	'so that we can work out how much tax we will be looking for in the future and we know who in the UK (the payer of the rent or your agent) we can collect it from.'
Question 10	'We want to know this to make sure we collect the tax on it in the future.'
Question 11	'because if he is in the UK he ought to continue to tax your salary under PAYE until we authorise him not to deduct UK tax; it is also an indication that you are likely to be remaining UK domiciled.'
Question 12	'The place of payment is completely irrelevant. It will not affect your UK tax liability in any way.* However, if you are

not being paid it all in the country you are going to you are probably trying to avoid tax there and we ought to consider tipping off our colleagues in that country; if it is going to be paid into an account in the UK this could suggest that you will remain UK resident.'

*It could if you are not UK domiciled but as the form does not ask questions about domicile this cannot be why they have asked for it.

Question 13   'because he ought to apply PAYE to it (possibly to your whole salary not merely the part paid here), unless we authorise him not to.'

Question 14   'because if not, we won't ignore available accommodation in the UK in determining your ordinary residence status.'

Question 15   'because if not, one full tax year abroad will not enable us to accept that you have ceased to be UK resident and ordinarily resident.'

Question 16   'because if it does not span a complete tax year we will similarly want to reserve judgement for three years.'

Question 17   'because if you are going to spend days off in the UK this could affect your residence position and if you will carry out any duties in the UK we need to form a view as to whether or not we should ignore them as being merely incidental.'

Question 18   'This will help us decide whether you are likely to be going abroad permanently (if we think you are we can provisionally rule you not ordinarily resident). We would also like to tuck the information away in case you claim at a later date to be non-UK domiciled.'

Question 19   'You may currently be getting some tax relief on these policies by deduction at source from the premium. You must pay the gross premium once you cease to be UK resident.'

Question 20   'because if you haven't done so we will!'

Declaration   'We would like you to complete this because although we cannot force you to give us the information you should appreciate that if you volunteer to do so we are entitled to charge penalties if a person "negligently ... makes any incorrect return, statement or declaration in connection with any claim for any allowance, deduction or relief in respect of income tax". Why do you think we told you about the possible tax repayment? That's right. You've filled in this form in connection with a claim.'

You also need to know the Revenue's internal procedure. When your local taxman receives the form P85 he will read through it to check that it has been fully completed and will ask any questions needed to resolve ambiguities. He will then send it to a specialist section, Claims Branch, which makes the decision on questions of residence and domicile. Claims Branch will tell the local taxman what further questions they want him to ask you and they will look at your file to try to work out whether any significant tax liability is likely to depend on their ruling. They will then either tell the local tax office what their ruling is or, if the case looks complex, could well correspond directly with you or, if you have one, your professional advisor.

If you do not tell the taxman that you have gone overseas he will probably write to you a few months after the end of the tax year asking who your current employer is as he will have been expecting another district to ask for the file.

This will be sent to your old address and, like all your mail, redirected to you. You will probably decide to ignore it. Alternatively, if you have not left a forwarding address the people who bought your house will either throw the letter away or send it back marked 'gone away'. The tax district will probably then retain your file for the next five or six years after which it will be sent to storage or destroyed. If you subsequently come back to the UK, the Revenue have another non-statutory form, P86. This asks about your connection with the UK in the prior five years. If you have been working abroad for the whole of this period they are unlikely to want to try to discover where your old file is.

Returning to the question of whether you should fill in the form, if you are intending to return to the UK within five years you are almost certainly going to need a ruling on your residence and ordinary residence during the period you spend abroad. If you will continue to receive UK income or you will be paid from the UK you will also probably need a residence ruling and you will not get this without completing the form. If none of these apply why bother to spend the time and trouble (and, if you employ a professional advisor, expense) of collating information for the Revenue's file which could need to be explained away at a later date if your intentions change after completing the form?

If you are going to complete it, when should you do so? The earlier you complete it, the quicker you will get a residence ruling. If this is important to you, ask the Revenue for a form P85. Don't wait for them to realise you have gone overseas. If you will clearly fall within the concession for full-time employment overseas, so that there is unlikely to be any argument over your status, it is sensible to seek an early ruling. If you are going to be paid from the UK, ask for the form. At the same time say that you are going abroad for a period spanning a complete tax year and ask them to issue you with a 'Nil Tax' (NT) PAYE coding on the basis that you will not be liable to UK tax on your salary either because you will be non-resident or because you will be working abroad for a continuous period in excess of 365 days (see Chapter 5). If you are going abroad in order to realise a capital gain and are intending to rely on the *Reed v Clark* decision and stay overseas for one year only, you will probably also want to seek an early ruling — although we would stress that we would not ourselves want to rely on that case.

If none of the above applies there is a lot to be said for waiting until you have been abroad for a year or two before completing the form. By that time you may be in a position to send a covering letter with the form telling them that you own a house in your new country, that your whole family is there with you, that you no longer own a house in the UK, and that visits to the UK since you went abroad were minimal; whereas at the time that you left, your wife may well have been still in the UK, you will probably have been house-hunting and your future visits were all a matter of conjecture. At the time you went abroad the Revenue would probably provisionally have ruled you as remaining ordinarily resident in the UK. By delaying the submission of the form you could well be ruled as provisionally not ordinarily resident because the available evidence at that stage points far more strongly to a long-term stay overseas. Either way the ruling will only be provisional. The Revenue will almost always write to you after you have been abroad for three complete tax years and ask for details of your visits to the UK up to the end of that period. They will then make a firm ruling.

It is worth remembering that the questions on the form P85, and any additional questions the Revenue ask you, are what they think they need to make a decision. Do not let this inhibit you from giving them additional information if you think that this will help you. If you own a house in your new country it is worth saying so. If there are specific reasons for visiting the UK it is worth explaining these. For example, if you visit the UK ten times in the first year for a week at a time the Revenue are likely to wonder whether you really ceased to be ordinarily resident. If you came here for hospital treatment and after the tenth visit don't have to come back for a year, why not explain this to the Revenue, as it will displace the inference that they are likely to draw from the simple list of dates that the form P85 asks for.

How do they know where I'm resident?

We are often asked how the tax men of the world can find out whether or not you are resident in their country, and how they can then tax you. There are many points to be aware of.

Firstly, in most countries it is your responsibility to make yourself known to the tax authorities if you are tax resident. If you are caught not declaring your tax residence, then you can be fined, or even jailed. In Spain, for example, the fine can be six times the tax plus interest plus a jail sentence.

Secondly, there is usually a huge amount of information which is automatically passed to a country's tax authority. This might include yacht registration, becoming a company director, buying a property, receiving bank interest. Often you need a tax reference number just to open a bank account! Under a new agreement being implemented by all members of the OECD (Organisation for Economic Co-operation and Development) each member state will automatically pass information to the other, and help to collect the other country's tax debt! So if you move from the UK to Spain, for example, your UK tax inspector might in the future be required to send full details of your assets, tax history etc. to the Spanish taxman. The UK has not yet signed this agreement, but, even now, most double tax treaties enable information to be passed to the other country, although it is not thought that this is done on an automatic basis.

Thirdly, many non-residents totally confuse tax residence with two other kinds of residence: for *immigration* and *exchange control*. The definitions of Tax Residence, Immigration Residence, and Exchange Control Residence are normally completely different. Being non-resident for exchange control or immigration purposes has nothing to do with your tax residence. Your tax residence is determined by completely different rules, and you must therefore make no assumptions, but take good professional advice to understand your position.

Fourthly, it is no good saying to the taxman in country A that you are resident in country B unless it is true. He will immediately ask for your tax identification number in country B, so that he can contact them to check out your story.

Fifthly, as you wonder how they can tell where you have been for the last 183 days (or whatever) as your passport is never stamped, think about the massive trail of paperwork which you leave behind you. Your telephone bills, electricity bills, bank statements, credit cards, parking fines, correspondence with professional advisers or files with doctors, dentists, etc. all stand by to give silent evidence of your whereabouts on a daily basis. Airline manifests are not sacrosanct. In Spain recently American Express have been forced to disclose to the tax authorities the names of all holders of their Gold Card. Most taxmen have power to obtain this information direct from third parties. Computers are phenomenally adept at storing and retrieving information easily.

Sixthly (as if you still need to hear more), remember the 'ex-factor'. Try firing your gardener, or divorcing your wife, upsetting a neighbour, or falling out with a business partner. Each of these sort of people are well known for shopping 'ghosts' (individuals who are tax resident in a country, but never declare themselves). In many countries e.g. Spain, there exists a system of 'denunciation' where individuals may be rewarded for passing on information to the tax or rating authorities.

Seventhly, most reasonably sophisticated tax authorities have the right to interview you, and possibly your spouse. Quite often the onus of proof can be placed on the taxpayer, rather than the tax inspector.

Eighthly, if you haven't been asked the right questions during your lifetime, your heirs may find that when your death certificate is filed, that an Inspector of Taxes becomes extremely interested as to how you managed to die in their country when you don't have a tax file number! You, of course, aren't too interested at this point. But your wife may find that the estate which you left disappears into paying large back taxes, penalties and interest.

Finally, if they catch you, they can freeze your assets in your country, making you bankrupt, and under new OECD rules being introduced, chase your tax debts into other OECD countries.

Take good professional advice to legally avoid tax — there is no need to follow the illegal route.

Tax planning points on UK residence

(*a*) Avoiding UK residence can be easy. If you work abroad full time, it is unlikely that you are resident in the UK. If you live mostly in a country with a double tax treaty you may have protection under that treaty. If you spend less than 90 days a year in this country, you will normally not be resident here.

(*b*) Avoiding UK ordinary residence is more difficult, but can be done by avoiding having available accommodation or by working full time abroad.

(*c*) Remember, protection from inheritance tax or wealth tax is often not given by the double tax treaty; other steps must be taken to avoid these taxes.

(*d*) Completing the form P85 on leaving the UK needs care. Innocent looking questions can have a major influence on your tax position. Advice should be sought in completing this form.

(*e*) Do not rely on Inland Revenue concessions on residence status. They will almost certainly be denied if you are trying to use them as protection against a tax bill.

(*f*) Note that a husband and wife's residence may be influenced by the residence status of the other — if your spouse is resident you may also be deemed resident even though you only visit the country in question occasionally.

(*g*) There is often a period when an individual is a fiscal nomad: not being tax resident anywhere. This can be your position after leaving the UK, but before officially becoming resident abroad. Advice should be sought as to how this can be used to advantage.

(*h*) If you are self-employed, a sole trader or in partnership, there can be considerable tax savings by careful timing of the cessation of your trade. Professional advice must be sought.

FOR COMPLETE OFFSHORE BANKING, TURN TO WALES...

...IN JERSEY.

•••HIGH-RATE MONEY-MARKET
CHEQUE ACCOUNTS
•••HIGH-RATE DEPOSIT AND
INVESTMENT ACCOUNTS
•••PROFESSIONAL TRUSTEE
AND CUSTODIAL SERVICES

BANK OF WALES plc
BANK OF WALES (JERSEY) LIMITED
BANK OF WALES TRUST COMPANY (JERSEY) LIMITED

Dept. EI, 31 Broad Street, St. Helier, Jersey, Channel Islands.
Telephone: 0534 73364 Fax: 0534 69038

Copies of the most recent Audited Accounts are available on request
A Member of Bank of Scotland Group

Registered under the Provisions of the Banking Business (Jersey) Law 1991.
Registered in Jersey No. 1868.

Chapter 3

UK income tax

Ceasing to be resident and ordinarily resident in the UK for tax purposes does not necessarily mean that you can wave a fond, or not so fond, farewell to the Inland Revenue. You will remain liable to UK tax on any continuing income arising in the UK.

Personal allowances

You will also remain entitled to claim the benefit of the tax personal allowances to reduce your UK taxable income provided that you are either

(*a*) a Commonwealth or Irish citizen,

(*b*) a Crown employee, a former Crown employee or the employee of a missionary society or of any State under British protection,

(*c*) a resident of the Channel Islands or the Isle of Man,

(*d*) a former resident of the UK who has gone abroad for the sake of his health or that of another member of his family, or

(*e*) the widow or widower of a former Crown employee.

You will not be entitled to claim the transitional relief under which a husband whose allowances in 1990/91 exceeded his income can surrender part of his allowances to his wife.

The form 12FR

The Inland Revenue have a special income tax return form, 12FR, for non-UK residents. It is not clear if there is an obligation to complete this if you have no UK income. There is probably not. In practice, if you send it back with a note to the effect that you have no UK income they will normally forget about you.

If your only UK income is the rental income from your house, and you are declaring this separately, the Revenue seem content for the form not to be completed provided that you are prepared to forgo your right to personal allowances. You can probably safely adopt the same strategy if all of your UK income suffers tax by deduction at source and is insufficient to bring you into the higher rate tax bands. However, although the Revenue do not appear to currently take the point, this could be dangerous. A non-UK resident is not, in general, entitled to claim the benefit of the tax credit that attaches to dividends from UK companies. There is a major exception to this rule; you are entitled to claim the tax credit if you are entitled to claim personal allowances and have in fact done so. The form 12FR incorporates your claim for personal allowances. For example, suppose that your only UK income is £10,000 of dividends from UK companies. If you complete the form 12FR you will claim the tax credit and your personal allowance. For 1993/94 the tax credit is 25% of the dividend, equivalent to 20% of the total of the dividend plus tax credit. Your tax position, assuming that you are single and under 65, will therefore be:

	Income £	Tax £
Dividends	10,000	
Tax Credit	2,500	2,500
	12,500	
Personal allowance	3,445	
	9,055	
Tax payable 2,500 at 20%	500	
6,555 at 25%	1,639	2,139
Repayment due		£ 361

If you do not complete the form and the Revenue turn nasty your position would be:

Dividends	£10,000	
Tax payable 2,500 at 20%	500	
7,500 at 25%	1,875	
Owed to the Inland Revenue		£2,375

For 1992/93 the tax credit was one third of the dividend—or 25% of the total of the dividend and tax credit—and the repayment significantly higher (£961).

	Income £	Tax £
Dividends	10,000	
Tax Credit	3,333	3,333
	13,333	
Personal allowance	3,445	
	9,888	
Tax payable 2,000 at 20%	400	
7,888 at 25%	1,972	2,372
Repayment due		£961

It should be noted that you are entitled to your full personal allowance and can set this wholly against your UK source income irrespective of whether you have other income that is not liable to UK tax. If your UK income exceeds £23,700 you are liable to higher rate tax on the excess in the same way as a UK resident — although, again, your non-UK income is ignored.

If you are liable to tax on UK income in any event, and not completing the form forfeits the right to personal allowance, why should you opt not to complete it? The answer is; firstly, that you are providing a great deal of information to the Revenue; secondly, a file on you is being maintained at the Inland Revenue's International Division, a specialist office, instead of details of income merely coming into one of the local Revenue offices; and thirdly, whatever information you provide to International Division is readily available to them to disclose to the tax authorities of your adopted country, whereas the existence of such information at a local office is not so readily known at International Division level.

The personal allowances for both 1992/93 and 1993/94, and the tax relief at 25% that you obtain are as follows:

	Allowance £	Relief £
Personal allowance — age under 65	3,445	862
65 – 70	4,200*	1,050
75 or over	4,370*	1,093
Additions for married couples, single parent families and recently widowed women	1,720	430
Additions for married couples age 65-75	2,465*	617
age 75 or over	2,505*	627
Blind persons relief	1,080	270

*   These reliefs are reduced where UK income exceeds £14,200. The reduction cannot reduce the allowances to below £3,445 for the personal allowance and £1,720 for the married couple's allowance.

In addition, the first £2,000 of taxable income for 1992/93, and £2,500 for 1993/94, is taxed at 20%, giving a further relief of £100 and £125 respectively.

Many people are prepared to forego these reliefs rather than remain indefinitely on the Inland Revenue mailing list.

Back to the form. The nasty part is section A. These questions are directed towards the review of your claim to non-UK residence. Some people when they leave the UK divide their time between several countries, spending three or four months in each and hoping to be resident in none for tax purposes. If this reflects your lifestyle it is best to try to give the same country every year in answer to question 1, as if you appear to be moving around this may cast doubt on whether you have ceased to be ordinarily resident in the UK. On the other hand, remember that all of the UK's double tax agreements contain provisions for the Revenue to exchange information with the tax authorities in the other country.

If you answer 'Yes' to question 2 and enter anything under question 3 you will be regarded as UK resident for 1992/93, unless your answer to question 4 clearly shows that you are working full time in the country where you live. Full time is not defined. The Revenue normally look for a minimum of at least 25 hours but if much tax hinges on your non-UK resident status you should aim for 30 — and not more than about four weeks holiday. The Revenue are likely to ask searching questions. From 1993/94 this question only affects ordinary residence.

Inland Revenue
Tax Return 1992-93

Income for year to 5 April 1992
Allowances for year to 5 April 1993

Reference

922/

National Insurance no.

Date of issue

Issued by
Inland Revenue
Claims Branch International
St John's House
Merton Road
BOOTLE
Merseyside, England
L69 9BB

You are required to make a full return of your income chargeable to income tax in accordance with the Taxes Acts.
You are required to complete this return form, sign the declaration on page 6 and send it back to me within 30 days.
Please read the enclosed guidance notes before you start to complete the form.

Ask me if you need any help or further information. If there is not enough space in any section please attach a separate sheet.

Section	A	**Complete in full**
Section	B	**Complete if claiming UK personal allowances and reliefs**
Sections	C and D	**Complete in full**
Section	E	**Complete if applicable**
Section	F	**Complete if claiming UK personal allowances and reliefs**

J.M. ATKINSON
HM Inspector of Taxes

Section A   **Residence status**   *See Notes 1 and 2*

1. In what country do you ordinarily reside?

2. Have you held any accommodation for your use in the UK during any part of the period covered by this return?   *Tick one box only*   Yes ☐   No ☐

   If 'Yes', please state its address and the period for which it was held.

3. Have you visited the UK during the period 5 April 1991 to date?   *Tick one box only*   Yes ☐   No ☐

   If 'Yes', please give the dates of your arrival in, and departure from, the UK.

4. If the answers to questions 2 and 3 are both 'Yes', have you worked full-time during any part of the year to 5 April 1992?   *Tick one box only*   Yes ☐   No ☐
   If 'Yes', please state
   • the dates between which you worked full-time

   • the nature of any duties performed in the UK, or

   • whether any part of a trade, profession or vocation was carried on in the UK

12FR(1992)   1

34

Section B	If you have not claimed before, please answer ALL the questions
See Notes 3 and 4	If you have claimed before, please answer questions 1 and 5

1. What is your nationality?

2. On what grounds do you claim this nationality?

3. Where were you born?

4. Are you a naturalised Commonwealth citizen (which includes a British citizen)?   *Tick one box only*   Yes ☐   No ☐

   If 'Yes', please state
   • the date of the certificate of naturalisation
   • its number
   • where it was issued

5. If you are not a Commonwealth citizen (which includes a British citizen) or a citizen of the Republic of Ireland, see Note 3 and say why you consider that you are entitled to claim

6. Have you ever been resident in the UK?   *Tick one box only*   Yes ☐   No ☐

   If 'Yes', please state

   • for what period(s) you were resident there

   • your last address there

   If 'No', please state what period(s) you spent in the UK in the three years before the period of your claim. Give the dates of your arrival in, and departure from, the UK.

Pensions information

Please also state here the current weekly/monthly/four weekly/quarterly rate of each Social Security or other pension you receive or expect to begin receiving before 6 April 1993. These details will help me to prevent arrears of income tax arising. *Tick the appropriate box in the final column if exemption from UK tax under a Double Taxation Agreement has been claimed for a pension.*	Nature of pension	Amount £	*State "Weekly", "Monthly", "Four weekly", or "Quarterly" and the starting date if after 5 April 1992*	"√" if exemption claimed

Do not forget to sign the Declaration on page 6

2

Section C	*See Note*	Income **liable** to United Kingdom income tax: year to 5 April 1992			*Amount for year*
		Details			
Trade, profession or vocation	6	*Nature*		*Business name and address*	£
Employments or offices	7	Earnings received *including fees, bonus, commission, tips etc*	*Occupation*	*Employer's names and addresses*	
	8	Benefits			
			If you received a taxed sum from the trustees of an approved profit sharing scheme enter "X" here and If the sum is included with other income above also enter "X" here	▶ ☐ ▶ ☐	
	9	Expenses in employment			
	10	Payroll deductions If any of these deductions have been made from your pay enter "X" here	Superannuation ▶ ☐	Payments to charity ▶ ☐ Profit related pay ▶ ☐	
Social Security pensions and benefits *include UK income even if relief under a Double Taxation Agreement has been successfully claimed for it*	11	Retirement pension or Old Person's pension			
	12	Unemployment benefit/Income support	*Enter the full taxable amount*		
	13	Widow's and other benefits	Nature of benefit ___ *see identity page of Order Book*		
Other pensions *include UK pensions even if relief under a Double Taxation Agreement has been successfully claimed for it*	14	Pension from former employer and other pensions	*Payer's name*	*Address*	

Husband and Wife	*If you hold a source of income in joint names please refer to page 4 of the Guide (before Note 15) before completing the rest of the form*

Property in the UK			Address	Gross income including premiums £	Expenses enclose statement £	
	15	Unfurnished lettings				
	15	Furnished lettings				
	15	Furnished holiday lettings				
	16	Ground rents and feu duties				
	17	Land				
UK interest from which tax has not been deducted	18	National Savings:	*Enter ALL the interest on each account or holding* NSB Ordinary account NSB Investment account Deposit or Income Bonds *including any purchased* Capital Bonds *outside the UK*	▶ ▶ ▶ ▶	
	19	Other UK banks and building societies	*Name of bank or building society*		
	20	Other UK sources *including War Loan, British Savings Bonds, other Government securities and loans to individuals*			

3

Section C cont'd	See Note	Income **liable** to United Kingdom income tax: year to 5 April 1992	Amount for year		
Interest from which tax has been deducted	21	Name of bank, building society or deposit taker	*(a)* *Gross amount of interest* £	*(b)* *Tax deducted* £	*(c)* *Net interest received* *(a-b)* £
		Totals			
Dividends from United Kingdom companies and tax credits *include UK income even if relief under a Double Taxation Agreement has been successfully claimed for it*	22	Name of UK company		*Amount of dividend* £	*Amount of tax credit* £
Other dividends, interest, trust income, annuities etc already taxed *include UK income even if relief under a Double Taxation Agreement has been successfully claimed for it*	23-24	Source *Show each separately* *Enter the gross amount for each holding, trust, etc.*	£		
Settlements	25	Include income and capital from settlements, parental gifts etc and transfers to be treated as your income			
Payments from estates	26	Include receipts from estates of deceased persons in Administration			
All other profits or income	27-34	Maintenance, alimony and aliment received Any other income not entered elsewhere *including* *accrued income charges and taxable gains on life assurance policies*			

Attach a separate sheet if there is not enough space in a section

4

Section D	See Note	Interest etc payable: year to 5 April 1992	Amount for year
		Details	
Payments out of foreign emoluments	35	Nature of payment Name and address of payee	£

Interest on loans *excluding bank overdrafts* **to buy or improve property in the UK or the Republic of Ireland**	36-39	**Only or main residence** *Tick if interest within MIRAS*

Loans made on or before 5 April 1988   Society   Account no.
a. UK building society
   Loan at 5 April 1992   *The society will advise me of the amount* ☐
b. All other lenders
   Name of lender   *Enclose interest certificates*   Account no. ☐

Loans made after 5 April 1988
Date advanced [   ]   Enter "X" if sharing with other borrowers apart from husband and wife occupiers
       Society   Account no. ☐
a. UK building society
   Loan at 5 April 1992   *The society will advise me of the amount* ☐
b. All other lenders
   Name of lender   *Enclose interest certificates* ☐

Building society loan paid off
in year to 5 April 1992   Name of society ☐

If you are married please read Note 36 which explains how relief is normally given and when it may be better for you to elect for a different split

36	Enter "X" if you are **married** and want a different split of the interest relief between you ☐
40	**Let property – no. of weeks let** ▶ [ ] *Enclose interest certificates*
	–address_____

Interest on other loans *excluding bank overdrafts*	41	**Qualifying loans** Name of lender *Enclose interest certificates*

Other outgoings	42	Covenanted payments to charities *Enter NET amounts paid*
		Covenants, bonds of annuity and settlements
	43	Maintenance, alimony or aliment
	44	UK property rents or yearly interest paid to persons abroad
	45	Accrued income purchased

Enter GROSS amounts before deduction of tax

Alterations since 5 April 1991 in untaxed income or interest etc payable out of income liable to UK income tax

46	Give particulars with dates

Section E	See Note	Income **not liable** to United Kingdom income tax: year to 5 April 1992	Gross amount of income £	UK tax deducted £
Income not liable to UK tax which has suffered UK tax	47			

Section F	**Claim for allowances for the year to 5 April 1993 (1992-93)**
	Before making any claim read the appropriate note

Personal allowance *Notes 48 & 49*   If you were born before 6 April 1928 give your date of birth ☐

Special personal allowance *Note 49* ☐

Married couple's allowance *Note 50*   *Please complete this section if you are a married man*

Wife's first names ☐   Enter "X" if you are living with your wife ☐

If you married after 5 April 1991 give **both**   Enter "X" if you separated from your wife before 6 April 1992 but are still married to her and have wholly maintained her since the separation ☐

• the date of your marriage ☐

• your wife's former surname ☐   If your wife was born before 6 April 1928 give her date of birth ☐

Additional personal allowance *Note 51*

Child's name _____   Child's date of birth _____
Surname first

Name of university, college, school or nature of training _____

Does the child live with you?   Yes ☐ No ☐

If child 16 or over on 6 April 1992 and in full time education or training   Is anyone else claiming the allowance for the child?   Yes ☐ No ☐

If you are living with a partner as husband and wife but are not married to each other **and** there is more than one child in your household please give your partner's name _____   If so give their name(s) and address(es) _____
Surname first

Do you want the allowance divided equally between you? Yes ☐ No ☐

If not how do you want it divided? _____

If you are claiming because your wife is unable to look after herself what is her illness or disability? _____   Is your wife likely to be unable to look after herself throughout the year to 5 April 1993?   Yes ☐ No ☐

Blind person's allowance *Note 52*
United Kingdom local authority or equivalent body in the UK with which registered _____   Date of registration _____

Married couples: transfer of surplus allowances *Note 53* Enter "X" if you want a transfer notice form for the year to 5 April 1993 ☐

Personal pension, free standing additional voluntary contributions and retirement annuity payments *Note 54*
Give the details asked for if you are
an **employee** and - pay for a retirement annuity or
- are liable at the higher rate and pay to a personal pension scheme or pay free-standing additional voluntary contributions (other than to your employer's scheme). Enter your **net** payments.

self-employed and - pay to a personal pension scheme or retirement annuity. Enter your **gross** payments.

Name and address of employer and PAYE reference or place of business and reference ☐

Name of approved pension scheme and scheme reference or contract or scheme membership number ☐

Name and address of scheme administrator ☐

Amount paid in year to 5 April 1992 £ _____   Your date of birth _____

Amount to be paid in year to 5 April 1993 £ _____   If you need a special form tick box ☐

Life insurance *Note 55* Name of company and address to which premiums paid	Who pays the premiums?	On whose life?	Date of policy or contract	Gross premiums to be paid in the year to 5 April 1993	Date final premium payable if before 6 April 1994	Premiums due in year to 5 April 1993 to be paid net of relief
				£		£

DECLARATION   To the best of my knowledge and belief the particulars given on this form
False statements can result in prosecution   are correct and complete

Signature _____   Date _____ 19 __
Please state after your signature whether you are single, married, widowed, separated or divorced

Private address _____
Use CAPITAL letters,
*include **postcode** _____*

Please enter your National Insurance number if it is not already shown on the front of this form ☐☐☐☐☐

© Crown copyright 1992   6   Printed in the UK for HMSO Dd. MAP0101156 2 92 C1160 52 0990 12521

UK income tax

Section B is ostensibly directed at your entitlement to personal allowances. However if you answer 'British' to question 1, or complete question 5, this is sufficient to establish that entitlement. So why do you have to answer the remaining questions? We don't know — the information sought seems much more relevant to your domicile status, which will not affect your UK income or capital gains tax position if you are not resident and ordinarily resident in the UK. The bit at the bottom of page 2 is a space-filler. There is no statutory requirement to complete it. As a rule of thumb it is generally safe to assume that if the Inland Revenue begin a question with 'please' you are not obliged to answer it.

Notice that section C only requires you to show income *liable* to UK tax. There is no need to declare any other income; income not arising in the UK. Take care with the first item; Trade, Profession or Vocation. If you are living in, say, Spain and receive income from customers in the UK, that is not income arising in the UK and does not need to be declared. This does not necessarily apply if you have an agent in the UK or business premises in the UK.

Note that the form specifically tells you to give details of UK income even if relief has been successfully claimed for it under a double tax agreement. It is doubtful if you can be required to do this. Prior to 1990 the position was clear. Your statutory obligation was to make a return of your income 'computed in accordance with the Income Tax Acts' and if an amount was exempt under a double tax agreement it could not be income for this purpose. This limitation has been included in the income tax legislation ever since Sir Robert Peel introduced income tax in 1842. John Major is obviously not a fan of Peel as one of the first things he did on becoming Chancellor of the Exchequer was to abolish this limitation. You must now make a return of such information as the Inland Revenue may require!

Section D is a claim for deductions. It is therefore in your interest to complete it regardless of whether you are required to or not. One item worth mentioning is covenanted payment (under Other Outgoings). If you make a payment under a deed of covenant the payment is treated as a net amount from which you have deducted tax at 25%. For example, a covenanted payment of £1,000 is treated as £1,333 less £333 tax. If your total UK income is less than £1,333 you owe tax on the difference to the Inland Revenue. For example, suppose your UK taxable income is £800. You will owe tax of £133 (£1,333 minus £800 = £533 at 25%). The Inland Revenue are unlikely to ask you for this as it is difficult for them to enforce payment. However if they owe you a refund they *are* likely to deduct the £133 from it.

Although section E asks for details of income not liable to UK tax, this is not what it seems. The first space is for income from which UK tax has been deducted. It is to claim a refund of tax on, for example, interest on those UK government stocks that are exempt from tax in the hands of a person who is not ordinarily resident in the UK. It is not clear what the second head, 'other overseas income' is intended to cover. The notes to the form specifically state that it is not necessary to provide details of income from overseas which is not liable to UK tax when received by a non-resident. We cannot think of any type of overseas income which would be liable to UK tax if the recipient is non-UK resident.

Income arising in the UK

The UK tax treatment of earnings is considered in Chapter 5 and that of pensions in Chapter 7. The treatment of rental income on letting your house is considered in Chapter 8. The same rules apply to rental income from other UK property both residential and commercial.

UK dividends

Dividends from UK companies constitute taxable income. However, they carry with them a tax credit. For 1992/93, this is 25% of the aggregate of the dividend and tax credit. This covers the shareholder's liability to basic rate tax.

For 1993/94 it is 20% of the aggregate figure. For example, a £100 dividend can be expressed as follows:

	Dividend	Tax Credit
1992/93	£100	£33.33
1993/94	£100	£25.00

Until 1994/95 the effective rate of tax credit was the same as the basic rate of tax in the UK. For 1994/95 onwards it is below the basic rate but (undoubtedly to save work for the Revenue) if you are liable to UK tax on dividends and are not liable to the higher rate of tax, the tax charge is at a special rate of 20%, so that there is no further tax to pay.

Under many double taxation agreements it is possible to claim a refund of part of the tax credit. The refund for individuals for 1992/93 is normally 10% of the dividend plus tax credit leaving a 15% effective UK tax rate but for 1993/94 the value of the tax credit is more than halved, i.e.:

	1992/93 £		1993/94 £	
Dividend	100.00		100	
Tax Credit	33.33	33.33	25	25.00
	133.33		125	
Reduced UK tax liability 15%		20.00		18.75
Tax payable		13.33		6.25

Credit is normally given in the foreign country for the 15% tax paid in the UK.

It is possible for a UK company to enter into an arrangement with the UK Inspector of Foreign Dividends to, in effect, pay the tax refund to non-resident shareholders covered by double tax agreements without their needing to make a formal claim. Many companies are unwilling to take on the increased administration and the liability to pay the Revenue any tax refunded to which it is subsequently discovered that the shareholder was not entitled.

UK income tax

UK Lloyd's underwriting earnings

Such earnings are liable to UK tax. Many individuals offshore reduce their UK tax exposure by giving a bank guarantee (secured by offshore assets) rather than depositing assets with Lloyd's (which increases the UK taxable income).

Bank and building society interest

If a non-UK resident receives interest from the UK without deduction of income tax no action is normally taken to pursue his liability to income tax in respect of that interest (Extra-Statutory Concession B13). This is a concession, not the law, but in practice it is safe to rely on it. There are, however, a number of exceptions. To qualify for exemption you need to show:

(*a*) that you are not UK resident for the whole year of assessment, i.e. the exemption does not apply to interest earned in the tax year that you either leave the UK or return to it;

(*b*) that the bank account is not under the direction or control of a UK trustee or guardian for an infant, person of unsound mind, lunatic, idiot or insane person;

(*c*) that the interest is not received by a branch or agent that you have in the UK, and

(*d*) that the Inland Revenue do not owe you money that they can set against tax on the interest.

The most common type of interest from which tax is not deducted at source is bank or building society interest. If anyone else in the UK pays interest to a non-UK resident they have an obligation to deduct income tax and pay it over to the Inland Revenue. If they omit to do so they will be personally liable for the tax. The concession also applies to discounts on bills of exchange, to profits on disposals of certificates of deposit and to payments representing investment made by a solicitor in respect of a general client account.

In spite of this concession it is inadvisable to leave funds on deposit in the UK unless you are working overseas for a year or two only. You need to sign a declaration to the bank that you are not UK resident. Although the bank is not obliged to declare the payment of the interest to the Revenue (as it must do with interest paid to UK residents which exceeds £150) provided that you specifically tell it in writing not to do so, mistakes do happen from time to time. If you have retired abroad and can establish a non-UK domicile you will also be subjecting the capital to UK inheritance tax on your death.

If you wish to retain funds in sterling you can do so and avoid these drawbacks by having your deposit in the Channel Islands or the Isle of Man. Indeed, it is difficult to see why an expatriate should keep funds on deposit in the UK when many UK banks and building societies also have branches in these offshore islands.

UK gilts

Gilts are publicly quoted stocks backed fully by the British Government. The name gilt comes from the original certificates which were issued with gilded edges. At no time has a British Government failed to meet any of its funded debt obligations, whether in the nature of capital or income. (This assumes that you accept the contention that when it issued 'War Loan 1952 or after' this did not mean that it would be repaid in 1952, but rather that it would be left outstanding indefinitely.) But don't be fooled into thinking that gilts are always safe. If you have to sell before maturity, you can lose a lot of money. How much you lose or gain depends on what has happened to interest rates since you purchased your stock.

When you buy a gilt, you are lending the Government money at a guaranteed interest rate (called the *coupon*). Repayment is normally due at a specified date, so you can work out exactly how much you will receive and when — although the Government have the right to repay some stocks at any time over a three - to five - year period. Rates of return are often higher than from a bank or building society, and the guarantee is stronger — the Government is even less likely to go bankrupt than Barclays Bank or the Halifax Building Society!

Interest on gilts is liable to UK income tax and the majority have tax deducted at source. However, there are a number of gilts on which there is no tax due, either on income or capital gain, if you are not ordinarily resident in the UK. It will be up to you to prove your non-ordinarily resident status, though; it is not enough simply to provide a foreign address, you may have to give details of your tax reference number in the overseas country. In order to obtain approval, you should obtain Form A1 from the Inspector of Foreign Dividends, Lynwood Road, Thames Ditton, Surrey, KT7 0DP. Unless you have already been cleared as not ordinarily resident, expect some searching questions about your long-term plans, duration of visits, location of home and so on.

The list of gilt stocks which are free of tax to residents abroad may be obtained from The Bank of England, Threadneedle Street, London EC2. These are specifically designed for non-residents and pay gross interest from the outset, subject to satisfactory evidence of non-resident status.

The list of such stocks at 1 March 1993 is:

9%	Conversion Stock 2000
9%	Conversion Stock 2011
9½%	Conversion Stock 2001
9¾%	Conversion Stock 2003
13¼%	Exchequer Stock 1996
6%	Funding Stock 1993
2½%	Index-Linked Treasury Stock 2024
5½%	Treasury Stock 2008/12
6¾%	Treasury Stock 1995/98
7¾%	Treasury Stock 2012/15
8%	Treasury Stock 2002/06
8½%	Treasury Stock 2000

UK income tax

$8\frac{1}{2}\%$	Treasury Stock 2007
$8\frac{3}{4}\%$	Treasury Stock 1997
9%	Treasury Stock 1992/96
9%	Treasury Stock 1994
9%	Treasury Stock 2008
$9\frac{1}{2}\%$	Treasury Stock 1999
10%	Treasury Stock 1993
10%	Treasury Stock 1994
$12\frac{1}{2}\%$	Treasury Stock 1993
$12\frac{3}{4}\%$	Treasury Stock 1995
$13\frac{1}{4}\%$	Treasury Stock 1997
$13\frac{3}{4}\%$	Treasury Stock 1993
$14\frac{1}{2}\%$	Treasury Stock 1994
$15\frac{1}{4}\%$	Treasury Stock 1996
$15\frac{1}{2}\%$	Treasury Stock 1998
$3\frac{1}{2}\%$	War Loan

Gilts are a good investment to meet a future known liability or to obtain a fixed return on capital. They can be useful as part of a portfolio, especially where it is felt that interest rates will fall. Index-linked gilts and low coupon gilts favour higher rate taxpayers. They can also be used to provide a do-it-yourself annuity to supplement income. This can be done by creating a portfolio of dated gilts maturing in consecutive years. As each matures, this cash released is used as additional income for the following year. However, small investors have avoided gilts for several reasons. First, they appear complicated. Gilts come in different shapes and sizes. They differ in prices, rates of return and maturity dates. The second reason why gilts have been avoided is inflation. In the years 1945 to 1980 gilts were a poor investment. Indeed, the real rate of return has sometimes been negative as inflation rates have far exceeded the interest rates earned. This is true of any fixed rate investment, including bank and building society deposits. Thirdly, gilts can lose you money if you sell them before maturity and interest rates have risen since you purchased your stock. They are nevertheless often useful as part of a portfolio, especially to pay large future tax liabilities.

There are a number of extremely successful high income producing off-shore funds investing exclusively in UK government stock. This will provide far more active and generally more successful management than holding stock direct. Where gilts are required to provide for capital growth as opposed to income, there are specific low coupon, short-dated, British Government stock unit trusts available within the UK which have certain advantages for off-shore investors.

UK royalties

Under some double taxation treaties, the maximum UK tax payable is reduced.

Maintenance and alimony

Payments between a divorced or separated husband and wife under voluntary arrangements have no tax effect on either payer or recipient. Neither do payments under an order of a foreign court.

If a legally binding contract or court order is made after 14 March 1988 the maintenance is again not income of the recipient or tax deductible by the payer. However, the person making the payments can deduct from his income the lower of £1,720 or the amount of the payments in calculating his tax liability. This applies both to payments to the spouse for her own benefit and to payments to her for the children's benefit. If no payments are made to the spouse but maintenance is paid to the child (or to the wife as guardian of the child) no deduction against tax can be claimed.

Tax relief may be due to the husband on all or part of the payments where the maintenance is paid under a pre-14 March 1988 agreement or order. If so, the wife is taxable on it. The payer (normally the husband) can elect to bring the maintenance payments into the new system in which case they will cease to attract a tax allowance and the wife will cease to be taxable on this. If the husband retires abroad and the wife remains in the UK, such an election is likely to be worthwhile.

Self-employment

If you are self-employed, going abroad can often provide an opportunity to escape tax on your income for the last year that you are in the UK — sometimes for up to the last 23 months. Your self-employed income will have been taxable on a preceding year basis. You probably look on this as meaning that you do not have to pay tax until some time after you have earned your profits. For example, if your accounts go to 30 April the tax on your profits for the year to 30 April 1991 will be payable half on 1 January 1993 and half on 1 July 1993, an average of 23 months after the end of the year in which the profits are earned. The reality is that the tax you pay in January and July 1993 is the tax due for 1992/93 but for convenience the tax system pretends that the profits earned in that year will be the same figure as you earned in your year to 30 April 1991 (i.e. in your accounting year ended in the previous year). The reason that this fiction was introduced was that the Inland Revenue would otherwise have to wait until you produce your accounts to 30 April 1992 and 1993 in order to work out your 1992/93 tax bill.

This fiction normally works reasonably satisfactorily while the business continues in existence. When it ceases there will be 23 months of profits that have not formed the basis of your tax bills for any year. Special rules apply to ensure that the profits that escape tax are the lower of the period of the 23 months up to the end of the tax year prior to that in which the business ceases or the 23 months ending two years earlier. For example, if the business ceases on 30 April 1993 the profits that escape tax will be the lower of those for

(*a*) the 23 months from 1 May 1991 to 5 April 1993, or

(*b*) the 23 months from 1 May 1989 to 5 April 1991.

Becoming non-UK resident does not affect the operation of these rules. Suppose that your business continues, you prepare your accounts to 30 April each year, and you are not UK resident throughout the tax year 1993/94. The position will be as follows:

Profits of	treated as	earned	Taxed in UK?
year to 30.4.1991	1992/93	in UK	Yes
year to 30.4.1992	1993/94	in UK	No
year to 30.4.1993	1994/95	in UK (mainly)	Yes
year to 30.4.1994	1995/96	overseas (mainly)	Yes

It will be seen that the profits for the year to 30 April 1992 escape UK tax. They will probably also escape tax in your new country as you are not resident there in the year you earned them. If these profits are exceptionally high — and in many businesses you have the ability to control the flow of work or receipts of money to maximise the income of a particular year — it is very attractive to be non-UK resident in the year for which they would otherwise have formed the quantum of your taxable profits. This is what Dave Clark did in 1978/79 (see Chapter 2).

Of course, as with Dave Clark, the Inland Revenue will try to show that you remain within the scope of UK tax if they can by claiming either that you were UK resident in your year abroad or that you went abroad solely for the purpose of occasional residence. If you do not set foot in the UK during your year abroad you are unlikely to be held to be resident here. Residence implies at least some degree of physical presence. If you visit the UK, even if you do not have property available for your use here, expect the Revenue to ignore their normal tests and claim that you remain at least UK ordinary resident. The Revenue refuse to apply any concession where they consider that it is being used, or in their view abused, for tax avoidance purposes.

If you do not stay in one location during your year abroad but travel around, the Revenue are likely to raise the occasional residence argument. This is probably why they did not take the *Clark* case to the Court of Appeal. They have drawn comfort from the stress that the judge laid on the fact that Dave Clark spent his whole year in Los Angeles. If you move around you could be the test case that the Revenue fight to try to win on the basis of this distinction. If you are intending to emigrate permanently, or for at least three tax years so that you will cease to be ordinarily resident in the UK from the day you leave, you will clearly not have left the UK for the purpose only of occasional residence. Accordingly, you will almost certainly escape tax on the profits earned from 1 May 1991 (in the above example). Of course there are other points you need to watch; in particular that you do not continue to carry on your trade through an agent in the UK. Nevertheless this is a tried and tested way to escape tax on profits earned while you were in the UK.

If you return to the UK after your year of non-residence there is a snag. You will be taxable in the UK on profits you earned while you were non-resident. This may not matter unduly. They may have already attracted tax in your adopted country and as the UK will allow you credit for such tax this may largely cover the UK tax liability. You may be able to ensure that profits are low, particularly if you brought forward into the previous year income that would have arisen during your year overseas.

Do not be tempted to cease your business when you go overseas. You do not want to bring the cessation rules into play — even if you are going abroad for three or more tax years. Using the example shown above, if the business ceased on 5 April 1993 the tax position would become:

Profits of	treated as	earned	Taxed in UK?
year to 30.4.1991	1990/91	in UK	Yes
year to 5.4.1992	1991/92	in UK	Yes
year to 5.4.1993	1992/93	in UK	Yes

The profits to escape tax will be those for the 23 months to 5 April 1990, not those of your exceptional year

Suppose you continue your trade overseas and cease it, while still living overseas, on 5 April 1994, i.e. after you have been abroad for a year. You still have problems.

Profits of	treated as	earned	Taxed in UK?
year to 5.4.1992	1991/92	in UK	Yes
year to 5.4.1993	1992/93	in UK	Yes
year to 5.4.1994	1993/94	overseas	No

The exceptional profit (that for the year to 30 April 1992) remains liable to UK tax. If the business ceases between 6 April 1994 and 5 April 1995 one-twelfth of the profit will still be taxable in the UK. A later cessation will not allow the Revenue to tax any part of it.

The arithmetic is different if you adopt a year end other than 30 April. This is generally the most favourable date to adopt (actually 6 April is better in theory but most people think it unnecessarily provocative). The least favourable date in normal circumstances is 5 April.

The best investment you might ever make...

An exclusive offer to all British expatriates. Just complete the form below and we will mail you, completely free of charge, the independent newspaper Expat Investor, published from London in an easy-to-read tabloid format.

Keep up to date with investment opportunities available throughout the world - shares, unit trusts, property, even classic cars and fine arts.

There's also an enticing travel and leisure section to help you spend your profit

More than just that, Expat Investor provides detailed but understandable data on the best performing unit trusts, bonds, currencies and equities, on a world-wide basis, to help you keep abreast of your own investments - and judge which new ones to buy. And it will help your choice of pension fund, mortgage, insurance, health care and UK schools. There's even help with taxation!

Expat Investor, a leader in its field and published six times a year, offers realistic financial information in a readable form. British expatriates only may apply for this special free subscription offer (except those based in North America). Complete the form now. The price of the stamp is your only cost. It could be the best investment you will ever make!

...absolutely FREE!

Return the coupon below to Tolley Publishing Co Ltd,
Tolley House, 2 Addiscombe Road, Croydon, Surrey CR9 5AF, England

I am a British Expatriate and wish to receive regular copies of Expat Investor without charge.

Name _____

Address (overseas only) _____

_____

Signed _____ Date _____

Chapter 4

UK capital gains tax

As indicated in Chapter 2, you will remain within the scope of UK capital gains tax if you are either resident or ordinarily resident in the UK. The meaning of these two terms is explained in Chapter 2. If you leave the UK to take up permanent residence abroad, or at least for long enough to cease to be ordinarily resident in the UK, the normal practice of the Revenue is to treat you as having ceased to be resident and ordinarily resident here from the day after you leave the UK. However, this is only a concession. Like all concessions the Revenue are likely to refuse to apply it if they think that it is being used deliberately to avoid tax.

Disposals after leaving the UK

It is therefore safer to realise capital gains in the tax year *after* you have left the UK (i.e. the year starting 6 April after you have left). There is no need to wait until you have been abroad for a sufficiently long period (normally three tax years) for the Revenue to have formally agreed that you have ceased to be ordinarily resident here. However, if you do sell an asset in the first three years, you need to be conscious that if for any reason you become UK resident again in the remainder of that period you may not be able to show that you were not ordinarily resident in the year in which you realised the gain. It is also important to remember that, even if you establish that you have ceased to be ordinarily resident in the UK, you will still be liable to capital gains tax on disposals in any year in which you are held to be resident here, e.g. because you are in the UK for more than 182 days.

The date of disposal

If you are emigrating to seek to avoid capital gains tax, or are taking advantage of your foreign posting to realise gains free of such tax, it is vital to know when the disposal of your assets is regarded as taking place. This is not when you get your money; it is the date when a contract for sale is entered into. This can be a month, or several months, before the completion of the contract. For example, in most property sales the contract is entered into a month before completion. Furthermore, a contract is not necessarily a document headed 'contract'. It is an agreement to sell. If a verbal agreement is entered into before the date of the written contract, it will be the date of that prior agreement that matters. If you were UK resident at that time, you are caught. The agreement does not have to be contained in a single document. Indeed, legally a contract requires one party to make an offer (to buy or sell your asset) and the other party to accept it. An offer and acceptance are frequently in separate documents, e.g. the offer may be in a letter from your purchaser's solicitor to yours, and acceptance in a letter from you to your solicitor that he faxes to the other solicitor. The contract does not even have to be legally enforceable. For example, a contract to sell land cannot be enforced unless all of the terms are contained in a single document signed by both parties. Nevertheless, the contract is no less a contract because these formalities have not been complied with. Remember also that the Inland Revenue has the right to see all correspondence, file notes, memos, etc., leading up to a contract, and could well request such documents from you, your accountant, your solicitor, the purchaser and even from the purchaser's solicitor.

Of course, having read this book, *you* are not going to fall into the trap of making an oral or an informal contract. Or are you? In the course of negotiations for the sale of a business, people rarely deliberately enter into oral contracts. The difficulty is that it is easy to do so unwittingly unless you are very careful. You will probably not know that you have done so until the Inland Revenue call for the correspondence and file notes, select a couple of letters or a couple of file notes of telephone conversations from it, and point out that together they constitute a contract.

You need to take particular care if you are selling your family company and emigrating to enjoy the proceeds without giving the taxman his share. If you emigrate before the negotiations start you are unlikely to get the best price as your solicitor or accountant or whoever else you leave to negotiate the price does not have the intimate knowledge of the business that you do. If you remain until the negotiations are at an advanced stage you risk unwittingly entering into a contract in advance of the solicitor drawing up the formal sale agreement. Furthermore, if you leave in the middle of the negotiations you risk them falling through without you there to smooth over relationships and make compromises. Of course, you can be on the other end of a telephone and fax machine in your Caribbean hideaway, or wherever, but, in practice, in a tough negotiation there is no substitute for face to face confrontation.

Options

A possible way around this dilemma is not to sell the business but to grant the purchaser an option to buy it which would not be exercisable until the tax year after you have emigrated. You can negotiate all the terms of the sale 'contract' with him, as you are not actually entering into that contract. You are entering into an agreement under which he is entitled, once you have emigrated, to call on you to sell him the shares in your company in accordance with the terms of the 'contract' that you attach to the option. An option, provided that it is subsequently exercised, is not a contract at the time it is granted but becomes a contract when it is exercised, i.e. when the purchaser formally requires you to sell him your shares in accordance with the option. Accordingly, your disposal does not take place until that date as far as the taxman is concerned. There are, however, a number of snags.

(*a*) You still have to take care to ensure that you do not enter into an informal contract to sell the shares prior to signing the option agreement. If you do the option will be ineffective.

(*b*) In many cases such an arrangement is impracticable. During the period between the grant of the option and its exercise who will run the business? You could stay in the UK until 5 April, but need to be overseas before the start of the year in which the option is exercised. The purchaser may not want to run the business before he owns the shares. Even if he does, you probably do not want him meeting your customers and suppliers and getting to know how your business operates, months before he has paid you. He may decide that with such knowledge he does not need your company, but can set up a new one in competition with it.

(*c*) The purchaser could decide in the interim that he does not want your company after all. You can guard against this by the use of cross options, i.e. he would have the right to call on you to sell him your shares and you would have the right to require him to buy them. However, this has its own problems. The Revenue have been known to contend that if both parties are able to enforce a sale at the same time these rights are equivalent to the option agreement constituting a contract for sale — which is what you are seeking to avoid. Even if you ensure that the options are exercisable at different times, what is your right really worth? How can you force someone to pay you money if he decides not to honour his obligation? You can always sue. But if he defends the case you may well have to come to the UK to give evidence — and that visit to the UK may be enough to enable the Revenue to say that you have remained ordinarily resident here.

(*d*) You may lose the sale. If a prospective purchaser has lined up finance from a bank or other lender they may be unwilling to commit to that money being available in six months time or whenever the option becomes exercisable. If your prospective purchaser has psyched himself up to buy your business he may lose interest very rapidly once you say that you would like to negotiate the terms but, having done that, he cannot actually buy the business for another six months. If the purchaser has lined up finance he may be committed to paying interest on a heavy borrowing for the next six months and having to leave the funds on bank deposit until the option is exercised. Guess who he will expect to bear the difference between the two interest rates?

Share exchanges

Another solution that is often suggested is to sell your shares not for cash, but for loan stock issued by the purchaser. This can only work if the purchaser is a company. There is an exemption from capital gains tax where one company acquires another in exchange for shares or securities (such as loan stock) issued by the purchaser company. The transaction is not a disposal for capital gains tax purposes; instead the law pretends that your new shares or securities are the same assets as your original shares in your family company.

UK capital gains tax

This solution can work if there is a spread of shareholders in the family company and you are the only one that is emigrating. It is unlikely to do so if you own the vast majority of the company. This is because the exemption applies only if both:

(a)   the share exchange (or exchange of shares for loan stock) is effected for bona fide commercial reasons, and

(b)   it does not form part of a scheme or arrangements of which one of the main purposes is avoidance of liability to capital gains tax.

The courts have given a very wide meaning to the word 'arrangements'. If you ask the purchaser for loan stock rather than cash, or if he suggests to you that you may prefer loan stock as he knows you intend to emigrate, you probably have arrangements one of the main purposes of which is to avoid capital gains tax.

There is a clearance procedure. Your company (or the purchaser company) can tell the Revenue before you enter into the sale contract that you are selling the business in exchange for loan stock and ask them to confirm that they accept that the two conditions above are satisfied. If they give such confirmation they cannot later claim that the transaction constituted a disposal of your shares, provided that the clearance application 'fully and accurately' disclosed all facts and considerations material for the Revenue to make a decision. If it did not, the clearance is worthless. You must form your own opinion on whether the Revenue are likely to accept that a sale in exchange for loan stock shortly before you emigrate, and thus escape the UK tax net, did not form part of an arrangement designed to avoid capital gains tax. We know how *we* think they will react!

If you do not tell them that you are about to emigrate, you could well get clearance. But it would probably be a complete waste of time, as it is difficult to envisage anyone accepting that your prospective departure was not a material fact that ought to have been disclosed.

Even if you can get over this hurdle, you will have to wait for your money. The Revenue will, in practice, not give clearance if the loan stock has a life of less than six months and normally expect a longer period. While you are waiting for repayment you are in the position where you no longer own your company but have in its place a piece of paper, which is usually unsaleable, issued by a company over which you have no control. In the 1980s a lot of people sold their family businesses to a publicly quoted company, British and Commonwealth Holdings Ltd, in return for loan stock. It subsequently went into liquidation and the loan stock proved worthless. If the vendors had not sought to avoid the tax, they would at least have ended up with 60% of the value of their businesses, instead of losing the entire amount. In most cases, with a little pressure — and probably a small reduction in the money you receive, to cover the bank's fee — it is possible for the purchaser's bank to guarantee the loan stock. This is a precaution that is well worth taking even if you end up paying the bank's guarantee fee yourself.

A trap — selling a business

Although one normally avoids capital gains tax by ceasing to be both resident and ordinarily resident in the UK prior to the sale, there is an important exception. A non-UK resident is liable to capital gains tax on assets in the UK used for the purpose of a trade carried on in this country. Accordingly, if you are self-employed or a partner, you cannot go overseas, sell the business and escape capital gains tax. The money you receive will be for the disposal of UK trading assets, such as goodwill, and thus within the scope of capital gains tax.

Example

Mr and Mrs Black owned a successful freehold hotel, which they operated as a partnership. They left the UK in February 1992 leaving a manager in charge of the hotel. In May 1992 the manager agreed to buy the hotel giving Mr and Mrs Black a capital gain of £430,000.

Unfortunately, Mr and Mrs Black remain liable for UK capital gains tax, even though they are both not resident and not ordinarily resident.

What if Mr and Mrs Black had gone abroad, ceased the trade and then sold the hotel as a property disposal? This would not have helped. The cessation of trading by a non-resident attracts capital gains tax as if the assets had been sold at their market value at that time. What if the trade had not been running a hotel but a hotel consultancy so that Mr and Mrs Black could have gone overseas and taken their goodwill with them? It would then cease to be a UK asset. The Government have thought of that too. Taking a trade asset out of the UK whilst the trade continues is also treated as giving rise to a disposal for capital gains tax.

You should note that capital gains tax is chargeable under this rule in respect of assets of both a trade and a profession.

It is also worth pointing out that letting a UK property held as an investment is not a trade, and therefore not liable to be taxed by this trap. Even disposals of short term holiday lettings — regarded as a trade for some sections of the Taxes Act — are not caught by this rule.

Is there anything that Mr and Mrs Black could have done? With advance planning they could have avoided UK capital gains tax by one of two methods.

(a) *Incorporation* — If the business had been incorporated while Mr and Mrs Black were still resident, the property could have been transferred to the new company or left in their own name, the sale of the shares and/or the hotel freehold would have been free of UK capital gains tax if sold in the tax year after leaving the UK, provided that Mr and Mrs Black remain both not resident and not ordinarily resident. There are two ways they could have achieved this. They could have put the property into the company with the business and sold the shares of the company. Alternatively, they could have let the property to the company (at a market rent) and sold both the shares and the company. The property would cease to be an asset used in a trade once it is let; it would have become an investment property. It is also important to incorporate in such a way that the incorporation itself does not give rise to capital gains tax. There are several ways that this can be done. Professional advice needs to be sought to determine which is the most appropriate. It is very important that the incorporation occurs *before* Mr and Mrs Black leave the UK.

(*b*) *Renting the freehold* — An alternative way would have been for Mr and Mrs Black to let the hotel to the manager. He signs a lease, paying a market rent. Later, having left the UK, and established non-residence and non-ordinary residence, they could have sold the rental property to him free of UK capital gains tax. Again, it is essential that the lease is granted before leaving the UK.

There is one word of caution about such tax planning. There have been several tax cases (in particular, one known as *Furniss v Dawson*) which enable the Revenue in certain circumstances to ignore steps in a series of transactions which have no real commercial purpose, other than the avoidance of tax — which may enable them to thwart the scheme that you have devised to avoid it.

Avoiding both UK and overseas capital gains tax

This chapter has explained the classic methods of avoiding UK capital gains tax, but clever avoidance of UK tax could end up becoming a case of 'out of the frying pan and into the fire'. You may also have to avoid paying tax on your gain in your new country. Unless you are moving to a tax haven, most countries nowadays tax capital gains realised by their residents.

There are several ways of achieving this; for example, by being a fiscal nomad for a few months. Alternatively, you can make your capital gains tax disposal whilst in a period when you are living in the new country *but* neither resident there nor in the UK. Another alternative plan makes use of the fact that some countries treat the individual as making a notional disposal and reacquisition at market value of all his assets at the time when he becomes or ceases to be resident there. Professional advice should be sought to ensure all taxes are properly avoided.

Foreign currency — a note

Gains on foreign currency are liable to UK capital gains tax. This is so even if the currency is used to acquire other foreign investments or to buy a foreign property without any conversion into sterling. The Inland Revenue treat transfers between foreign currency bank accounts as one account, so that capital gains tax does not then arise (see Inland Revenue Statement of Practice SP 10/84). The tax treatment of foreign currency accounts is a trap for the unwary.

Payment dates of UK capital gains tax

The normal date of payment is 1 December after the end of the tax year in which the gain was made, or 30 days after the issue of the assessment, if later. Penalties can be charged if the capital gain is not reported to the Inland Revenue well before 1 December. Interest can be charged on tax paid late.

The tax can be paid by instalments where the proceeds of the sale are received by instalments over 18 months or more and paying the tax in one sum would cause hardship. However, as the instalments attract interest this is unlikely to be attractive.

Capital gains tax on death

No capital gains tax charge arises on death — is this the ultimate tax plan? The Inland Revenue has conceded that death is not a tax planning technique!

Retirement relief and rollover relief

Retirement relief is given to individuals aged 55 or over. The first £150,000 of capital gains is tax free, and only 50% of the difference between £150,000 and £600,000 is taxable.

Rollover relief enables an individual to sell business assets and 'roll over' the proceeds into certain specified new assets without paying UK capital gains tax. However, you cannot roll over your gain onto an asset that is itself outside the scope of capital gains tax. Accordingly, reinvestment into an overseas business will not normally obviate the need to pay the UK tax.

The March 1993 Budget introduced a new form of roll-over relief where an entrepreneur sells shares in an unquoted family trading company and reinvests the proceeds in shares in a new unquoted trading company. This relief is not identical to the roll-over relief for business assets. It merely defers payment of the tax until a future date. Although such payment will normally be triggered by the sale of the shares in the new company, it will also be triggered by emigration. Accordingly, where the relief is claimed, a subsequent emigration will not save the tax.

These are complex reliefs and professional advice should be sought.

Chapter 5

Working abroad for short periods

You do not automatically escape the UK tax net, even on your earnings for non-UK work, simply by working abroad. A UK resident is liable to tax on his worldwide income. The course of action you need to take in order to cease to be UK resident is considered in Chapter 2. For the person working full time abroad this normally requires:

(*a*) a contract of employment extending over one complete tax year,

(*b*) no work under the contract being done in the UK (other than merely incidental duties such as reporting back to your UK boss), and

(*c*) visits back to the UK not exceeding an average of 90 days (if they did it is doubtful if the contract could be regarded as a full-time one in any event).

Where these tests are not met, it may still be possible to establish non-residence under one of the other tests outlined in Chapter 2. However, this will involve either spending at least three years abroad or, possibly, staying abroad for an entire tax year, i.e. not coming back even for a single day and basing yourself in a single location during that year.

Tax relief under the 365-day rule

If it is not practical to establish non-UK residence, but you will work abroad for at least a year (or, with a little planning, for at least ten months) it may still be possible to avoid UK tax on this salary for the work done in that period. This is because there is a special relief that applies where:

(*a*) a person works abroad in an office or employment the duties of which are performed wholly or partly outside the UK, and

(*b*) those duties are carried out in the course of a 'qualifying period' which consists of at least 365 days.

In calculating UK tax on the earnings the employee is allowed a special deduction of 100% of the earnings for that period. This effectively exempts those earnings from tax. Indeed, in some ways it is better than exemption. As the earnings are theoretically still liable to UK tax they will count as earnings for pension purposes and in some cases the fact that the earnings are 'taxed' in the UK may exempt them from overseas tax.

It should be stressed that this special relief applies only to employments (and directorships). If you are self-employed, or a partner in a firm, you will be taxable in full on your non-UK earnings unless you can shed your UK residence. If you are self-employed and obtain a contract that will require you to work for several months overseas, consider whether it might be sensible to form a limited company to take on the contract so that you can work overseas as an employee. There are a great many factors to take into account in making this decision and you ought to seek professional assistance in deciding whether, in your particular circumstances, it is worthwhile.

Qualifying period

You do not need to spend the entire 365 days outside the UK. A qualifying period for the purpose of the relief is a period of consecutive days which either:

(*a*) consists entirely of days spent overseas, or

(*b*) consists partly of such days and partly of 'intervening days'.

Intervening days are days in the UK which are preceded by a qualifying period and followed by a further qualifying period. However, the UK period between overseas trips must not be longer than 62 days and the total number of days in the UK from the beginning of the 365-day period to the date you next return to the UK must not exceed one-sixth of that entire period.

This probably sounds very complicated. It may be easier to follow with an example.

Example

Joe leaves the UK on 12 May 1993 to take up a one-year contract in Singapore. He returns to the UK on 18 July 1993 for 30 days during his children's school holiday, on 18 December for 13 days over Christmas, on 4 February 1994 for 9 days for his wife's birthday, on 29 March 1994 for 8 days for Easter, and finally returns to the UK on 14 May 1994.

(i) The period 12 May 1993 to 17 July 1993 is a qualifying period under (*a*).

(ii) The period 17 August 1993 to 17 December 1993 is a relevant period under (*a*). Accordingly, provided that the 30 intervening days in the UK do not exceed the one-sixth maximum, the whole period from 12 May 1993 to 17 December 1993 can be treated as a single qualifying period under (*b*). That period consists of 219 days. One sixth of 219 is 36. As the 30 intervening days are less than 36, the period counts as a single qualifying period.

(iii) The period 31 December 1993 to 3 February 1994 is a relevant period under (*a*). There is a previous qualifying period from 12 May 1993. Accordingly, the entire period 12 May 1993 to 3 February 1994 will be treated as a qualifying period provided the one-sixth maximum is not exceeded. The total days in that period is 266, one-sixth of which is 44. The total days in the UK are 30 on the first trip and 13 on the second, a total of 43. As this is less than 44, the entire period from 12 May 1993 is a single qualifying period.

(iv) The period 13 February 1994 to 28 March 1994 is a relevant period. There is a previous qualifying period. Accordingly the entire period 12 May 1993 to 28 March 1994 will be treated as a qualifying period provided that the one-sixth limit is not breached. The total number of days in that period is 319, one-sixth of which is 53. The cumulative number of days in the UK is 52 so again the limit is not breached.

(v) The period 6 April 1994 to 14 May 1994 is a relevant period. As there is a previous qualifying period the entire period 12 May 1993 to 14 May 1994 will be a qualifying period provided that the one-sixth limit is not breached. The total number of days in the UK, 52 plus 8 which is 60, is less than a sixth of 367, so the entire period is a single qualifying period.

The effect of these rules is to allow you to return to the UK for up to two months a year on average and still qualify for the 100% deduction. However, great care needs to be taken, as, if there are a number of visits back to the UK, it is easy to break the qualifying period. If this happens, the relief will be lost for all the previous time overseas (unless the period is already at least 365 days by the time of the offending visit) and the job will probably not last long enough for you to start a new 365-day period. The relief is very generous and the Inland Revenue apply it very vigorously. It is therefore wise to keep some permitted days back in the UK in hand in case you need to return suddenly in an emergency.

There are a number of points that need to be borne in mind.

(*a*) The legislation looks at days of absence from the UK, not days spent working overseas. It does not matter what you are doing while you are overseas.

(*b*) The 62-day figure looks only at days in a single trip. If you are overseas for, say, 540 days you can come back in aggregate for up to 90 days provided that no single trip exceeds 62 days.

(*c*) The one-sixth test is applied by reference to days up to the time you come back to the UK for your second or subsequent visit, not the time you leave the UK to go abroad again. Thus, it does not matter that when Joe, in the earlier example, goes to Singapore after Easter he has at that stage spent 60 days in the UK out of a total of 337 days since 12 May 1993 (one-sixth of which is 56). Accordingly, it does not really matter how many days you spend in the UK on a visit (provided it is less than 63) if you then stay abroad for a sufficient period to bring the cumulative UK days below one-sixth of the total.

(*d*) Going abroad for a very short period and then returning to the UK can be very dangerous. Suppose Joe in the example had taken his wife to Paris on 8 and 9 February as a birthday treat. Those two days would form a relevant period so the one-sixth test would have to be applied after that trip. At that stage the total period from 12 May 1993 would be 272 days of which 43 plus 4, or 47, would have been spent in the UK. This is greater than one-sixth of 272 (which is 45). Accordingly, the period 12 May 1993 to 9 February 1994 cannot be a qualifying period. The effect is that the earnings for the period 12 May 1993 to 3 February 1994 would be fully taxable as that qualifying period is one of less than 365 days. A new qualifying period would start from 31 December 1993 as the 4 UK days in the 41-day period 31 December 1993 to 9 February 1994 are less than one-sixth of that period. However, unless Joe remains overseas until 31 December 1994, that new qualifying period would again be less than 365 days so no relief would be due.

(*e*)   There does not appear to be any requirement for the employment to exist throughout the qualifying period. All that is required is that overseas duties are performed 'in the course of' the qualifying period. Accordingly, in theory Joe could simply stay overseas after his employment ceases in May 1994 until such time as he has built up a 365-day qualifying period and thus at least obtain relief for his earnings from 31 December 1993 onwards.

(*f*)   It is specifically provided that a person cannot be regarded as absent from the UK on any day unless he is absent at the end of it, i.e. at midnight. [*ICTA 1988, 12 Sch 4*]. It does not matter that you do a full day's work overseas; if you catch a late flight arriving into the UK that evening, the day will be treated as a day of presence in the UK. The converse does not hold good. If you are overseas at midnight it is a question of fact whether or not the day is a day of absence from the UK. If you leave in the early morning it probably is; if you leave late at night it probably is not. In practice, the Revenue treat any day on which a person is overseas at midnight as a day of absence. However, a person who uses up all his available intervening days in the UK would be unwise to rely on this.

Attribution of salary

Once a 365-day qualifying period is established, it is next necessary to ascertain the part of your salary attributable to that period. If the duties of your employment (the relevant employment) or of any other employment you hold which is 'associated' with that employment are not performed wholly outside the UK, a limitation applies. The amount of salary attracting the 100% deduction is not to exceed such proportion of your salary for that year from the relevant employment and the other employment (if any) as is shown to be reasonable — having regard to the nature of, and time devoted to, the duties performed outside and in the UK respectively and to all other relevant circumstances. In other words, if you have two related employments, for example one for UK work and the other for overseas work, you must add together the two salaries and attribute to the days spent overseas such part of that total as is reasonable on a consideration of all the facts.

For this purpose two employments are associated if they are with the same person or with persons associated with each other. Two companies are associated with one another if one has control of the other or both of them are under the control of the same person or persons. A sole trader or partnership is associated with another person (including a company) if one of them has control of the other or both are under the control of the same person or persons — but in applying this test a sole trader is not to be treated as under the control of any other person. If you have a single employment the salary must be apportioned between the qualifying period (including the intervening days) and a period of UK employment before or after the qualifying period on a reasonable basis.

In practice, if a person has a single employment embracing both UK and overseas duties the Inland Revenue will rarely accept that any method other than a straight time apportionment is appropriate to ascertain the earnings qualifying for the deduction. If there are separate employments for UK and non-UK duties it is more difficult for the Revenue to mount a challenge under this provision, particularly if the earnings from the non-UK employment can be shown to be directly related to the profits of the overseas employer, e.g. the employee is paid on a commission basis.

It has been held by the courts that the split of the salary of a single employment between UK and overseas duties must be made by reference to the employee's contractual rights (subject to the ceiling described above). When the contract does not specifically allocate part of the remuneration to the overseas duties, it legally accrues on a day-to-day basis under the Apportionment Act 1870. For this purpose the daily salary is 1/365th of the annual salary, irrespective of the number of days in the year that you are contractually required to work.

Where there is a single employment with both UK and non-UK duties, it is the salary attributable to the qualifying period that qualifies for the deduction, not that attributable to the duties performed abroad. In other words, the emoluments for intervening days spent in the UK qualify for the 100% deduction, even if the employee works in the UK on those days. For this reason it can be better to have a single employment for both UK and overseas work if the job involves UK duties and there are no special circumstances which could justify a far higher proportion of your salary being attributed to overseas work than would apply on a strict time basis.

It should be noted that the deduction applies to emoluments attributable to (i.e. earned in) the qualifying period. The relief will, of course, be given in the year that those earnings are assessed where they are received in a later year to that in which they were earned.

Where a person has a separate overseas employment, consideration needs to be given to the wording of his employment agreement. For example, if it is wished to pay him, say, 80% of the company's income this could either be 80% of the amounts received in the year (in which case the payment qualifying for the deduction would include funds generated for the company in earlier years when the employee was working wholly in the UK); 80% of the amounts earned in the year (which could again include the exploitation of the fruits of previous years' work); or 80% of the amount generated from the employee's services during the year (which, if the exploitation of such work generates royalties, could accrue over a very long period). The latter is, of course, far easier to justify. On the other hand, it can involve a great deal of record keeping to ascertain the earnings. The fact that remuneration may be received 10 or 20 years after the year in which it was earned does not prevent the Revenue assessing it. Under the new system of taxing emoluments remuneration is, of course, in any event taxable in the year of receipt irrespective of when it was earned.

The salary attributable to a qualifying period includes any terminal leave pay for a period of leave immediately following it. This can create an interesting tax planning opportunity on the employee's return to the UK. When the tour of duty overseas ends, the employee could have a period of paid leave as part of that employment before taking up his new appointment. By leaving the overseas country before the paid leave begins he will probably no longer be taxable in the foreign country. Any income arising in the period of leave is not taxable in the UK either, if the individual does not return to the UK until after the leave period has ended. *It is possible to return before the leave period ends, but professional advice should be taken.*

If an employment is, in substance, one the duties of which fall in the year of assessment to be performed in the UK, any duties performed overseas which are merely incidental to UK duties must be treated as if they were performed in the UK. However, it is difficult to envisage a person spending a continuous period of 365 days abroad if the substance of his employment consists of UK duties. Duties which a person performs on a vessel or aircraft engaged on a voyage or journey beginning or ending outside the UK (or on part of a journey beginning or ending outside the UK) are to be treated as performed abroad notwithstanding that they may be performed on a UK-registered ship or aircraft — except, where the journey or any part of it both begins and ends in the UK (including the Continental Shelf), to the extent that they are actually performed in the UK.

A special, very limited relief applies to certain people who would have qualified for the 100% deduction but for the intervention of the Iraqi invasion of Kuwait on 2 August 1990. To qualify the taxpayer must

(*a*) have been in Iraq or Kuwait at any time between 2 June 1990 and 2 August 1990 performing the duties of an employment which were to be performed to a substantial extent in one (but not, apparently, both) of those countries,

(*b*) have returned to the UK after the time mentioned in (*a*), and

(*c*) satisfy the Revenue that, having regard to all the circumstances, it is likely that his period of absence from the UK would have been part of a qualifying period of 365 days but for the events leading up to, or arising from, the invasion.

In such circumstances the period up to the time of the return to the UK is treated as a qualifying period of 365 days so that the 100% deduction applies to it. [*FA 1991, s 46*]. If the taxpayer subsequently returned to Kuwait (or Iraq — if anyone did so) but the period of his contract is such that there are insufficient days left for the rump of his contract to constitute a qualifying period, no similar exemption applies. Nor will the exemption apply to salary paid after the employee's return to the UK if the employer continued to pay him, even if it only paid him to sit at home waiting until it was opportune to return to Kuwait. A seafarer is entitled to this special relief if he was in Iraq or Kuwait at any time between 5 May 1990 and 2 August 1990.

Non-UK domiciled employees

A person who is resident but not domiciled in the UK is taxable on a 'remittance basis' on earnings from an employment carried on wholly outside the UK for an employer who is himself not resident in the UK. This means that he is taxable on such earnings only if and when he brings them into the UK. The courts have given a wide meaning to remittances. This is an area in which professional advice is essential. With care, the remuneration can be brought into the UK without attracting UK tax in a tax year after the employment ceases.

If you are resident but not domiciled in the UK, you should consider having two separate employments — preferably with different employers, e.g. two different companies in your employer's group of companies — one for UK work and the other for non-UK work. There are a number of points that need to be watched.

(*a*) The employments must be genuine. It is no good entering into an employment agreement that requires you to work for six months of the year outside the UK if, in reality, you are only going to spend the odd day abroad. The employment will be a sham and the earnings will be treated as additional earnings under the UK contract.

(*b*) The split of salary between the two employments needs to be realistic. The Revenue have power to aggregate and re-apportion them.

(*c*) If you need all of the earnings in the UK there is no advantage in splitting the employment unless you have capital outside the UK which you can remit to meet your living requirements and replace by accumulating the overseas earnings.

(*d*) You cannot claim both the relief under the 365-day rule and the remittance basis of assessment for the same earnings. If you can qualify under the 365-day rule that will normally be the preferable route. To do this you need to ensure either that you have a UK employer for your overseas work or that the employment involves some UK duties.

(*e*) You must be able to separate the UK and overseas duties. If you perform any UK duties under your overseas employment contract, e.g. you write a letter or make a phone call in the UK that relates to the overseas work, the whole of the salary will become liable to UK tax. This requires discipline and good legal advice in defining the duties to be performed under each contract, as well as the overseas duties being distinct from the UK ones. There is no exception to permit incidental duties to be performed in the UK.

(*f*) Remember that the employer under the overseas contract must be non-UK resident. For UK tax purposes a company is resident in the UK if it is either incorporated in the UK or controlled and managed from the UK, and a partnership is resident in the UK if it is controlled and managed in the UK. If the overseas employer has little substance apart from the contracts on which you will be working overseas, great care is needed. The easiest way for the Inland Revenue to seek to tax your overseas earnings is to show that, in reality, your employer is controlled and managed in this country.

(*g*) The relief does not apply at all if the employer is resident in Ireland.

Working abroad for short periods

There is another special relief that applies to people who are resident but not domiciled in the UK and work for a non-UK resident employer. This applies even where some or all of the duties are performed in the UK. If you make payments overseas out of those earnings which correspond to items that would have attracted tax relief in the UK, the Revenue will normally allow such payments to be deducted to arrive at the taxable emoluments. This is intended to cover overseas pension payments, overseas alimony in certain circumstances, and possibly overseas mortgage interest.

The tax maze

If you will remain resident in the UK follow the maze below to determine whether your earnings from your overseas employments are liable to UK tax.

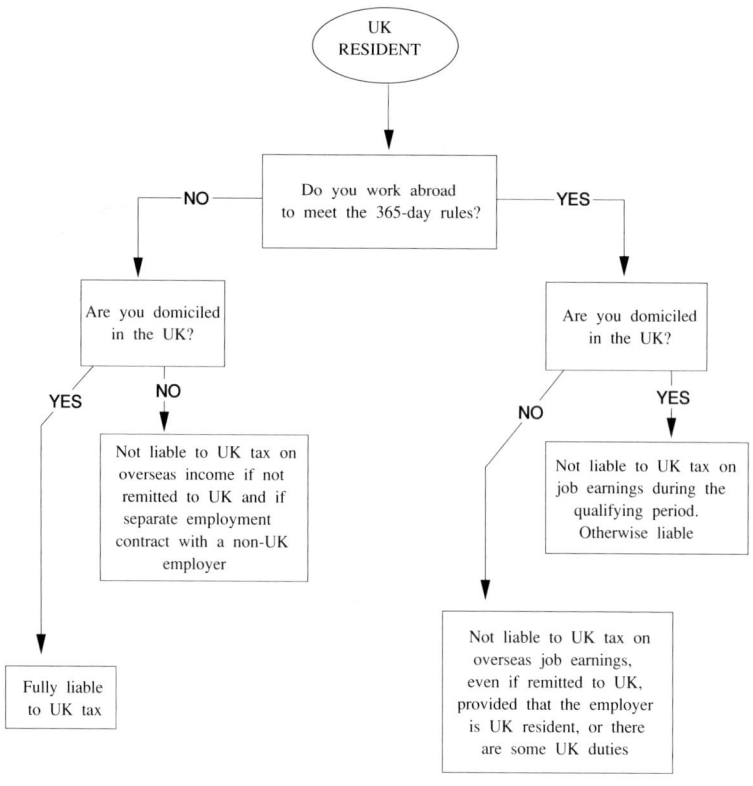

Travelling expenses

Normally, travelling expenses to one's place of work constitute personal expenditure as far as the taxman is concerned. If your employer pays such expenses you are taxed on the cost as a benefit in kind. This would be somewhat harsh if the employment is overseas. Accordingly, there is a special relief which applies to a person who is resident and ordinarily resident in the UK. The travelling expenses to the overseas place of employment on its commencement, and on returning to the UK on its termination, are treated as a business expense. They will, therefore, not give rise to a benefit in kind if paid by the employer and will qualify as a deductible expense if paid by the employee himself. This relief does not apply if the employer is non-UK resident and the employee is non-UK domiciled. As indicated above, in such circumstances the emoluments of such an employment are taxable on a remittance basis, so with a little care the employee should be able to incur the expenses overseas, thus reducing the amount of income which he can remit.

This relief does not apply to travel to and from the UK during the course of the employment — there is a separate relief for some such travel. This is described below under the heading of family travel.

If a person has more than one employment simultaneously, travel between the different employments is similarly treated as a business expense of the employment to which he is travelling where the travel is entirely outside the UK, or to or from the UK. There is no limitation on the number of journeys to which this applies.

The cost of board and lodging outside the UK is also not taxed on the employee provided that the employer bears the cost and the payment is for the purpose of enabling the employee to perform the duties of an employment which is performed wholly overseas. It should be noted that no tax relief is given if the employee pays the cost himself and is not reimbursed by his employer.

If your job involves both UK and overseas duties (within a single contract of employment) these special reliefs do not apply. The travel and board and lodging will normally be in the course of the duties of the employment and thus will attract tax relief as business expenses under the normal rules. Where they do not, for example if you return to the UK for personal reasons and then return to your overseas job, tax relief for the expenses can be claimed provided that you can show that the overseas duties could not be performed within the UK.

Family travel

A special relief is given for expenses of an employee's family incurred in visiting him, or of the employee in visiting his family, where the employee is working overseas for 60 days or more. You must be absent from the UK for a continuous period of 60 days or more for the purpose of performing the duties of one or more offices or employments. 'Continuous' means that even a single day back in the UK, for whatever reason, will debar the relief (or start a fresh 60-day period after you return overseas).

If travel facilities are provided for your spouse or infant children and the cost is borne by or on behalf of your employer (or you incur the expense and it is reimbursed to you by your employer) the expenditure is allowed as a deduction in calculating the tax on your salary. The effect is that you will not be assessed on a benefit in kind in relation to the expenditure.

This relief applies only to travel between a place in the UK and the place of performance of the duties (or any of them) outside the UK, being either

(*a*) a journey by the employee's spouse or any infant child of his accompanying him at the beginning of the 60-day period or to visit him during that period; or

(*b*) a return journey following a journey falling within (*a*).

It applies to not more than two outward and two return journeys by the same person in the same year of assessment. A child includes a stepchild and an illegitimate child, but must be under 18 at the beginning of the outward journey.

Example

On 1 January 1993 Keith is sent by his employer to work on a contract in Indonesia. The contract lasts until 31 October 1993. Keith's employer pays for the following trips for Keith's wife, Katie, and his children Ken and Kelly. Ken is 16 and Kelly's eighteenth birthday is on 12 September 1993.

> 1 January 1993 initial visit by Katie and Ken
> 15 January 1993 return trip by Katie and Ken
> 10 February 1993 visit by Ken and Kelly
> 21 February 1993 return trip by Ken and Kelly
> 31 March 1993 visit by Ken and Kelly
> 14 April 1993 return trip by Ken and Kelly
> 9 September 1993 visit by Katie and Kelly
> 18 September 1993 return trip by Katie and Kelly

(i) Travel for both Katie and Ken on 1 January 1993 and 15 January 1993 qualifies for relief.

(ii) Travel for both Ken and Kelly on 10 February 1993 and 21 February 1993 qualifies for relief.

(iii) Travel by Kelly on 31 March 1993 qualifies for relief. That for Ken does not as Ken has already made two return journeys in 1992/93. It is assumed that there was no previous overseas tour (in the same or a different country) by Keith in 1992/93. If there had been, any trips by Katie, Ken or Kelly during that previous tour would have to be taken into account to determine which visits breached the two-trip limit.

(iv) Travel by Kelly on 14 April 1993 qualifies for relief. It is not clear whether that by Ken does. It probably does. Although it is his first trip in 1993/94 the expression 'two outward and two return journeys' could be interpreted as requiring both the outward and return journey to qualify to obtain relief for either.

(v) Travel by both Katie and Kelly on 9 September 1993 and 18 September 1993 qualifies for relief. It does not matter that Kelly is over 18 on 18 September 1993 as she was under that age on 9 September.

It should be noted that the visit must be to the place of performance of the duties. Thus, if Keith had been worried about Ken and Kelly coming to Indonesia and has suggested that instead they all fly to Singapore to see one another, the relief would not apply and Keith would be assessed on the cost of Ken and Kelly's fares. Indeed, if he had suggested they visit him in Djakarta, the capital of Indonesia, rather than going to the remote jungle site where Keith was actually working, it again appears that the relief would not apply, as Djakarta would not be 'the place of performance' of the duties.

Self-employment

There are few special reliefs for the self-employed (which includes a partner in a partnership) who work abroad for significant periods but remain resident in the UK. The relief for family travel described above also applies to the self-employed. At least, that is the intention. The relief is actually expressed to apply only if the trade is carried on wholly outside the UK, which would not normally be the case. It may be that the Government think that the taxpayer is carrying on his trade wholly outside the UK during any period that he is physically outside the UK. If so it is doubtful if this is right in law.

There is also a specific relief for travelling expenses and for board and lodging whilst the self-employed person is working overseas. It is doubtful if this is wide enough to cover board and lodging overseas where the trade is carried on partly in the UK and partly overseas, although we have not known the Revenue to take this point.

Overseas tax

If you are working overseas you will normally be liable for income tax on your earnings in the country in which you work — although if your employer does not have an office there you will, in practice, probably not be taxed by default as the tax authorities will not be aware of the earnings.

Most of the UK's double taxation agreements exempt a UK resident from overseas tax on earnings in the overseas countries in limited circumstances. Income from an employment or directorship cannot normally be taxed in the overseas country if

(a) you are not present in that country for more than 183 days during the year (i.e. the overseas country's fiscal year),

(b) your employer is not a resident of that country, and

(c) your salary is not borne by a permanent establishment of your employer in the other country, e.g. it is not charged to a branch office there, the profits of which are taxable in that country.

If all three of these conditions are not met, you can be charged to local tax.

If you are self-employed, the other country can normally tax your earnings only if you have a fixed base regularly available to you in that country.

As with all reliefs under double tax treaties, it is important to refer to the treaty to check the terms of the relief as some differ from these standard rules. For example, the agreement with Montserrat, which is a 1947 agreement, requires the employer to be a UK resident (whereas (*b*) above permits him to be a resident of a third country), and requires the salary to be taxable in the UK.

Double tax treaties normally contain special rules for entertainers and athletes (to allow the country where the artiste performs to tax him); directors fees — i.e. for acting as a member of the board as opposed to remuneration for acting as an executive — (to allow the country of residence of the company to tax them); government employees (they are normally taxable only in the employing country); teachers (may be exempt from tax in the country where they work if the job is for under two years and there has not been a previous employment in that country) and students (may be exempt from tax in the country of study on income arising overseas). If you fall into one of these heads you should check the treaty to clarify your tax position.

Where overseas tax is paid, the UK tax authorities will allow relief for it against the UK tax on the same income. They will require a receipt or similar evidence to prove that the overseas tax was paid. If no UK tax is payable because of the relief under the 365-day rule, no relief for the overseas tax can be claimed in the UK.

Chapter 6

Working abroad as a non-UK resident

If you become a non-UK resident you are obviously not liable to UK tax on your overseas earnings. If you carry out duties in the UK you are taxable here on your earnings for such duties unless they are merely incidental to your overseas work. It should be noted that merely incidental does not mean insignificant or of a minor nature. It means that the duties must not be an integral part of the work that you do. For example, coming to the UK once a month to report to your boss would normally be incidental. Coming to the UK for a day a month for a meeting of branch managers would probably not be. Coming to the UK for a day a month to review what is happening in the UK office if you are in charge of European operations would certainly not be merely incidental.

The Inland Revenue have indicated that they regard visits to the UK by an overseas representative of a UK employer to report to the employer or to receive fresh instructions as incidental. They also accept that time spent undergoing training in the UK is incidental to the overseas employment provided that this does not exceed 91 days in a year and no productive work is done in the UK during that time (Booklet IR 20, para 6.8).

If the country in which you have taken up residence has a double tax treaty with the UK this could well prevent the UK charging tax if (in most cases)

(*a*) you spend less than 183 days in a tax year in the UK,

(*b*) the salary is paid by a non-UK employer, and

(*c*) the salary is not borne by a permanent establishment or a fixed base of the employer in the UK.

Where you work for a UK employer, full UK tax would be payable.

There can be special rules for artistes, entertainers, students, teachers and government service. Reference needs to be made to the treaty concerned to find the precise rules.

UK directorships

It is unwise to retain any UK directorship if you intend to establish non-UK residence and ordinary residence, but to do so is not necessarily fatal. What you must not do is attend board meetings or the AGM or perform any other statutory duties in the UK. This is because such tasks, however minor, being fundamental to a directorship cannot be merely incidental to overseas duties. If you retain a house available for your use in the UK, these UK duties will remove the protection from UK ordinary residence where an employment is carried on full time abroad. Because of the importance of being able to show that none of the duties of the directorship are performed in the UK, it is advisable to minute the fact that you will not be able to attend board meetings or carry out any statutory functions in the UK. You also need to review the company's Articles of Association to check that a director is not required to attend a minimum number of such meetings.

If you will be working abroad for a sufficiently long period to establish non-UK residence it is generally advisable to do so. However, instances can occur where it is better to remain UK resident even though you are working full time abroad. In particular this can protect you from overseas tax if you spend less than 183 days in any other overseas country. The tie-breaker clause of a double tax agreement could well result in your being treated under the agreement as not resident there (even though you could be under that country's domestic law), and the employment clause of the agreement will then exempt you from tax there if your salary is not charged to a local branch. If the relief under the 365-day rule described in Chapter 5 effectively exempts the earnings from UK tax, this would put you in an attractive position. The problem is how do you remain UK resident if you are working full time abroad. The answer in the past was frequently to become a director of a UK company, make sure that you perform some duties of the directorship in the UK, retain accommodation for your use in the UK, and ensure that you visit the UK, preferably for several weeks during each tax year. However, this probably no longer works after 5 April 1993.

Taking advantage of your non-UK residence

If you are sent overseas by your employer, particularly if you will be employed there by a different company in the group, your period of non-residency may provide an opportunity to escape tax on amounts that are not part of your normal salary. For example, the tax charge on the exercise of an unapproved share option will not apply if the option is exercisable by virtue of the overseas employment, and the value of that right may well not be taxable in your new country of residence. The special rules that impose a tax charge on the removal of restrictions attaching to employee-held shares will also normally not apply if the taxpayer is non-UK resident at the time. If you have approved share options, exercising the option while you are not UK resident or ordinarily resident will normally take the gain out of UK tax and it will probably not be taxable in your new country either.

In some countries there may be scope for paying part of the salary either as an inducement payment after leaving the UK and before becoming resident in the new country or as a terminal bonus after leaving the country.

Other employment considerations

Company pension schemes

If you are still employed by a UK company or another company in the same group you should check how long you can continue to contribute to your UK company pension scheme.

If you are seconded from your UK company you can normally remain in the UK scheme for at least three years. After that your employer needs to seek Inland Revenue approval.

If you are sent abroad to work for any other type of employer, including the non-resident subsidiary of a UK group, you should consult your employer and a professional adviser.

You will probably find it beneficial to remain in your UK scheme. If that is not possible you should consider transferring your UK scheme entitlement to an overseas scheme.

Finally, you should check whether your employer's pension contributions, if you are subject to tax in the new country in which you will be working, are taxable in that country. *Previously, as a UK taxpayer, you would not have been taxable on your employer's contributions.*

Personal pension schemes

Check with your independent financial adviser whether it is best for you to continue with your personal pension scheme and for how long and what other conditions and/or restrictions may apply.

Life assurance

Ask your employer or the pension scheme trustees to check the policy if they have taken out death in service cover for you. You may not be covered for death in service while you are abroad. Consider taking out extra cover, perhaps term life assurance, to cover your foreign stay because of your changed circumstances.

Your overseas remuneration package

Discuss with your employer whether he is prepared to contribute towards your cost of living overseas. Many employers are willing to pay for, or contribute towards, accommodation, children's education, family travel, subscriptions to an expatriate social club in the country where you will work, medical insurance and similar expenses. In many countries these benefits are either not taxable or attract a tax charge on a far lower figure than the equivalent cash salary. Another benefit that is often provided is payment of fees to obtain tax advice both on your UK tax position and on your tax position in your new country. Your remuneration package ideally needs to be reviewed completely. For example, a company car may not be much use to you if you are being posted to somewhere like Hong Kong. It would probably be an inappropriate benefit if you are being posted to the USA where the provision of company cars is a far less common benefit than in the UK and so could cause problems with your colleagues.

Tax equalisation

Does your employer operate a tax equalisation scheme under which you will be compensated for any excess of the tax payable in your new country over that which you would have paid in the UK? Don't forget that many countries have higher tax rates than the UK. If there is a tax equalisation plan, the timing of payments to you under it can determine whether they are taxable in the country in which you will become resident.

Place of payment

We are sometimes asked whether there are problems in part of a person's salary while they are overseas being paid to them in the UK. In general there are not. Once a person ceases to be resident and ordinarily resident in the UK he falls out of the UK income tax net except in relation to UK income. Accordingly, the receipt by such a person of funds in the UK does not create UK taxable income.

However, in most cases it also does not take the money out of charge to tax in the country where it is earned. It may avoid the imposition of a payroll withholding tax on that part of the earnings but there is usually an obligation to declare the receipt. In some cases the deferral of receipt until after the overseas job has terminated may avoid the overseas tax.

If you have continuing commitments in the UK, or are saving out of your earnings to invest in the UK, the receipt of part of your salary here also minimises any currency exchange risk. As you will be receiving part of your earnings in sterling, the currency in which you will spend the money, on a monthly basis, you are effectively converting it into sterling as you go along.

Self-employment

There are no special considerations to bear in mind if you are self-employed while you are overseas and are abroad for a sufficiently long period to become non-UK resident. You may need to take care not to cease your self-employment in the first two or three years if your trade or business started while you were in the UK. The reason for this is dealt with in Chapter 3. You may also need to consider ceasing your business, perhaps by incorporating it, if you subsequently return to the UK.

You also need to bear in mind that the Revenue concession on ordinary residence described in Chapter 2 under the heading 'Going overseas to work' does not apply to the self-employed. If you obtain a particularly lucrative overseas contract, consider incorporating your business, i.e. transferring it to a company, before you leave the UK so that you can bring yourself within this concession.

Chapter 7

Pensions

State retirement pension

The state retirement pension and widow's pension will continue to be paid to you while you are abroad. You need to have met the qualifying contributions record during your 'working life'. This means the period from 6 April 1948 (or your 16th birthday if later) until you reach 65 (60 if you are a woman). Broadly speaking, to get the full pension you need to have a full contributions record for 44 out of the 49 years of your working life (39 out of 44 if you are a woman). If you have not yet reached pension age it may be worthwhile paying voluntary national insurance contributions until you do so in order to meet this condition.

Unless you are within four months of retirement age, the Government will give you a forecast of the pension to which you are entitled (at current rates) assuming that you continue to make contributions until retirement age. You need to obtain a form BR 19 from your local DSS office and send it to the Retirement Pension Unit in Newcastle. If your state pension will be an important part of your retirement income you ought to do this at an early stage in your planning to go abroad if you are leaving before you start to draw your pension.

Once your pension starts to be paid it is normally fixed at the current rate; you do not get future pension increases. You will, however, be entitled to future increases in the benefit if either you remain ordinarily resident in the UK (which is unlikely) or you are living in another EC country or in Austria, Bermuda, Cyprus, Finland, Gibraltar, Guernsey, Iceland, Israel, Jamaica, Jersey, Malta, Mauritius, Philippines, Sark, Sweden, Switzerland, Turkey, USA or Yugoslavia. If you are already in receipt of your pension you need to tell the DSS before you go abroad so that they can make the necessary arrangements to pay you overseas. War pensions and war widow's pension can also usually be paid anywhere in the world.

The state pension is chargeable to UK tax. The Inland Revenue will generally allocate your personal allowance against this so you may well not be asked for tax on your pension, but remember that this will have utilised your personal allowance so this is no longer available to set against other UK sources of income.

Occupational pensions

If you are entitled to an occupational pension from your (or your late spouse's) former employer, this will normally be paid under deduction of UK tax. Such

Pensions

pensions fall into two types, those paid direct by the former employer or by a self-administered pension scheme operated by that company, and those paid in the form of an annuity from an insurance company. The first type will be subject to PAYE in the same way as your salary used to be. If the 40% higher rate of tax is payable on this pension, the PAYE system will deduct this. If your pension takes the form of an annuity, tax will be deducted from this at the 25% basic rate only. You will, accordingly, owe an extra 15% tax if you are liable at the 40% rate.

If you were formerly employed by the UK Government, your pension will always be paid net of tax. Most double tax agreements give the UK the right to tax UK Government pensions and exempt the pension from tax in the country where the pensioner has taken up residence.

If you have not yet started to draw your pension, consider whether it might be sensible to take the maximum tax free lump sum and either use it to purchase an annuity or invest it overseas as a lump sum. If you are in a company pension scheme which is not fully funded it may be possible to take the whole of your pension entitlement as a lump sum. If you are not in such a scheme, the maximum amount that you can withdraw will be limited to 25% (slightly more under retirement annuities).

A pension paid under one of the following schemes is exempt from UK tax if the recipient is not resident in the UK.

— India, Pakistan, Myanmar (formerly Burma) and Colonial statutory schemes.

— Pension funds for former public service employees of overseas territories.

— The Central African Pension Fund.

— The Overseas Service Pension Fund.

— Pension funds set up for overseas employees of UK employers.

This is because these are pensions for overseas work which, for administrative reasons, are paid from the UK. It would clearly be unreasonable to tax a non-UK resident on his pension where the sole connection with the UK is that it is paid from this country. A pension from a non-UK employer is, of course, also not liable to UK tax in the hands of a non-UK resident as it is not income arising from a UK source.

Double taxation agreements

If you are in a country with which the UK has a double taxation agreement, this will probably exempt your pension from UK tax — unless it is a UK Government or local authority pension, when it may instead exempt it from tax in your country of residence. The exemption for pensions normally also applies to annuities, including purchased annuities. This does not apply under all the UK's double tax agreements. It is essential to check the position for the country to which you are emigrating. A list of countries with which the UK has a double tax agreement is given in Chapter 2.

If you can claim the benefit of a double tax agreement and tax on your pension is deducted under the PAYE system, you should ask the Inland Revenue to issue a NT (nil tax) code number to you. You need to tell them the country in which you are resident and that you wish to claim the benefit of the exemption for pensions under the double tax agreement. There is no special claim form; simply write a letter to the Revenue. If you have not completed a form P15, they will require you to complete one and will also ask questions to satisfy themselves that you are indeed resident in your adopted country. If you have completed a tax return in your new country which shows that you are being taxed there on the pension, sending them a copy of that return may save time.

Pension contributions

If you are working abroad and are a member of an occupational pension scheme (i.e. a company pension scheme) and your employer is a UK company, you are entitled to remain a member of that scheme and both you and your employer can continue to make contributions to it. If your employer is a non-UK resident, you cannot normally contribute to a UK occupational pension scheme. There is an exception to this. If you are employed overseas by a non-UK company which is in the same group of companies as your former employer, you can remain a member of your group pension scheme if you will remain resident in the UK and are not entitled to the 100% deduction under the 365-day rule. This exemption will therefore only apply to relatively short trips overseas. It is unlikely to apply very often as, in such cases, it is rare to switch employments; you are more likely to be seconded by your UK employer to the overseas company.

If you remain an employee of your UK employer and it seconds you to another group company during your time overseas (i.e. you remain an employee of the UK company but work for the overseas one), the Revenue will want to satisfy themselves that the UK company retains control over your movements. Furthermore, if the period of secondment exceeds three years, they will normally insist that contributions to the pension scheme cease after that time.

If you are not a member of an occupational scheme, you can continue to make payments into a personal pension scheme (or a retirement annuity scheme that started before 1 July 1988) only if your earnings, in the year of assessment in which you make the payment, are chargeable to UK tax. If they are effectively exempted under the 365-day rule they are nevertheless technically chargeable to tax, so you can, if you wish, continue to make contributions — although, as the tax relief can be given only against earnings, you will not obtain relief for the contributions unless you have other taxable earnings.

The maximum percentage of earnings that can be paid into such schemes depends on your age, as illustrated below.

Pensions

Age	Personal pension	Retirement annuity
Under 36	17½%	17½%
36 to 45	20%	17½%
46 to 50	25%	17½%
51 to 55	30%	20%
56 to 60	35%	22½%
61 or over	40%	27½%

Although the personal pension rules appear more generous there is a major snag for high earners: there is an overriding limitation that contributions can be made only in respect of the first £75,000 of earnings. There is no such limitation on retirement annuities. However, it has not been possible to take out a new retirement annuity since 1 July 1988; contributions can now only be made to plans that were in existence on that date — and even then only if they permit further contributions to be made. Because of the differences in the contribution limits, problems can arise in mixing the two. In particular, a person whose earnings exceed the £75,000 'earnings cap' who contributed to retirement annuities should not take on a commitment to pay regular annual contributions to a personal pension. As many life assurance policies are written under the personal pension rules, care needs to be taken when considering life assurance, to avoid unwittingly making a personal pension contribution.

It is possible to elect to treat a retirement annuity or personal pension contribution as having been paid in the previous tax year or, if you had no earnings of any sort taxable in the UK in that year, in the year before that. Accordingly, if you cease to be UK resident you can use your salary in the first two years abroad to fund pension contributions to utilise unused relief of earlier years. The election has to be made by 5 April in the year in which the premium is actually paid, i.e. an election to carry back contributions made in 1993/94 must be made by 5 April 1994. In the case of personal pension contributions, a further three months' grace is allowed, i.e. the election could be made at any time up to 5 July 1994.

Example

Joe is aged 46. He has been employed by Yewkayco Ltd for many years. The company does not operate a pension scheme and Joe has been paying £2,000 a year into retirement annuities up to 1990/91 and £3,000 thereafter. On 31 July 1992 Joe left Yewkayco and went to work for Overseas Trader in Hong Kong for three years at a salary of £60,000 p.a. Joe's salary from Yewkayco in recent years has been:

	£
1987/88	20,000
1988/89	22,000
1989/90	24,000
1990/91	26,000
1991/92	28,000
1992/93 (to 31 July)	8,000

	UK Salary	17 ¹/₂% thereof	Premium	Unused Relief	Cumulation
	£	£	£	£	£
1987/88	20,000	3,500	2,000	1,500	1,500
1988/89	22,000	3,850	2,000	1,850	3,350
1989/90	24,000	4,200	2,000	2,200	5,550
1990/91	26,000	4,550	2,000	2,550	8,100
1991/92	28,000	4,900	3,000	1,900	10,000
1992/93	8,000	1,400	3,000	(1,600)	8,400

Joe can obtain relief for his premiums in full, including those paid in 1992/93 after he left the UK. He can obtain no tax relief for any premiums paid in 1993/94 as he has no UK taxable earnings in that year. If he pays a contribution in 1993/94 he can, however, elect to treat it as having been paid in 1992/93. If the contribution does not exceed £5,000 he would then get full relief for it. If it exceeds £5,000 the balance would be unrelieved as he has only £8,000 of taxable earnings in 1992/93 and thus cannot get relief for more than £8,000 of premiums. Suppose Joe pays £3,000 in 1993/94 and elects to treat it as paid in 1992/93. Suppose also that he elects to treat the contributions actually paid in 1992/93 as having been paid in the previous year.

The position for 1991/92 and 1992/93 would now become:

1991/92	£28,000	£4,900	£6,000	(£1,100)	£7,000
1992/93	8,000	£1,400	£3,000	(£1,600)	£5,400

If Joe were then to pay a further £5,000 in 1994/95 he could carry this back to 1992/93 (as he has no UK taxable earnings in 1993/94) thus utilising the bulk of the available relief, i.e.

1992/93	£8,000	£1,400	£8,000	(£6,600)	£400

The same principle applies where a person retires abroad. Pension contributions made in the two years after leaving the UK can be related back to earnings earned whilst in the UK.

Purchased annuities

If your pension is inadequate to meet your needs but you have capital, you could supplement your income with a purchased annuity. You pay a capital sum to an insurance company in return for which they agree to make you a monthly or quarterly payment. For UK tax purposes, each payment is split into a capital and an income element. The capital element represents a return of capital and is tax free. The income element is taxable as income. The advantage of purchasing an annuity rather than simply living off capital is that the annuity payments will continue for the rest of your life, but the capital payment you make has been calculated on the assumption that you will only live for your current life expectation (taken from published mortality tables). Accordingly, if you live longer you will continue to receive payments even though the amounts you have received up to that time have exhausted the capital payment you made plus the income it generates. In fact, you benefit doubly. The capital element is fixed at the time the annuity is purchased and thus part of the annuity continues to be tax free. If you die early, the insurance company benefits. However, this may be an acceptable price to pay to give you the peace of mind that if you live longer than average you will continue to receive the annuity payments to assist in meeting your living requirements.

It is best to defer purchasing an annuity as long as possible, partly because the older you are the greater is the capital element and partly because the shorter the period for which (in accordance with their mortality tables) the insurance companies expect to have to be paying you, the larger the annuity they can offer. In general, annuities are not normally attractive for people under about 70.

It may be possible to obtain a better return by purchasing an annuity from a Channel Islands or Isle of Man insurance company which is outside the scope of UK tax — although, as most types of income are likely to suffer withholding taxes before they are received by the insurance company, the rates are unlikely to be significantly better.

Many newly-retired people would like to supplement their income without eating into capital in the short term, before committing themselves to the purchase of an annuity. One way of doing this is by purchasing a Jersey Investment plan. This is a Jersey-based insurance bond (Jersey is used to avoid UK tax) combined with a capital protected annuity, i.e. one which is guaranteed to pay out for a fixed (but limited) period even if you die. These are obviously more expensive than standard annuities as the insurance company cannot benefit from your early demise. The concept is that you put, say, 40% of your capital into buying the annuity and 60% into the bond. The annuity is payable for a fixed period of five years. This will supplement your income as the return should be superior to the investment income which your funds currently produce. The bond will grow back to the current value of your capital (and hopefully more) over the five-year period. The percentages given above are merely to illustrate the principle. The actual percentage put into the product depends on a combination of your age and the annuity rates offered by insurance companies at the time you enter the plan.

Chapter 8

Your UK home

One of the biggest decisions you need to make is what to do about your UK home. Should you sell it, let it or leave it unoccupied? The answer is likely to depend on how long you expect to be abroad. If you are retiring abroad you will probably need to sell it as you will want to buy accommodation in your new location. If you are going abroad for two or three years you may well be content to live in rented accommodation overseas — particularly if your employer will pay the bill.

In such a case you probably want to retain your UK house, partly because you will want to return to the same neighbourhood and renew your friendships after your stay abroad and do not want to risk not being able to find a house in the locality at that stage, and partly because, having started to climb the housing ladder, there is a reluctance to get off it. In the past this was because of a worry that house price inflation was increasing at such a pace that one would not be able to afford to climb back on to the ladder after a couple of years of absence, and also because it was hard to find an investment to match the growth in real terms in value of the house. It is now more likely to be either because of a reluctance to sell the house at a figure below its value in 1989 — albeit that most people think that it will take at least three more years before most houses reach such values again — or because of an inability to find a buyer at a price that you regard as acceptable. In any event, in the current market you are unlikely to be financially better off selling your house, investing the money while you are overseas, and buying a new house when you return, so why take the risk, however unlikely it may seem, that house prices could start to move upwards again while you are overseas?

If you are going abroad for ten years you will probably want to buy a house in your new location, and may well not intend to return to your old home at the end of that time as your lifestyle will probably have changed and your family may have grown up. Accordingly, unless you look on it purely as an investment, you are probably going to decide to sell your UK home and acquire one in your new country. If you will be abroad for between three and ten years the decision as to what to do is more difficult. Most people are likely to decide to let the house, at least initially, and review the position after a couple of years.

Leaving your home vacant

Unless you will only be abroad for a few months, possibly up to a year, this is not generally a good idea. Empty houses are vulnerable to burglars and, far worse, to squatters. If it is obviously empty, a house can also be a source of amusement to vandals. If you have a neighbour who is prepared to keep an eye on the house, or, better still, a relative or friend who is looking for temporary accommodation and is willing to house-sit for you, you may be able to avoid these problems. Otherwise the risk is too great.

In any event most people need the house to produce income to meet the mortgage interest. Even if you can afford to pay this out of your overseas salary, why leave the house idle? If you don't need the rental income to meet current expenses why not generate it nevertheless and invest it?

Letting your home

Dealing with the tenant

The biggest problem in letting your home is finding a reliable tenant. The second biggest is satisfying his demands. The third is doing both of these things while you are living in another country. Although I have friends who have done all these successfully, it normally requires a combination of luck, unannounced visits to the house whenever you visit the UK, and an arrangement with a builder or handyman whom you have learnt to trust before you left the UK. The best advice is don't try. Put both the letting and the management of the property into the hands of a local estate agent. Of course you will resent his taking a hefty letting commission when you might have found a tenant by putting an advert in the local paper. You will resent even more the, say, 15% of the rent that he takes each month for banking the tenant's cheque and sending you the balance (or, more likely, 75% of the balance to create a reserve for tax). Look on this expense as an insurance policy against things going wrong.

How can you judge the reliability of a potential tenant who answers your ad? How do you know what is the right rent for your house? How will you do this from, say, Australia in three months time if the tenant has decided that the house wasn't really what he wanted and left? Your estate agent's letting commission is the price for avoiding these problems. He is experienced in signing up potential tenants. His reputation depends on getting it right most of the time and doing something about it on those occasions when something goes wrong. If he lets you down you will almost certainly tell your friends back home and they will tell their friends. The estate agent knows this; he also knows that many of the people to whom the tale is told are potential customers. He would much rather they were being told how efficient you found him and how helpful he was when the tenant walked out.

Similarly with management. Do you really want the tenant on the telephone to you when things go wrong — particularly if he is oblivious to the time differential between the two countries? Most tenants expect the landlord to do everything, even the very small jobs like replacing the washer on the leaking tap, or the cracked window, that an owner-occupier would do himself. You don't want the aggravation of his problems. To avoid this you might give him the phone number of the builder, plumber, electrician etc. that you normally use. Do you really want them to decide between them what work should be done and to send you the bill? If the workmanship is shoddy do you want him to get the tradesman back and send you another bill? If the tradesman goes out of business do you want the tenant to find his own replacement, no matter how expensive he may be, as you are paying?

If the answer to these questions is 'No' the only realistic alternative is either to persuade a friend or relative to stand in your shoes and deal with the tenant's problems on your behalf or to pay an agent to do this, and to inspect the house regularly and to take some action if the rent cheques stop coming.

When my brother moved from Connecticut to Montreal he let his house in Connecticut and did not use an agent to collect the rents. One day the rent cheques stopped coming. He tried to contact the tenant by phone. Eventually he took some time off work and travelled down to Connecticut and unravelled what had happened. The tenant, the son of a friend, had shared the house with friends, they had fallen out and the original tenant had left. One day the new tenant turned on the tap and no water came out, so he decided to stop paying the rent. He didn't bother to complain to my brother, in the same way as the original tenant had not bothered to tell him that he had moved out and left the house to a stranger. The reason no water had come out of the tap was that a pipe had burst in the cellar. Losing the rent was the least of my brother's worries; he was left with about £10,000 worth of damage to the house as the burst pipe was not the only problem the tenant had ignored. Admittedly this was America. Nevertheless I like to think that if he had used an agent the problems would have been discovered and dealt with long before the damage was done.

The lease to the tenant

It is advisable to engage a solicitor to draw up the lease to your tenant. The estate agent may have a standard form of lease into which he inserts the tenant's name and the length of the tenancy, but property law is complex and it is unwise to rely on this as there may be something special in your particular case to make it inappropriate.

You will undoubtedly have read 'horror stories' in the papers about people letting their houses for short periods and then finding that the tenant refused to leave when he said he would and that the courts uphold his right to stay. In fact, security of tenure has been significantly reduced in recent years. With a few exceptions that are unlikely to be relevant to you, leases entered into after 14 January 1989 are not subject to the Rent Act 1977 which provided strong protection to the tenant.

There are now two main types of residential letting, the assured tenancy and the assured shorthold tenancy. Under an assured tenancy the tenant is, in general, entitled to remain in possession at the end of the lease, but at a market rent. Even if the tenancy is for a fixed term, the landlord cannot evict the tenant; he must obtain a court order to do this. Provided that at the time you enter into the lease (or earlier) you serve a notice on the tenant to the effect that you are likely to seek possession at some stage because you require the house for your own occupation or for that of your spouse, the court *must* order the tenant to vacate the premises. It is important that notice on the correct form is given at the correct time. If this is not done it does not mean that you cannot regain possession, the court still has a discretion to terminate the tenancy, but you may have to prove that you have a greater need for the property than the tenant does. You must have occupied the house as your main residence at some time before the start of the tenancy or bought it with the intention of occupying it as the main residence of yourself or your spouse at some future date, e.g. you buy the house in preparation for returning to the UK. However, this protection to enable you to regain possession of your own house will not apply if you buy the house with the tenant already there. There are various alternative grounds on which you can ask the court to terminate the tenancy, but this is the easiest one. The assured tenancy protection for tenants does not apply to very large houses.

An assured shorthold tenancy is an assured tenancy which is granted for a fixed term (of at least six months) and in respect of which before the lease was granted the landlord served a notice on the tenant stating that the tenancy was an assured shorthold one. The notice must be in a specific form and the procedure needs to be followed strictly. This is another good reason for using a solicitor who will know exactly what needs to be done. If the parties agree to allow the tenancy to continue after the end of the fixed term it will remain an assured shorthold tenancy in most cases. Again, the landlord cannot evict the tenant but, provided that he gives the tenant at least two months notice, the court must do so, assuming, of course, that the agreed term has expired.

The building society

Under the terms of your mortgage, you will no doubt discover that you are obliged to inform your building society that the property will no longer be occupied by yourself and your family. If you tell them that you intend to let the property, the building society may refuse their permission. However, they will probably agree if you are leaving the UK for less than three years and have paid all your mortgage payments on time. They will almost certainly put up your interest rate. They will probably want to review the tenancy agreement and they would insist on the following.

(*a*) That no tenant enjoying diplomatic immunity be accepted. This is because you cannot sue such a tenant to get them out of your house.

(*b*) The tenancy agreement must not allow the tenant to sub-let or part with possession of any part of the property, either with or without your consent.

(*c*) The rent agreed must be paid either weekly or monthly.

(*d*) The rent must be sufficient to cover all outgoings.

The permission — if granted — is likely to be only for a period of three years, with your having to re-apply at the end of the three years if you are still abroad.

Insurers

You must inform your insurers that you intend to let the house, otherwise the policy may be void. An extra premium may be payable. They may insist, if the house is empty for any period of more than 24 hours, that the water tank be drained. You must read the small print carefully. The policy will only pay out on theft if there are signs of forcible entry. You will not be covered for theft by your tenants, unless you pay an increase in the premium to cover larceny or take out a separate policy.

Furniture

The better a house is furnished the higher the rent it is likely to command. On the other hand, the more expensive the furniture the more annoying any ill treatment of it and damage to it will be. If you have furnished your home with expensive antiques it is safest to remove them before you let the house. If you know that the tenant can afford to pay for damages — and you are confident that you will be able to enforce payment — you could leave the antiques in place as they will almost certainly enhance the rent that the house will produce (assuming that it is of a size that is consistent with being furnished with antiques). If you have family heirlooms or gifts to which you have a sentimental attachment do not take chances; remove them from the house before it is let. Some people put all their valuable furniture into one room, lock it and exclude it from the lease. If for any reason the tenant gets upset and decides to vandalise the house, a locked door will not stop him; indeed the locked room may be a great temptation to the unscrupulous tenant. It is far better to take valuable personal effects out of the house completely.

Taxation of the rental income

If you decide to continue to own your UK house, but to let it, you will continue to be liable to UK tax on the rental income even if you are not resident and not ordinarily resident in the UK. The UK includes England, Northern Ireland, Scotland and Wales.

Rent receivable

The income is not the rent received; it is the rent due under the terms of the lease in any tax year (6 April to 5 April). No adjustment is to be made for pre-paid rent. The accounts must always be drawn up for the year to 6 April (although, in practice, the Inland Revenue do not always insist on this). Only if it can be shown that unpaid rent due is irrecoverable, after all reasonable steps have been taken to recover it, can the income be reduced to take account of unpaid rent.

If the property is let at a low rent to a friend or relative, the Revenue can only tax you on that amount, not on the market rent that you could have got for the house. However, if the property is let at a figure below a commercial rent (which is not defined but is probably the figure necessary to cover all the expenses) you cannot claim relief for mortgage interest.

Deductible costs

The following costs can usually be deducted against the income.

— Council tax (and for earlier years the collective community charge) to the extent that this is borne by the landlord.

— Water rates where paid by the landlord.

— Agent's fees.

Your UK home

— Legal fees relating to the letting (including VAT).

— Repairs and redecorations (see below).

— Postage and telephone costs directly relating to the letting.

— Wear and tear (see below).

— Other services such as electricity, gas, TV, paid by the landlord.

— Insurance.

— Inventory fees.

— Ground rent.

— Valuation fees for insurance purposes.

— Gardening costs or window cleaner, if imposed on the landlord by the lease.

— Accountancy fees.

— Travel to the UK if you have to come to sort out problems with the tenancy.

— Interest costs (see below).

— VAT charged (see below).

Repairs and redecorations

Repairs and redecorations must be 'normal' (i.e. any outlay necessary to protect the property from dilapidation or to make good dilapidation which has already occurred). This cannot include expenditure on improvements, additions or alterations to the premises. The repairs and redecorations must be incurred and the work carried out when the tenant is in occupation, or between lettings, not before or after the tenancies. Furthermore, expenditure on making good dilapidation occurring before you begin to let the property cannot qualify as repairs.

Wear and tear

An allowance for wear and tear on furniture, carpets, fittings etc., may be claimed by concession. The Inland Revenue permit this to be calculated by one of two methods at your option:

(a) 10% of the gross rental income less water rates and services (such as gas, electricity and TV) supplied directly to the tenant, or

(b) the net cost of replacements, but nothing for initial purchases.

If you are likely to let the property for only two or three years you are unlikely to need to replace furniture so method (b) is unlikely to be of help. Most people use the 10% of rents method.

If the letting is treated as a trade, the allowance is in the form of capital allowances, currently 25%. However, the Inland Revenue scrutinises such claims closely and it would be very unusual for a non-UK resident to be able to establish his lettings as a trade.

Value added tax (VAT)

Although you may live overseas, any invoices relating to the property (e.g. agent's fees, repairs, surveyor's fees, legal fees) have to carry VAT if the supplier is VAT registered. The VAT can be deducted as a cost in arriving at the taxable profit.

Deducting interest

Interest is not strictly deductible in arriving at the net taxable income from the letting. However, provided that it meets a number of conditions, it can be deducted from the net income which, for all practical purposes, amounts to the same thing.

Interest on a loan is deductible against the rental income if:

(*a*) the loan was used only to purchase or improve the property,

(*b*) the property is let at a commercial rent, not at a low rent to a friend or relative,

(*c*) it is let for at least 26 weeks in a 52-week period which includes the interest payment date, and it is either available for letting or under repair for the remainder of the period,

(*d*) in most cases, the interest is paid to a UK bank, building society or other lender not an overseas one, and

(*e*) the interest is payable on a loan not an overdraft.

If these conditions are met, there is no limit on the loan, unlike the £30,000 limit that applied to your home mortgage when you lived there. Similarly if you are liable to higher rate tax, relief will no longer be restricted to the basic rate. However, relief for the interest can be given only against UK rental income (not necessarily from the same property). It cannot be claimed against any other UK income.

The following points require particular consideration.

(i) If you increased your mortgage after 6 April 1988 to raise funds for home improvement, that part of the interest will not currently qualify for relief, but interest paid on that borrowing after you have ceased to use the property as your residence and put it in the hands of letting agents will normally do so. It might be worth investigating whether you can delay payment of interest due until shortly before you move out. It is the date the interest is paid, not when it became payable, that matters.

(ii) A loan to replace an earlier loan to purchase or improve the property will also qualify for relief provided the previous loan met all of conditions (*a*) to (*e*) above. If you borrowed money interest-free from relatives for improvements or towards the purchase of the house you could reduce the UK tax bill by taking a mortgage now to replace that interest-free borrowing. Bear in mind that this will also reduce your income unless the relative is prepared to make the funds released available to you or your children.

(iii) Most people find that they have to spend money on redecorations and possibly on buying some new furniture in order to let the house. Interest on a loan to meet these costs is not deductible.

(iv) If you changed your main residence after 15 March 1993 and, in addition to interest on a loan to buy the new residence, obtained interest relief for a mortgage transferred from your old home under the special rules for transfer of negative equity introduced in the March 1983 budget, that transferred loan will cease to qualify for relief once the house is let.

Losses

If your allowable expenses and interest exceed the rental income, the resultant loss can be carried forward and set against future rental income. A furnished letting loss can be set against any other Case VI income that you may have.

Income tax payment dates

There are two kinds of lettings:

(*a*) unfurnished letting — taxable under Schedule A;

(*b*) furnished letting — taxable under Case VI of Schedule D.

In both cases the tax is payable on 1 January in the year of assessment. For example, the tax on the rental income for the year to 5 April 1994 is payable on 1 January 1994. As the taxable income is not known at that date the tax is normally based on an estimated figure and adjusted later. For unfurnished lettings the law provides that the tax should be based initially on the previous year's income and adjusted to the correct figure after the end of the tax year. In both cases the amount of allowable interest is also normally estimated to arrive at the initial payment.

Tax deducted at source by tenant

If the tenant pays you the rent direct, he is required to deduct UK tax at 25% on the gross rent and pay that to the Inland Revenue. If, on the other hand, a UK agent collects the rent, the tenant does not deduct tax. The agent is then responsible for the tax on your net renta' income if you do not pay it.

As the agent is responsible for the tax, he would normally ensure that a reserve is made out of your rental income in order to pay the Inland Revenue. If you use a relative as your agent you should warn him that he will receive the tax assessments in his name and will be personally liable for the tax. Where no agent exists the Inland Revenue will enforce their collection rights upon the tenant even if he omits to deduct the income tax. It is not unusual for such a person to withhold future rent until his loss is made good. A good agent will know the likely tax payable and only reserve the minimum, paying you the balance.

Even if you decide not to engage an estate agent to manage the property, it would be sensible to have someone in the UK to act as your agent for this purpose. This could be a relative. Strictly speaking, the agent ought to receive the rent. In practice, the Inland Revenue do not enforce that. If someone in the UK puts himself forward as your agent they are normally happy to assess him as such. Even if you use an estate agent there can be cash flow advantages in appointing a relative as your tax agent as the estate agent will then probably be prepared to pay you the full rent (less his commission) with no reserve for tax, and the relative will probably be content to rely on you to pay the tax bill when it arrives. You will therefore have the use of the tax money — and depending on where you are living may be able to invest this tax free until the Revenue demand it. If the estate agent still insists on making a reserve for tax ask him to pay the rent into a bank account in the name of your UK relative and let the relative pay over the money to you.

If you do not use a UK agent at all, the 25% deduction is, in effect, a payment on account of your tax liability on the rental income. If it turns out to be excessive the balance will be repaid. You will, however, effectively pay tax quarterly on the gross income and will not obtain any tax relief for your expenses and mortgage interest until you produce your statement of income after the end of the tax year. Apart from the earlier payment of the tax that this gives rise to, it will mean that you are asking the Revenue for a refund. If there are any disputed items, or they have not yet agreed your non-resident status, this puts you in a weaker negotiating position than if you owe them money.

Furthermore, the Revenue do not have to pay repayment supplement to a non-UK resident (they have to pay this to a UK resident if they delay the tax repayment for more than a year). There is, therefore, an incentive to the Revenue to delay the repayment.

Holiday lets

Special tax rules apply to furnished holiday lettings. The letting is taxed as if it were a trade. This makes it easier to obtain a deduction for certain types of expense. More importantly, tax relief can be obtained for interest paid even if the rules for deducting interest set out above are not met. For a letting to qualify, the property must be let on short term lettings as holiday accommodation. It must be so available for at least 140 days in the tax year and must actually be let for at least 70. The property can be let for a longer period during the remaining five months of the year, e.g. a single tenant can occupy the property 'out of season'. Of course, it is difficult to find a series of short term tenants while you are abroad. However, there are organisations, such as English Country Cottages, that will do this for you.

Working abroad and MIRAS

Keeping a house in the UK will not in itself affect your UK tax residence status. You may still even be able to continue with your MIRAS relief.

Mortgage interest on house loans can be paid after deduction of tax at the basic rate (currently 25%), for the income tax year in which the payment becomes due, if the interest is:

Relevant loan interest paid by you being a

Qualifying borrower to a

Qualifying lender.

Your UK home

(*a*) *Relevant loan interest* is interest paid and payable in the UK to a 'qualifying lender' if it is interest on loans for the purchase of a residence, including a residential caravan, or houseboat in the UK, which, when the interest is paid, is used wholly, or to a substantial extent, as the only or main residence of the borrower. Before 5 April 1988 relief was also available for the purchase of a residence for a dependent relative or separated or former spouse and for home improvements. Interest relief will continue for such loans until they are repaid *or* replaced.

(*b*) A *qualifying borrower* is any individual who pays 'relevant loan interest'. There is an exception to this. If you, or your husband or wife, receive earnings that are exempt from UK tax, e.g. from certain Crown and Foreign Office appointments, neither of you can qualify for MIRAS. There are very few tax-exempt occupations.

(*c*) A *qualifying lender* includes a building society, a local authority, the Bank of England, an insurance company authorised to carry on long term business (e.g. life assurance) in the UK, a trustee savings bank, and any recognised bank or licensed deposit-taking institution authorised by the Treasury. MIRAS can only apply to interest on the first £30,000 of a loan to buy your principal private residence.

Even though you, as an expatriate, are no longer living in the UK and may have no UK income, you can still obtain MIRAS relief under an Inland Revenue concession. Where you are required by reason of your employment to move from your home to another place, either in the UK or abroad, for a period not expected to exceed four years, any property being bought with the aid of a mortgage which was being used as your only, or main residence *before* you went away, will be treated as remaining as such, provided that it can reasonably be expected to be so again on your return. If you will be away for more than four years you *cannot* claim this relief for the first four years of your expected absence; the maximum period is four years. But if there is a further temporary absence *after* the property has been reoccupied for a minimum period of three months, the four-year test will apply to the new period of absence *without* regard to the previous absence.

If you are already working abroad and purchase a property in the UK in the course of a leave period and use that property as an only, or main, residence for a period of at least three months *before* your return to the place of your overseas employment, you will be regarded as satisfying the condition that the property was used as your only, or main, residence before you went away.

If you let your property at a commercial rent whilst you are away, the benefit of the concession may be claimed if this is more favourable than a claim for relief against letting income. It will rarely be beneficial to do this.

If you go abroad but leave your family living in your UK house, MIRAS relief will not be subject to the above mentioned four-year time limit.

Capital gains tax

If you decide not to let the house but to sell it, no UK capital gains tax is payable provided that the house is your principal residence and has been such throughout your period of ownership. If the house does not satisfy this exemption, for example because you have two houses, or because it was let for a period, you should try to delay the sale until after you have gone abroad — or preferably, to be safe, until after 5 April following your departure from the UK. This is because if you sell the property in a tax year in which you are both not resident and not ordinarily resident (these terms are defined in Chapter 2) no UK capital gains tax is payable. Similarly, if you are planning to return to the UK and have a potential UK capital gains tax liability on your house, you may be better off selling it in the tax year before you return when you are not resident and not ordinary resident. In that way, you will avoid UK capital gains tax.

Provided a house has been your only or main residence at some time, the part of the gain attributable to the last three years of ownership is always exempt from capital gains tax.

There are a number of other rules about avoiding capital gains tax on a principal private residence (your own home) which are rather complex, but worth setting out in detail as this is often a key point for the working expatriate. Note that the capital gains tax rules for determining whether a property is your main residence do not apply to mortgage interest relief. That is a question of fact. Accordingly if you have two properties it is perfectly possible for one to be your principal residence for capital gains tax purposes, but for the other to qualify for mortgage interest relief.

More than one residence

If you own (or have available to you) more than one residence, you can elect which property should be regarded as the principal private residence for capital gains tax exemption. Such an election, which must be in writing, cannot apply for a period starting earlier than two years prior to the election. The election can be varied at any time, by giving a fresh notice, but again the variation cannot apply to any period over two years before the date of the new election. If no election is made, the Inspector of Taxes will choose, on the basis of what appears to him on his examination of the facts to be the main residence at the time. A second property which you let to bona fide tenants (or keep available for letting) is not treated as being available to you.

It must be borne in mind that you can have two residences available to you without owning them both. A home which you rent counts as a residence. An overseas flat or house — whether owned or rented — is also a residence. In practice, the Revenue tend to ignore your overseas residence for a period in which you are neither resident nor ordinarily resident in the UK. This is probably because that property is not within the scope of UK capital gains tax and is thus not another residence eligible for the exemption.

Your UK home

Time limit for election

The Revenue consider that the time limit for making the election is two years from the date on which the second residence first becomes available. Many people doubt this interpretation of the legislation and in practice elections are often accepted outside this limit (but not so as to operate more than two years retrospectively). It is understood that the Revenue have lost a case on this point before the Special Commissioners (a sort of tax appeals court which sits in private and whose decisions are not published) but intends to appeal to the High Court against the decision.

The Revenue have stated that where the taxpayer's interest in one of the properties has 'no more than a negligible capital value in the open market' and the taxpayer was unaware that an election could be made, they will extend the time limit to a reasonable time after the individual first becomes aware that he is entitled to make an election. They will then treat it as having effect from the date on which he acquired the second residence (Inland Revenue Extra-Statutory Concession D21). This concession is intended to cover the position where one of the properties is rented and the taxpayer did not realise that it constitutes a residence.

Husband and wife

A husband and wife can only have one main residence between them whilst they are living together. Where a private residence election affects both (e.g. joint ownership or where they each own a house) it must be given by both.

The capital gains computation

If you let your house (or leave it unoccupied) and sell it in a tax year when you are resident (or ordinarily resident) in the UK, you may have a capital gains tax liability for the period that it was let (or unoccupied). The part of the gain which remains free of capital gains tax is:

$$\text{total gain} \quad \times \quad \frac{\text{Number of weeks owned as principal private residence}}{\text{Number of weeks owned altogether}}$$

Remember that the number of weeks which count as your owning the house as your principal private residence always includes the last 36 months even if the property was let in that period. If you acquired the house before 31 March 1982 the period before that date is ignored, both in calculating the period during which you used the property as your private residence and in calculating the total period of ownership.

Periods of absence

For the purpose of the calculation above, certain periods of absence can also count as being periods when the house is your principal private residence, even though factually it was not (it can even have been let during that period).

These periods of absence are:

(*a*) Any period (or periods) not exceeding three years in total.

(*b*) Any period during which you worked overseas as an employee and all the duties of your employment were performed overseas. There is no time limit. If the husband works, but the wife does not, she would still be eligible for relief for her part ownership as long as she is living with her husband. This exemption does not apply if you are self-employed, nor does it apply if *any* of the duties were performed in the UK, however incidental they might be.

(*c*) Up to four years in total where your job requires you to live elsewhere (usually means more than 100 miles away).

There are several major traps if you want to take advantage of these periods of relief. You must meet each of the following three conditions:

(i) The house must be your main residence before the start of the period of absence.

(ii) It must be your main residence at some time *subsequent* to the period of absence. This means you must reoccupy the house before you sell it. There is no legal limit on the minimum time the house must be occupied. Some say that even one week is sufficient, so long as you have no other residence available. The Inland Revenue have stated that they believe the minimum period is three months, but their view has not been tested in the courts. There is one exception to having to reoccupy before you sell. There is an Inland Revenue concession where you are forced by your job to live somewhere else in the UK on your return.

(iii) You must have no other residence eligible for relief during the periods of absence. Of course, whilst overseas you are bound to have your overseas house available for your use as a residence. It is not at all clear if this is a residence 'eligible for relief' if you are not resident or ordinarily resident in the UK throughout the time you own it. In practice, the Inland Revenue tend to ignore it, although there is no guarantee that they will continue to adopt this approach. To be on the safe side, it is advisable to submit a written election to the Inland Revenue within two years of going overseas that your UK home is to be treated as your principal private residence.

Separation or divorce

Where a married couple separate or are divorced and one partner (usually the husband) moves out and subsequently, as part of a financial settlement, disposes of the home (or his interest in it) to the other, it can be regarded as continuing to be the husband's main residence during the period up to the date of the transfer providing that it continues to be the wife's main residence throughout that period and the husband does not have another property which he is claiming as his main residence (Inland Revenue Extra-Statutory Concession D6). It should particularly be noted that this applies only where the house is ultimately transferred to the wife. If it is sold and all or part of the proceeds paid to her, the concession will not operate. In such a case it may be preferable to transfer the property to the wife and allow her to sell it.

Buying whilst overseas

An expatriate who buys a UK house whilst he is overseas will not be able to meet the rule of using the house as his principal private residence both before and after a period of absence. Whilst the house may be eligible for relief for interest purposes, it cannot qualify for relief for capital gains tax purposes. Instead the expatriate should consider selling the house in the tax year before he returns, whilst he is both not resident and not ordinarily resident, when he is exempt from all capital gains tax. By concession, if you work full time overseas, the Revenue will regard you as both not resident and not ordinarily resident until the day you return to the UK, in which case it would appear unnecessary to sell the house in the tax year before you return; selling before you return, even in the same tax year, would be sufficient. However, if possible, you should not rely too heavily on this concession as it can always be refused.

Avoiding capital gains tax and keeping the house

As an alternative to selling to a third party in the tax year before return, you could transfer the house to a trust for yourself and your wife's benefit. The transfer into the trust will be tax free if you are not resident and not ordinarily resident in the UK at the time of the transfer, and any subsequent disposal by the trust will also be tax free if the property is occupied by you under the terms of the trust.

Appointing an accountant in the UK

It is well worth appointing an accountant who is experienced in lettings and capital gains tax to ensure that you minimise your tax liability. In addition, the accountant can take the responsibility of dealing with the Inland Revenue and minimising the amount of tax deducted at source by your agent. He can also receive all tax assessments direct from your Inspector of Taxes, ensure that appropriate appeals are made within the statutory 30-day limit, which can be difficult to meet from overseas, and prepare your annual UK tax return if you are required to submit one.

UK house, tax and financial planning

(a) *Expenses* — If you rent your house, ensure that you claim as many expenses as you can; including repairs, redecorations, telephone costs, gardener, wear and tear, accountancy costs.

(b) *Interest unlimited* — When you rent your house, the £30,000 loan limit does not apply. You can claim interest on an unlimited loan, as long as it meets certain requirements, i.e. it is a loan *not an overdraft*, from a UK bank and was only used to purchase or improve the property. A UK bank includes a UK branch of a foreign bank. However, part of the interest may be disallowed if the loan is not on usual commercial terms (a borrowing in excess of 70% of the valuation of the property may not be on usual commercial terms).

(c) *Repairs and redecorations* — Avoid carrying out any repairs or redecorations either before you first let the house or just after you have permanently stopped letting, as the costs will not be deductible. Only redecorate between lettings (or whilst the tenant is in occupation).

(*d*) *Avoiding capital gains tax* — There are lots of ways of avoiding capital gains tax, yet numerous pitfalls exist for the unwary. In particular, you ought to make an election, in writing, within two years of leaving the UK, that your UK house is to be regarded as your principal private residence.

(*e*) *MIRAS* — You may be able to continue with MIRAS if you are working abroad. See above for details.

(*f*) *Insurers* — Do not forget to inform your insurers of your moving plans, or you will be uninsured.

(*g*) *Lease* — Use a lawyer! There are too many pitfalls.

Chapter 9

The concept of domicile

Residence and ordinary residence are transitory concepts. It is easy to change one's residence and relatively easy to change one's ordinary residence. It is also possible to be both resident and ordinarily resident simultaneously in more than one country. Domicile is a different matter.

Unlike residence where different meanings have been given to the term for different purposes, domicile is a basic legal concept applying not only to tax but to other branches of the law such as the validity of marriages, legitimacy, adoption and intestate succession. A person's domicile connects him (for the purpose of UK law) with a particular legal system, that of the country in which he is domiciled, and limits the extent to which the UK courts can intervene in some aspects of his personal life. It would cause immense confusion if a person could be domiciled in more than one place simultaneously or if his domicile could alter from year to year. It needs to be an almost permanent concept, so that a person's domicile will change only if there is a radical and permanent (or, rather, likely to be permanent) change in the country with which he is connected.

This is probably an appropriate place to mention that whilst it is convenient to talk of the country in which someone is domiciled, and this book adopts that convention, it is not strictly correct; the purpose of domicile is to tie someone to a particular system of law rather than a country. For example, if a person leaves England to retire in Wales he will not change his domicile; England and Wales have a common legal system so one is domiciled in England and Wales rather than an individual one of those countries. On the other hand, a person who leaves England to retire in Scotland or in Northern Ireland may well change his domicile as those countries have separate legal systems. A person cannot be domiciled in the UK; he must be domiciled in England and Wales, in Scotland or in Northern Ireland.

This distinction can be extremely important if one moves to a country that is organised on a federal system. For example, you cannot be domiciled in the United States; you will be domiciled in one of the individual States. If a person leaves the UK to retire to Florida and after a few years decides to move to New England, and perhaps later moves to California, he is likely to find that he will remain UK domiciled. Even though he has no intention of returning to the UK or, indeed, of leaving the USA, he will not have demonstrated an intention to reside permanently in any one American State and will therefore have retained his UK domicile.

It will be apparent that domicile is not the same thing as nationality. Nationality is an accident of birth. Changing your nationality is indicative of a change of domicile, but will not necessarily bring about such a change.

The meaning of domicile

The basic rule is that a person is domiciled in the country in which he has his home permanently or indefinitely. This is often described as the country which a person regards as his homeland. It is frequently described as the place where a person intends to die. This is why an emigrant is sometimes advised to buy a burial plot in the country in which he wishes to establish his domicile — although it is doubtful if in practice this will influence the Inland Revenue's view, apart from acting as an indicator that the person is worried that he remains domiciled in England.

Your place of domicile does not have to be the country with which you have your closest personal association. A person can live in a country for many years and still remain domiciled elsewhere. For example, it was fairly common in the past for an expatriate to spend his working life in Africa or India intending to return to the UK to retire. Such a person remains UK domiciled. It is very difficult to establish a change of domicile.

A person has a *domicile of origin*, which is normally the domicile of his father at the time of that person's birth. If your father's domicile changed before you reached age 16, then you will have acquired his new domicile. A woman who married prior to 1 January 1974 automatically acquired her husband's domicile — effectively as a domicile of choice.

The domicile of origin can be altered to become another country, called the *domicile of choice*. However, this is not easy. Furthermore, if you lose your domicile of choice, e.g. by leaving your adopted country and moving to a third country, you automatically re-acquire your domicile of origin. The sort of things that the Revenue look at to consider where a person is domiciled are the country of which he has a passport, or a driving licence, or in which he has made a will, has arranged to be buried, is a club member, owns credit cards, personal insurances, bank accounts, and property, and has family.

Domicile is largely a question of intention. Unlike with virtually all other aspects of tax, where it is up to the taxpayer to disprove the Revenue's claims, it is up to the person alleging a change of domicile to establish it. If you are domiciled in England and retire to Spain you must prove that you have ceased to be domiciled here. If you were initially domiciled in Norway, came to England and retired in Spain it is up to the Revenue to show that you acquired an English domicile when you came here. If they can do this it is then up to you to show that you lost it when you moved to Spain.

If you are going abroad to work, even if the job looks set to last indefinitely, you are unlikely to cease to be English domiciled; you will need to show that you are emigrating permanently to the new country.

The concept of domicile

It is clearly easier to establish a change of domicile if you are retiring abroad, as the act of retiring is itself an indication that you intend to make the new country your home for the remainder of your life. Even then it is by no means a foregone conclusion that you will be able to shed your UK domicile. And remember that domicile is only likely to matter in such a case for inheritance tax purposes — so when the Revenue challenge whether you abandoned your English domicile you will not be around to explain what your intention was. Thus, courts will have to draw a conclusion from other available evidence. Take especial care what you say to your friends and business colleagues. They may be called upon to give evidence after you have died!

George Furse was an American. He brought his wife and family to the UK in 1923 following the death of her parents as her doctor had recommended a change to help her over the loss. They bought a farm in Sussex and George lived there for the rest of his life. He died in 1963 aged 80. George remained a US citizen. He frequently visited the USA. Right up until 1963, the year of his death, his visits were for between one and two months a year. From 1946 to 1964 his eldest son worked in New York. The family home in America which his wife had inherited from her parents and where George and his wife had lived prior to coming to the UK was retained throughout and they visited it regularly. The house was let on short leases to enable George and his wife to resume residence on short notice when they decided to return to the US. When they were driving away from the house in 1963 George had remarked to his son that when he came back and lived in the house he would have to install a new central heating system as the present one was too expensive. There could not have been much more evidence to show an intention to return to the US; yet George was held to have died domiciled in the UK.

Why? George's US bank manager was called to give evidence. He said 'I personally was convinced that he was coming back to the United States ultimately and I . . . would always ask him "When are you coming back?" and he always wanted to stay a little bit longer. He liked his farm very much, but he did talk about coming back to the United States to live here until he died'. He later said 'I was convinced that he was coming back. Personally, I thought he was postponing it too long, but there was no doubt in my mind that his intention was to return'. The judge concluded, largely on the basis of what the bank manager had said, that George did not have a real intention of returning to the United States; he had left it too long for this to be a serious possibility. It was a vague notion; coupled with the congeniality of his farm in Sussex it was not even a hope to return. George had indicated that he would go back to America when he was no longer able to live an active physical life on the farm, but the judge felt this was such an indefinite concept that it could not be regarded as imposing any clear limitation on the period of his residence in the UK. If George had not become so friendly with his bank manager the result might well have been different!

In late 1977 Sir Charles Clore took up residence in Monaco. He took professional advice as to what he needed to do to show that he had abandoned his English domicile and acquired a Monagesque one. He followed that advice. He put both of his UK houses up for sale. He retired as chairman of the English public company, Sears Holdings. He took steps to strengthen his association with Monaco, bought a large apartment there and moved furniture and objets d'art from his former house in the UK to furnish it. The judge admitted that if these factors had stood alone it might have been enough to satisfy him that Sir Charles had formed a settled intention to remain permanently in Monaco and had thus become domiciled there.

Unfortunately they did not stand alone. The friends he had left behind were there to damn him. Lady Milford Haven said that for two years before his death Sir Charles was unwell and that he was unhappy in Monaco and had often said that he would really like to return to England permanently and accept the tax consequences. Mr Jarvis Astaire said that Sir Charles had told him that he was thinking of changing his mind and returning to live in England regardless of the tax consequences, and added the opinion that he believed that Sir Charles had meant what he had said and would have returned to England had he lived. Mr Leonard Sainer, who besides being a close friend of Sir Charles was his solicitor and in that role presumably intimately involved in the scheme for him to change his domicile to Monaco, said that Sir Charles was always changing his mind about where he wanted to settle and that after leaving England he never settled in one place. For good measure he volunteered his personal opinion that Sir Charles did not in fact acquire a domicile of choice in Monaco. The judge concurred with that opinion. He held that Sir Charles had died domiciled in England. If Sir Charles had kept his thoughts to himself instead of voicing his misgivings to his friends it is probable that he would have been found to have acquired a Monagesque domicile.

Proposed changes to the law on domicile

In the mid 1980s the Law Commission reviewed the law of domicile. They reported to the Government in 1987, setting out some suggested changes.

Like the reports of many government Commissions, it looked as if this had been quietly buried somewhere in Whitehall. However, the Government recently announced that they have accepted the recommendations of the Law Commission and would introduce legislation as soon as parliamentary time permits.

The likely changes

The main recommendations of the Law Commission were as follows.

(*a*) The domicile of a child should be that of the country with which he is most closely connected. This would normally be the country in which his parents are domiciled and, if he lives with one parent, would be the country in which that parent is domiciled. (At present a child's domicile follows that of his father.)

(*b*) The normal civil standard proof of a balance of probabilities should apply in all disputes about domicile. (At present it is for the person who is seeking to establish a change of domicile to prove that such a change has taken place.)

(c) No higher standard of proof should be required where it is contended that a person has changed his domicile of origin, i.e. his domicile at birth, than where it is claimed that he has changed a domicile of choice. (At present a domicile of origin has a far more enduring character than a domicile of choice, so it is more difficult to show a change.)

(d) If a person intends to settle in a country for an indefinite period, this should suffice to show that he has acquired a domicile in that country. However, there should be no presumption that once a person has stayed in a country for more than seven years, he should be regarded as having become domiciled there. (In recent years the Inland Revenue have tended to apply the test of intention to settle for an indefinite period under the current legislation in any event.)

(e) Where a person acquires a domicile of choice and leaves the country in which he is domiciled, that domicile of choice should continue until he obtains a new domicile elsewhere. (At present his domicile of origin, i.e. his domicile at birth, revives when a person loses a domicile of choice.)

(f) Amendments to the law of domicile should not have retrospective effect. However, they should apply to determine a person's domicile from the time that the legislation comes into force.

(g) If a person settles in a federal country but not in a particular subdivision of it (e.g. a US state), he will be treated as domiciled in the subdivision with which he has the closest connection.

Domicile is a concept that applies in many areas of family law and the Law Commission specifically recommended that the legislation should not be implemented until some months after Royal Assent, in order to give taxpayers and their advisers full opportunity to consider how the change might affect their individual circumstances. In most cases, the proposed changes are unlikely to affect a person's domicile for tax purposes. The main changes relate to the domicile of children, although there is a little more emphasis than at present on the concept that an intention to stay in a place indefinitely is indicative of a domicile in that country. The Revenue have said that the changes would take place from a 5 April, probably the one after the date on which the Act is passed.

Establishing your domicile

How can you be certain that you have succeeded in abandoning your UK domicile and acquired a new domicile elsewhere? Unfortunately you can't! The Inland Revenue's policy is not to give a ruling on a person's domicile unless and until it becomes relevant for tax purposes. It is relatively easy for a person who is resident in the UK and who claims to be domiciled elsewhere to make the question relevant; he can generate some overseas income and not remit it to the UK. If he is UK domiciled the income will be taxable. If he is not then it won't. The Revenue will therefore have to rule on his domicile (unless the amount of income is so small that they simply say that they won't tax it but reserve their position on whether he is UK domiciled). If you are non-UK resident and ordinarily resident you are not taxable on overseas income or gains in any event so domicile is irrelevant. You could make a gift of a non-UK asset but the value would need to exceed the inheritance tax nil rate band and the gift would need to be to a company or certain types of trust to generate a tax liability and thus make the question of your domicile relevant.

You could, alternatively, become UK resident again for one year by breaking the 183-day residence rule and test your domicile position during that year. However, this could be a self-defeating strategy. Becoming resident could itself cast doubt on whether you have really abandoned your UK domicile.

If you can find a way to make your domicile status relevant for tax purposes the Inland Revenue will send you a domicile questionnaire. Their standard questionnaire is reproduced below.

HMIT

REF:

NAME:

In order that your domicile may be determined, please provide the following information –

a. Where and when you were born.

b. In what country your father was domiciled at the date of your birth.

c. What changes, if any, took place in your father's domicile during your minority.

d. If your father is dead, please state his full names and place of his death.

e. In what country you consider yourself to be domiciled and on what grounds.

f. Is any accommodation retained for your use in that territory and, if so, what is the address, nature of the accommodation and is it kept in a permanent state of readiness for occupation by yourself.

g. Your business, personal, social or other connections (if any) with that country.

h. If you are married, the date of marriage, where your spouse and children (if any) reside.

j. i. Date you took up residence in UK.

   ii. What periods you have spent in the UK during each of the past 10 years.

k. i. Whether you have a place of abode in the UK.

   ii. Is accommodation retained for your use in the UK and, if so, the address and type of accommodation.

   iii. If accommodation was held as an owner or tenant.

   iv. If the latter, was the letting furnished and what was the period of the lease?

l. i. If you were born abroad, your reasons and object in coming to the United Kingdom, or whether in connection with business or employment here, or the education of your children.

   ii. Dates of birth of children concerned and/or details of the business or employment and nature of position held.

m. Your intentions for the future and if not to stay in the UK the circumstances in which it is envisaged that residence will cease.

Signed ....

Full Name ....

Date ....

NOTE: In the case of a country with a federal system, the particular State, Province, etc. should also be stated.

The reasons for questions (*a*) and (*b*) are obvious. Question (*c*) is directed towards finding if you changed your domicile as an infant — you will automatically have acquired your father's new domicile if he changed his. The date of your father's death is relevant if you were an infant at the time but probably not otherwise. His place of death should not affect your own domicile; the Revenue probably want this as, if it is somewhere other than the place where you claim he was domiciled when you were an infant, they may want to look more closely at your claim. This is particularly likely if he died in the UK.

Question (*e*) is, of course, one of the key questions. If you do not feel that you can answer it adequately in the half inch space that has been provided for your answer it is better to give a full answer on a separate sheet of paper than to try to encapsulate an explanation in two lines. Questions (*f*) and (*g*) are very important and should be answered as fully as possible. Again, you probably need more space. The place of residence of your spouse and children is important only insofar as it could cast doubt on your professed domicile since you might be expected to want to live with them. However, as domicile is a question of long term intention, their short term residence ought not to affect the position. If the answer is unhelpful to your case, try to explain it away when you complete the form rather than leaving the Revenue to build up their suspicions first.

Question (*j*) is directed towards showing that you are domiciled in the UK. However, the questions are really more appropriate to test your residence. Accordingly, there is no need to be too concerned about the answers, but it is sensible to answer them in such a way as to point out that you are temporarily resident in the UK and to stress the temporary nature of your stay. Question (*l*) is another important one. This looks at whether your stay in the UK is for a specific purpose which will come to an end, or if it is indefinite. If it is the latter you will almost certainly be regarded as UK domiciled. Take care with this answer. If you say that you are in the UK to educate your children you may have a problem if you remain here after they have finished their schooling. It is best to try to give more than one reason if possible.

The final question, (*m*), is the most important. Do not say that your intentions are uncertain. Do not say that you intend to remain here indefinitely. You need to say that you intend to return to the country where you claim to be domiciled on the occurrence of a specific event, such as when your working life is over.

Chapter 10

UK inheritance tax

Inheritance tax is a cross between death duties and gift tax. It is payable on the value of all of the assets that you own on death — plus those that you have given away in the previous seven years. It is also payable on certain lifetime gifts — in particular, on gifting assets to trustees when you set up a discretionary trust. If you have a life interest in a settlement (or a *right* to receive the income from a settlement) you are also treated as owning the assets in the settlement for this purpose. The value of those assets will be added to the value of your own assets to calculate the tax due.

Inheritance tax liabilities have nothing to do with whether or not you are resident or ordinarily resident in the UK. Instead, UK inheritance tax (which we shall call 'IHT') is based on your domicile.

IHT may be payable by your estate on your death and on gifts made in your lifetime.

Domicile is explained in Chapter 9. You are domiciled in the country that you regard as your homeland. If you are domiciled in the UK, then no matter where you live you are liable for IHT on your worldwide assets, *including all of your assets in your new country or elsewhere*.

It is very, very difficult to change your domicile. If you are not domiciled in the UK but in, say, Spain, you can still be liable to IHT, but only on assets located in the UK.

If you intend to return to the UK at some stage, however far in the future, you are unlikely to shed your UK domicile. You should assume that you will die domiciled in the UK and that IHT will have to be paid on your worldwide assets on your death. If you are emigrating to another country it is possible to become domiciled there — but you will need to take active steps to build up evidence to show that you have severed your connections with the UK and now regard your new country as your homeland. The more trips back to the UK you make, particularly to visit friends and relatives, the harder it will be to convince the Inland Revenue that you have ceased to be UK domiciled.

Even if you manage to change your domicile, you must not then die too quickly. This is because, for inheritance tax purposes only, you will be taxed as if you were domiciled in the UK if you were UK domiciled at any time *in the three years prior* to an 'event' (i.e. gift or death). In other words, UK domicile for inheritance tax purposes persists for three years *after* the acquisition of a new domicile.

It should be emphasised that this special rule does not apply for income tax or capital gains tax purposes. (You are also deemed to be domiciled in the UK for inheritance tax purposes if you are *resident in the UK for 17 of the 20 consecutive tax years* ending with the tax year in which there is an 'event' (gift or death).) Residence has the same meaning as described earlier. However, this special rule applies to people coming to the UK rather than to those leaving it (other than non-UK domiciled individuals who have been resident in the UK for 16 years and are going abroad for four years to avoid breaching this condition).

If you feel confident that you have ceased to be UK domiciled, remember that this is not sufficient to avoid IHT. You also have to make sure that you do not own any assets in the UK — or at least that such assets do not have a combined value of £150,000 or more. Non-UK domiciled persons are liable to UK inheritance tax on all assets located in the UK, even if they've never visited the UK! A UK asset will include a loan to a person who is resident in the UK, shares in a UK company (unless they are registered in a foreign register or they are bearer shares and the share certificate is held outside the UK) and money in a UK bank account, (although there is an exception for accounts maintained in a foreign currency) as well as a house or other property in the UK.

If you need to invest in UK assets they can be insulated from inheritance tax relatively easily by putting them into an offshore company — as the assets you will then own will be the shares of the company or a debt due from the company, neither of which are UK assets. However, you need to weigh the potential IHT liability against the costs of running the company for the 10, 20, 30 or whatever years until you die. You should also be conscious that maintaining a large proportion of your assets in the UK, even if indirectly through an offshore company, will make it more difficult to show that you have severed your connection with the UK; if you have not done so you will not have shed your UK domicile at all.

Rates of tax

IHT bites quickly and hard. It is not only a tax for the very rich, as quite modest estates are liable to the tax.

1993–94 rates

Cumulative chargeable

Gross transfers	Rate %
£1 — 150,000	0
over £150,000	40%

Thus, the tax on a £500,000 estate is £140,000.

The amount taxable at nil per cent is generally referred to as the nil rate band. There are technical reasons why the Government should have chosen to impose tax at nil per cent rather than exempt the first £150,000 from tax. An affidavit certifying the assets you own has to be submitted to the Inland Revenue by your personal representatives or the donees or trustees and the tax paid (with some exceptions) before a grant of probate of your will can be obtained, and therefore before any of your assets can be distributed to beneficiaries.

IHT is not payable on a death to the extent that the assets pass to a surviving spouse. Accordingly, if both husband and wife leave all their assets to one another no IHT will be payable until the second death. However, as this aggregates all of the assets in the hands of the last to die, it can be an inefficient solution as (unless lifetime gifts are made by the surviving spouse who also continues to live for a further seven years) it will increase the overall tax burden and thus reduce the money passing to your children. If one spouse is domiciled in the UK and the other is not, the exemption does not apply on the death of the UK domiciled spouse. Only the first £55,000 of assets passing to the surviving spouse is exempt in such a case (and even that is reduced if gifts were made to the spouse in the previous seven years).

Shedding your UK domicile

In order to shed his UK (or rather English, Welsh, Scottish or Northern Irish) domicile a person will need to build up evidence to show both that he has abandoned his UK domicile of origin and that he has acquired a new domicile of choice. If a person emigrates to another country where he then lives permanently until he dies, it is generally easy to show that he has acquired a new domicile of choice. However, most people who emigrate for tax reasons do not do this. They tend to use the new country as a base and spend significant amounts of time in other countries including England, etc. Indeed, many emigrants leave with the firm view in mind that they are allowed to visit England for up to 90 days a year. Whilst, in general, this is true as far as income tax is concerned, such a pattern of life is likely to be taken as a strong indication that the taxpayer has not abandoned his UK domicile of origin. Saving tax, particularly death duties, should not dominate a person's life and unless an emigrant has a genuine intention to sever his connection with England it may be sensible to accept that he will not shed his UK domicile and will have to give the Inland Revenue their due at the end of the day. If a person wishes to safeguard his estate he needs to accept that this is likely to require a radical change in his lifestyle and that he will need to genuinely sever most of his connections with this country. The acquisition of a domicile of choice is not easy. Even if one is acquired it is held on a slender thread and constant vigilance may be needed to ensure that it is not lost and the domicile of origin automatically revived. The prospective emigrant should take as many as possible of the following steps in order to evidence the abandonment of an English domicile and the acquisition of a new domicile.

(a) Dispose of all private residences in the UK. If a person has a residence here this is suggestive of an intention to live here at least some of the time and thus casts doubt on the intention to die elsewhere.

(b) Buy a private residence in the new country. If a person stays in hotels or guest houses this suggests that he is living temporarily in the new country and has not made a firm decision not to return to England.

(c) Make a will under the law of the new country. This is suggestive of an intention that one's assets will be primarily in that country on death, one's trusted executor will be there and so will one's personal records. Many people recommend buying a burial plot in the new country. I am personally sceptical of this. Burial plots are generally cheap and the acquisition of a plot is just as likely be looked on by the Revenue as a device to pretend that one is domiciled in the new country (and that accordingly one is worried about being regarded as English domiciled) as to be seen as evidence of an intention to die in the new country.

(*d*) Take the nationality of the new country. At a minimum, if permission is needed to live permanently in that country, ensure that this is obtained.

(*e*) Give up British nationality even if the new country permits dual nationality.

(*f*) Join clubs and social organisations in the new country. The place where a person spends his social life is likely to be the place he regards as home.

(*g*) Resign from clubs and social organisations in the UK.

(*h*) Dispose of UK investments — or at least reduce them to a small percentage of overall investments.

(*i*) Acquire investments in the new country. This is not, of itself, of great importance as a prudent person will invest his funds where he feels that they are safe and produce a good return. Nevertheless, if a person leaves the bulk of his assets in England this casts doubt on his intention to give up his English domicile.

(*j*) Do not take out subscriptions to English newspapers and magazines. This suggests a reluctance to abandon the taxpayer's English domicile.

(*k*) Close English bank accounts.

(*l*) Maintain a bank account in the new country. This is probably a practical necessity in any event.

(*m*) Try to build up a circle of friends in the new country. An involvement in local affairs suggests an intention to become part of the local community in the new country.

(*n*) When visiting England avoid giving an impression of homesickness: after your death your family and friends may be called to give evidence of your attitude to the UK.

(*o*) Do not retain directorships of UK companies.

(*p*) Do not retain business interests in the UK.

(*q*) Do not vote in UK elections.

(*r*) Exercise any right to vote that you may have in the new country.

(*s*) Consider what other steps, in the light of your particular circumstances, can be taken either to sever all connections with the UK or to build up connections with the new country. Social, political and personal connections are generally more important than business connections.

None of the above is vital in itself. However, the courts will seek to look at all the factors that can be put in evidence to determine whether there is a settled intention to reside permanently in the new country. Connections with England that are retained militate against the existence of such an intention unless it can be shown that there are specific investment, commercial or family reasons for any such connections. Unless the courts find convincing evidence of a settled intention to reside permanently in the new country they will hold that the emigrant remained domiciled in England.

As one of the major problems with establishing domicile is generally lack of evidence it may also be worth considering making a Statutory Declaration notarised to the effect that one is leaving the UK with the intention of living permanently abroad and that, whilst one may in the future make occasional visits to this country, there is no intention ever to resume residence here.

Sixteen ways to avoid or reduce UK inheritance tax

(1) *Giving it away tax free* — If you give away no more than £150,000 there is no inheritance tax to pay. After seven years you can give a further £150,000 (and so on every seven years and one day). Both husband and wife each have their own £150,000 limit. In addition, each year, you (and your wife) can give away £3,000. Thus, over a period of seven years and one day you can give away:

	Husband	*Wife*	*Total*
2 x £150,000	£300,000	£300,000	£600,000
8 x £3,000	£24,000	£24,000	£48,000
	£324,000	£324,000	£648,000

(2) *Giving away 'in consideration of marriage'* — Each parent can give away an additional £5,000 to a child or £2,500 to a grandchild and £1,000 to anyone else on the recipient's marriage. The rules are very strict and professional advice on how to arrange the gifts should be taken — in advance of the marriage.

(3) *Normal income expenditure* — Regular amounts can be gifted as 'normal expenditure out of income' representing perhaps as much as 10% — 50% of annual income free of IHT. Careful use of this exemption can significantly reduce, even eliminate, your IHT problem. You must be left with enough income to live on. You cannot give away all of your income under this exemption and live off capital.

(4) *Unlimited lifetime transfers to individuals or trusts* — You can give unlimited amounts to any other individual during your lifetime or to some trusts (but not discretionary trusts). The gift could be money, shares in a company, or any other asset. However, if the donor is not both non-UK resident and non-ordinarily resident, the gift may attract capital gains tax. In some cases an election can be made not to pay tax on the gain (with the recipient of the gift undertaking to pay it when he sells the asset). Professional advice should be taken if substantial gifts are contemplated. In the event of the donor dying within

seven years, there will be IHT to pay but at reduced rates. If he dies within three years of the gift, there is no tax reduction. Trusts can be very useful for giving wealth to grandchildren under the age of 25.

(5) *Avoid 'reservation'* — gifts 'with reservation' will not be exempt from tax under (1) to (4) above. The gift must be given absolutely. A gift where the donor enjoys any interest or retains any rights is not acceptable. Thus, the gift of a house with rights for the donor to reside in it is not an absolute gift, nor is the gift of shares with the right to an exceptional salary from the company. This is a very technical area. It is possible to carve out for oneself a right to reside in the house prior to making the gift. Professional advice should be sought before attempting such a gift.

(6) *Tax discount* — Even if you are going to pay the tax, if you give away at least three years *before* your death the tax rates are reduced (maximum 32% instead of 40% after 3 years, 24% after 4, 16% after 5 and 8% after 6 years).

(7) *Keep the back door open* — You could give away any amounts into a discretionary trust where you are not a beneficiary but other relatives — including your wife — are the named beneficiaries. By appointing yourself a trustee you could remain in effective control of the assets in the trust. As long as your gifts are within the limits set out in (1) above, there will be no IHT due. Careful draftsmanship and planning is required in this area.

Your wife can also establish a similar trust or series of trusts.

(8) *Life insurance* — Life insurance can be a surprisingly cheap way of covering any eventual IHT bill. For example, if your estate were worth £350,000, you and your wife were aged 50 and you leave all your assets to her on your death, the IHT payable at the second death would be £80,000. For an annual outlay of about £900 p.a, a tax free benefit under trust of over £90,000 can be obtained, and indeed, is projected to be worth over £220,000 on the death of the survivor at the age of 85.

Alternatively, at age 65, you could invest £25,000 in a last survivor investment bond (under trust) with life cover of a sum assured at second death of just under £100,000.

These costs can be reduced considerably by purchasing term life insurance which provides cover for a fixed number of years only. You choose how long. During the time you pay regular premiums; if you die, the policy pays out a fixed amount. If you survive to the end of the term, you get nothing back and premiums cease.

The problem with such insurance is ensuring that you die during the term of the policy! It can be very expensive for an elderly person to take out life assurance cover if you need to start a new 'whole of life' policy after your term policy has expired. Term assurance is best for relatively young people who can obtain a higher level of cover than they could afford under a whole of life policy. It can also be useful if you are planning to pass surplus assets to your children when you reach retirement age, but are reluctant to do so until you are in a position to assess how much you need to retain for your retirement.

Life insurance should not be written for your own benefit, it should be for the benefit of your wife or children or other beneficiaries. If this is not done, the insurance proceeds will themselves be liable to inheritance tax on your death, so 40% will be wasted. Life assurance premiums normally qualify as normal expenditure out of income even if you die before paying the second premium so that a 'gift' of the policy to your wife in this way will not attract inheritance tax.

As well as providing funds to pay the tax, life assurance will often produce cash for your widow more quickly than cash in your estate can be made available to her, as the money in your estate cannot be utilised until after probate has been obtained.

(9) *Equalising estates* — If the husband's estate is worth £500,000, then the IHT payable is £140,000, leaving £360,000 as the net estate. If the estates are equalized between husband and wife, i.e. the husband transfers £250,000 of assets to the wife so that their estates are of equal magnitude and each wills their estate to children/grandchildren/relatives, then the IHT payable is reduced to £80,000, saving £60,000. This is the maximum saving (i.e. 40% of £150,000 — the wife's nil rate IHT band). If the combined assets exceed £300,000 there is, in fact, no point in transferring more assets to the wife than is needed to bring the value of her estate up to £150,000. The gift to the wife obviously needs to be genuine: there must not be strings attached to it.

(10) *Residential property* — If a donor gifts a property and continues to stay in it, or even visit it for other than short periods, the gifts will normally give rise to a reservation of benefit (see (5) above) unless a commercial rent is paid.

Various solutions are possible. If a leasehold can be created on a freehold property, it is possible *but not certain* that the gift of the freehold interest will be outside the donor's estate. However, once the leasehold has expired, the donor would have to vacate the property or pay a commercial rent.

If a property can be sold and the proceeds gifted, the beneficiary may be able to purchase a new property and allow the donor to live there rent free without there being a reservation of benefit.

(11) *Company shares, business assets and woodlands* — Private company (i.e. close company) shares are eligible for a special 100% business relief, i.e. the value is reduced by 100% for IHT purposes, thus in effect exempting it from the tax, for a controlling interest (which is defined as a shareholding of at least 25% for this purpose) or 50% for a lesser interest. The property must have been owned for at least two years before it attracts this relief. Another way to reduce the value is to form another company (owned by the ultimate beneficiaries) and build this new company up in preference to the existing one. Assets used in Lloyd's

underwriting or in any other business you carry on are also eligible for the 100% reduction.

Certain other property used by a private company or a partnership is also eligible for business relief at 100%. Similar rules apply to agricultural property. Woodlands can also qualify for the relief. In addition there is a special relief for growing timber (although it is often not attractive to claim it as there is a sting in the tail — you can pay IHT ultimately on a higher amount). It is more beneficial to gift other assets during your life in preference to assets attracting these special reliefs.

(12) *Giving away shares in newly formed companies* — Making gifts of assets likely to appreciate is an effective way of reducing your estate. A gift is valued at the date it is gifted so even if you pay IHT on the gift, e.g. because you die within seven years — you are giving away the subsequent growth in value free of tax. Giving away shares in a newly formed company to trusts for your children's benefit can make sense. Even where the asset qualifies for the 100% business relief, are you confident that this relief will continue indefinitely?

(13) *Giving away when cheap* — One of the few benefits of 1987's stock market crash was that it reduced values for IHT purposes. The same thing has happened to property values currently. Look for opportunities to give assets away while prices are depressed as, if IHT became payable, the gift will be valued at the lower level.

(14) *Generation skipping* — If your own children are already wealthy, pass your estate onto your grandchildren instead. This skips a generation and thus avoids IHT on the same assets on your childrens' death.

(15) *Writing in trust* — Life insurances and death benefits from pension schemes may form part of your estate for IHT purposes. You can set up the policy to pay the benefits direct to your children, in which case they do not attract IHT. If you are concerned that your wife, should she survive you, should receive the benefit, you can write the policy benefits in trust for your children unless your wife survives you by 30 days, in which case she receives the benefit.

(16) *Interest free loans* — An interest free loan is not a gift as long as:

(*a*)   the loan is documented;

(*b*)   the loan is repayable on demand or on very short notice.

Gifts into settlements

Inheritance tax on settlements (or trusts, the two words are for all practical purposes interchangeable) is very complex and professional advice needs to be sought if you intend to use a settlement in relation to inheritance tax planning. If someone has an interest in possession, i.e. a right to income from the settlement (as opposed to being entitled to it only at the discretion of the trustees) he is treated as owning all of the assets in the settlement for IHT purposes. A discretionary settlement is itself within the scope of IHT. It pays IHT on distributing assets to beneficiaries and every ten years has to pay IHT on all of the assets that it then owns. The tax is at a special rate — which is graduated but is a maximum of 6% of the value of the assets. This can be looked on rather like a parking fee — you pay 6% of the value of the assets on each tenth anniversary of the creation of the settlement as a fee for being able to park the assets outside the scope of IHT, as they will not come into the estate of any individual on his death. Special IHT privileges attach to a hybrid form of trust called an accumulation and maintenance settlement. This is basically a discretionary settlement for the benefit of children under 25 which automatically converts into an interest in possession settlement for the child when he reaches 25. The ten-yearly discretionary settlement charge does not arise.

Because of the way the charge is calculated, no tax is normally payable on payments to beneficiaries from a discretionary settlement, or on the conversion of the settlement to an interest in possession trust, during the first ten years if the original value of the assets settled (before business or agricultural property relief) was less than the IHT nil rate band. Such a trust can be useful in holding assets in suspense for up to ten years as beneficiaries will then be older, their needs or ambitions may have become clearer, and you will then be in a better position to decide what you want to happen to the funds. If you want to settle assets for your grandchildren there can be advantages in starting with a discretionary settlement and converting this into an accumulation and maintenance settlement shortly before the end of the tenth year.

An overseas settlement is within the scope of inheritance tax to the same extent as a UK one. There is one major exception. If the settlor was not domiciled in the UK at the time that he created the settlement, IHT does not apply to non-UK assets of the settlement. Accordingly, if you are going permanently overseas and are likely to cease to be domiciled in the UK, creating a settlement whilst you are UK domiciled may not be a good idea. The same applies to a settlement created in the first three years after going abroad as, for IHT purposes, you are deemed to remain UK domiciled in that period.

Wills

This may be a convenient point to mention wills. The consequence of dying without a will can be serious. A UK will made before a marriage, or remarriage, is normally ineffective — you have to make another one. If you die, without a will and domiciled in the UK, there are set rules as to where your estate goes (called the Intestate Succession provisions). The advantage of having a will is that your estate will be distributed as you want it to be, the administrators of the estate will be chosen by you, and the estate is likely to be distributed faster and at lower costs. The statutory rules can give rise to an unnecessary inheritance tax liability. They are also unlikely to deal with your assets as you would have wished. For example, many people believe that if they die without a will all of their assets will pass to their widow. This is not the case unless the total assets are less than £75,000 if one has children, or less than £125,000 if there are no children.

Professional advice should be taken to ensure that all of the estate is properly disposed of and partial intestacy is avoided. Careful consideration should be given to what would happen if the person to whom you are leaving your estate (e.g. your wife) were to die just before or just after you. You should also be aware that in the UK a dependant has a right to make a claim against the estate if reasonable financial provision is not made for that person and this right can override the provision of you will. You may wish to create a trust on your death if, for example, you want the income to go to your spouse but the capital to go to your children when your spouse dies.

A special kind of UK will, called a discretionary will trust, enables you to alter your will without going through all of the formalities of drawing up a new will as circumstances alter. A similar result, with a more favourable IHT position, can be obtained by your will creating a trust with a revocable interest in possession to your widow. The usefulness of these techniques in your particular circumstances should be carefully discussed with your professional advisers.

If you have put assets into settlements during your lifetime, these assets are not governed by your will; they will continue to be dealt with in accordance with the trust deed. However, when deciding how you want your estate to be divided on your death do not overlook such settlements; you may want to coordinate the two. For example, if you want to leave substantial legacies to people other than your spouse, it may save IHT if you make them beneficiaries of your settlement and provide in your letter of wishes to the trustees (see Chapter 11) that payments should be made to them on your death. You may want to include them in your will in case there are insufficient assets in the settlement at that time. If so you will want to provide that they should benefit under your will only if, and to the extent that, they do not benefit under the settlement.

If you have foreign assets, you also need to take account of the inheritance laws of that country. For example, whatever you may say in your will, if you own a house in France it will pass in equal shares to your widow and surviving children. Accordingly, your will should take account of this in relation to the disposition of other assets.

Dying without a will

If you die without having made a will, your assets in England will be distributed according to the rules of intestacy. These rarely reflect what you are likely to want to happen to your estate. The intestacy rules in England are:

(*a*) *Deceased is married with no children*

The widow or widower receives:

(i)   all personal possessions;

(ii)   first £125,000;

(iii)   one half of everything else.

The remaining half goes to the deceased's parents. If no parents are alive, the individual's brothers and sisters (or their issue) will share the half-share.

If there are no such relatives, the widow or widower will take the entire estate.

(b) *Deceased is married with children*

The widow or widower receives:

(i) all personal possessions;

(ii) first £75,000;

(iii) a life interest in a trust of one half of everything else.

The remaining half passes to the deceased's children in equal shares. They will also inherit the first half when the surviving spouse dies. The surviving spouse may redeem the life interest, i.e. surrender it in return for a part of the capital when all the beneficiaries are adults so the whole estate may then be distributed.

If the deceased leaves children but no spouse, the estate is divided among the children equally.

(c) *Unmarried, no children*

The entire estate passes to the parents. If no parents are alive, the estate passes to the nearest surviving relatives in the following order:

(i) brothers and sisters,

(ii) children of (i),

(iii) grandparents,

(iv) aunts and uncles,

(v) the Crown.

If anyone is alive in category (i) the whole estate is divided between those people. If there are none it is instead divided between everyone in category (ii) who is alive, and so on.

(d) *Common law wives*

They do not benefit under the intestacy rules in the UK, though anyone dependant on the deceased can make a claim for financial provision under the Inheritance (Provision for Family and Dependants) Act 1975.

A foreign will

It is usually advisable to also have a will made in your new country (dealing only with assets in that country) so that assets there can be dealt with more quickly and easily. Your UK will should cover all assets in the UK and elsewhere other than in your new country of residence, although if you have substantial assets in a third country, a local will in that country to deal with such assets may be desirable. As with settlements, it is important to coordinate the two wills to ensure that you do not duplicate legacies but at the same time do not accidentally cut out beneficiaries because the proportion of your assets held in each country changes.

It is also vital to ensure that the lawyer who draws up each will knows that the others exist. If your main will is, say, a Spanish one and you have a secondary will for UK investments, the UK solicitor is likely to automatically include wording to the effect that the will revokes all previous wills unless you tell him that you want your existing Spanish will to remain in effect, as this is a standing precaution 'just in case' you may have overlooked an earlier English will. You also need to make sure that one of the wills clearly covers any odd assets you may have in other countries where you have not made a separate one.

If you are seeking to show that you have ceased to be UK domiciled and have acquired a domicile in your new country, your main will should be made in that country. This is a strong indication that you expect to spend the rest of your life in that country, and die there. In such circumstances careful consideration should be given as to whether you should also have a UK will to deal with UK assets. If you have a UK will and UK executors, this might be taken as a strong indication that you still regard yourself as primarily connected with (and therefore domiciled in) the UK. It may therefore be preferable to have only a foreign will dealing with all your assets, including those in the UK, even though this may make dealing with the UK assets by your executors more difficult.

It also needs to be borne in mind that whilst a UK will is perfectly acceptable elsewhere, it will probably need to be translated if the language in your adopted country is not English. This can give rise to delays in dealing with the assets. Different wills for the assets in each country also keeps a degree of confidentiality if you appoint different executors under each will.

Chapter 11

Offshore trusts and companies

Offshore trusts have been used for many years as a way of avoiding tax and, for individuals, are probably the single most effective tool for this purpose. Offshore trusts enjoy many valuable tax privileges, and a close study of them can reveal many ways of how they can be used to advantage. Trusts are complicated and professional advice must be sought.

Before we discuss the ways in which these trusts operate, here is an explanation of the meaning of some of the technical terms which will be used in this chapter.

Glossary of terms

The Trust — A separate legal entity which holds assets, which is managed by the trustees and is governed by a document (the trust deed) which was drawn up by the settlor. You can have a trust without a trust deed but this is inadvisable, particularly with an offshore trust where the trustees are not well known to the settlor. A settlement is the same thing as a trust. The two words are, in practice, interchangeable (although 'settlement' can have a restricted legal meaning in some circumstances).

The Settlor — The person who set up the trust.

The Trustees — The people who own the assets put into the trust. They can only use or exploit those assets in accordance with the trust deed. The settlor can be a trustee, and can have power to appoint or remove other trustees (provided that this power is set out in the trust deed). However, unless he is himself non-UK resident the settlor should not normally be a trustee of an offshore trust.

The Beneficiaries — The lucky people who may, or will, eventually, be given income or capital from the trust. There is nothing to stop the settlor (or the settlor's spouse) being one of the beneficiaries, although this will often have adverse tax consequences. The beneficiaries are usually either listed in the trust deed or defined by reference to a class of persons (e.g. 'relatives of X' or 'all children of X'). In order to preserve flexibility, many offshore trusts will give the trustees power to add extra beneficiaries. Sometimes an offshore trust will name a couple of charities as the only beneficiaries, but give the trustees power to add extra beneficiaries. Take care if you are offered one of these. Make sure that the trustees do not have power to add relatives of theirs as beneficiaries and then appoint all the assets to them instead of to your family as you intended.

Discretionary Trust — A trust where the trustees are given power to decide who will receive income or capital. They will also, in theory at least, pay regard to a 'letter of wishes' from the settlor.

Letter of Wishes — A letter written by the settlor to the trustees setting out his wishes as to how the trust is to be managed and who is to benefit from it. Such wishes can be ignored by the trustees who are not legally bound to follow the wishes (although with careful selection of your trustee this is a remote risk). Verbal wishes may also be made. If the trustees are professional trustees you cannot expect them to know what the needs of your family are, what are the personal relationships, and who you would really like to have the funds in the event of your death. A letter of wishes enables you to give them some guidance. This is so important that some professionals refuse to accept appointment as trustee without a letter of wishes.

Protector — If you are giving the trustees wide discretionary power, particularly a power to add beneficiaries, it is advisable to appoint a protector. His role is to exercise a right of veto over major decisions of the trustees. The power of a protector will depend on what degree of unfettered control you are willing to leave to the trustees. The protector needs to be someone in whom you have complete trust. Normally this means he will either be resident in the UK or perhaps be resident with you in your new country. If his powers are too extensive this could create a risk that he could be held to control the trust. This could make it resident where he lives thus defeating the object of the exercise.

Trust with Interest in Possession — A trust where the income has to be paid to one or more individuals, and the trustees have no discretion as to how the income is distributed. The right to the interest in possession is sometimes known as the *life interest*, and the person with the life interest sometimes referred to as the *life tenant*.

Reversionary Interest — The entitlement to the trust assets after the person(s) who have the interest in possession.

Offshore Trust — A trust controlled from a tax haven — normally an island off the shore of a country which imposes taxes at a comparatively high rate (hence the name); i.e. Isle of Man, Channel Islands, etc. To ensure that the trust is controlled from the tax haven, the majority of the trustees should be resident in the tax haven.

The discretionary offshore trust

Most offshore trusts are discretionary. Usually all (or a majority) of the trustees are not resident and not ordinarily resident in the UK. In addition, none of the administration takes place in the UK or your new country of residence. This does not prohibit the trust from using UK resident advisers, such as chartered accountants, investment managers or stockbrokers. The final decisions must be taken by the offshore trustees and the administration must not be undertaken in the UK.

Most trust deeds provide that in the event of political unrest, the trust is to be relocated in an alternative tax haven — sometimes the deed will contain provisions to ensure that this happens automatically.

Usually, there are no government reporting requirements for trusts located in tax havens. Thus, there is no register of trusts and no tax to pay in the tax haven provided that none of the beneficiaries are resident in the tax haven and no income arises in the tax haven itself.

If structured carefully, there will be no taxes to pay within the trust, thus allowing income to be reinvested tax free (or in some cases subject only to withholding tax imposed in the country in which it arises).

If the settlor dies, the assets in the trust are usually free of all capital taxes (but not UK IHT). The enjoyment by beneficiaries of the trust income and capital remains at the discretion of the trustees, who will usually have regard to the wishes of the deceased settlor. Thus, there are no complicated foreign probate regulations to deal with.

If a beneficiary goes to live in a highly taxed area, he can request that the trustees reduce the level of payments to him.

An offshore company

An offshore company is usually one which is incorporated in a tax haven (e.g. Jersey). Many people mistakenly believe that such a company will automatically be free of tax in the UK. This is not so. For example, even though a company is incorporated in, say, Jersey, it can still be tax resident in the UK. It is a matter of where, in reality, the company is managed and controlled which usually determines its residence. If you live in Spain, for example, and own a Jersey company which is managed and controlled by you, then that company can be liable to Spanish taxes on its worldwide income.

In theory, a company is managed and controlled by directors and resident in the country in which its directors meet to make their management decisions. However, the Inland Revenue are not naive. If, in practice, the directors merely rubber stamp decisions that you make, they will contend that you manage and control the company even if you are not yourself a director. What matters is what happens in practice, not what the constitution of the company says ought to happen, nor what the board minutes purport to have happened (although board minutes will normally be accepted as evidence).

It cannot be stressed too strongly that the directors will also make the management decisions. You can offer them advice and make suggestions. You can draw investment opportunities to their attention. However, you must not instruct them what to do.

Usually, an offshore company is owned, managed and controlled by an offshore trust. This breaks the legal ownership chain between the settlor or beneficiaries and the company. The offshore company does not have to be incorporated in the same country as that in which the trustees are resident. Indeed, often the two are different, although there are advantages in the trustees and directors being the same people. As well as taking whatever decisions are necessary in relation to the investment of the company's assets, the directors will ensure that shares are issued, hold regular meetings, update the company's statutory and accounting records and manage the company's bank account properly.

The offshore company can be a trading or an investment operation. A company, rather than the trust itself, is often used to own assets as it is a clear separate legal person and usually a simpler medium in which title to assets can be bought and sold. If borrowings are to be secured on the assets and professional trustees are used, they will often insist on the interposition of a company between them and the borrowing as, otherwise, they may find themselves with personal liability for the borrowing.

Protecting your assets

It is important to keep tax avoidance in perspective. In the UK it is only 40% of your wealth (in the case of inheritance tax), your gain (in the case of capital gains tax) or your income (in the case of income tax). The rate is higher in some countries. It will rarely be 100%, however! When creating a trust you are giving assets, in many cases a substantial part of your wealth, to someone who lives in another country and who you may have never met, and you are going to have to trust him to deal with those assets in accordance with your wishes. It is not unheard of for trustees to disappear with the funds.

We are not seeking to discourage you from using an offshore trust or company, but simply to stress that you need to consider what steps are available to you to ensure that your money is safe. Some things that you might consider are listed below.

(*a*) Appoint a protector.

(*b*) Make the protector a signatory on the bank account — and make sure that the bank mandate requires him to sign all cheques and other instructions over a certain figure.

(*c*) Appoint a company owned by a major bank as trustee — if you know that the trustee has millions of pounds of assets and, in the last resort, cannot escape being sued by disappearing out of sight, it is unlikely to run off with your trust's, to it, minuscule assets. However, banks may not be as flexible as independent trust companies and are unlikely to want to manage active companies where a lot of work is required. We would stress that this is not intended as a reflection on other trust management companies. There are many very good ones around. Indeed, there are some that we ourselves recommend clients to. The point we are seeking to make is that you need to do something to protect your assets. Choosing a very rich company is just one of the possible ways to achieve this.

(*d*) Alternatively, insist that share certificates and other documents of title are held by a bank — and that the bank has a copy of the trust deed so they know the extent of the trustee's powers.

(*e*) Limit as far as possible the discretion that you give the trustees. In particular, require them to seek your consent or, preferably, the consent of a protector before adding additional beneficiaries to the trust deed or before making capital distributions to beneficiaries. Also make sure that the trustees are not the people who have power to appoint new trustees. We have even seen cases where the trustees were given power to appoint the protector, i.e. they could choose who is to look over their shoulders.

(*f*) Use the trust as a conduit, passing the funds to you personally as soon as they arise in the trust. This depends on what you are seeking to achieve from the trust. It obviously cannot be done if one of the objectives is to direct income from the investment of the funds away from you.

(*g*) If the trustee is not a company owned by a reputable bank, check that it has fidelity insurance cover — and that this extends to fraud by directors.

(*h*) Try to get someone that you trust to recommend a trust company to you.

(*i*) Locate your trust somewhere where there is strong government regulation to protect investors.

UK inheritance tax ('IHT')

If the settlor of an offshore discretionary trust is UK domiciled, then gifts into the trust over the £150,000 nil rate inheritance tax band are liable to UK IHT. If the gift is subject to business property relief, an unlimited value of shares can be transferred into the trust. However, the trust itself may be liable to IHT — and you should not simply assume that it will be entitled to the business property relief.

If the settlor is not domiciled in the UK, IHT does not arise unless UK assets are put into the trusts.

As explained in Chapter 10, unlimited gifts can be made into trusts which have an interest in possession for someone other than the settlor. As long as the settlor survives for seven years there is no IHT payable.

Where the settlor himself has an interest in possession (called a *settlor trust*) there is no IHT due. However, IHT would be payable on the settlor's death, as a person with an interest in possession in a trust is effectively deemed to own the trust assets for inheritance tax purposes.

UK income tax and capital gains tax

If you are emigrating from the UK and will become and remain resident and ordinarily resident outside the UK, there is unlikely to be a liability to UK income tax and capital gains tax on the trust assets if all the members of your family go with you. However, if you are likely to return to the UK at some stage, it is important to realise the UK tax implications of the overseas trust once you return. Similarly, if some of the potential beneficiaries of the trust will remain resident in the UK, tax could well be payable in the UK in relation to income and capital gains of the trust.

Income tax

Not surprisingly, there are a large number of anti-avoidance provisions designed to thwart the avoidance of tax by the use of overseas trusts by UK residents. If the settlor or his spouse are beneficiaries or potential beneficiaries of a trust (whether UK or offshore) the settlor is taxable on the trust income. This rule is supplemented by a further provision that will enable the Revenue to tax the settlor on income of a company owned by the trust or which increases the value of assets owned by the trust. If, however, the settlor and his spouse are excluded from benefit, for example the trust is for the benefit of his children and grandchildren, the trust income remains free of UK income tax while it is retained within the trust (except, of course, to the extent that it arises from UK sources). If it is subsequently distributed to a UK resident beneficiary — or such a beneficiary receives any benefit from the trust — the amount distributed (or the value of the benefit) will be taxed as income of the beneficiary at that stage, up to the amount of the accumulated income. Accordingly, if the trust property is invested overseas and the income is accumulated the trust will achieve a deferral of UK income tax. If at some stage the beneficiary ceases to be both resident and ordinarily resident in the UK, the accumulated income could be distributed to the beneficiary at that time without a UK tax liability arising.

Capital gains tax

The capital gains tax anti-avoidance provisions in relation to overseas trusts were altered radically in the 1991 Finance Act and are now very complex. Overseas trusts can be divided into three categories:

(a) those created after 18 March 1991 (and some earlier ones) in which the settlor has an interest,

(b) those of which the settlor is not UK domiciled, and

(c) the rest, i.e. most trusts created before 19 March 1991, trusts created after 18 March 1991 in which the settlor does not have an interest, and trusts created after 18 March 1991 where the settlor has died.

Trusts in which the settlor has an interest

Where a settlor has an interest in the trust, its gains are treated as gains of the settlor and taxed on him if he is resident or ordinarily resident in the UK. A settlor has an interest in the trust if any of the following are possible beneficiaries, either currently or at some future date (with some fairly minor exceptions):

(i) the settlor himself,

(ii) the settlor's spouse (but it is alright to include the settlor's widow),

(iii) any child (or step-child) of the settlor or his spouse — including an adult child,

(iv) the spouse of a child,

 (v) a company controlled by one or more of the people in (i)–(iv),

(vi) a company that is associated with one within (v).

It will be apparent that this is a very wide spread of people and includes most of those that a person is likely to want to benefit. It does not include

(A) the widow of the settlor (i.e. you can include your spouse indirectly, provided that she cannot benefit during your lifetime),

(B) grandchildren of the settlor,

(C) the parents of the settlor, or

(D) a brother or sister, or nephews or nieces of the settlor.

The capital gains of a trust set up for the benefit of all or any of the people in (A) to (D) above will not be taxable on the settlor provided that none of the people in (i) to (vi) above can benefit from the trust in any circumstances.

The tax charge on the settlor normally applies only to settlements created after 18 March 1991. It will, however, also apply to a settlement created before that date if, after that date

 (I) any property is added to the settlement,

 (II) the settlement was resident in the UK at that date and overseas trustees are appointed to it,

(III) the terms of the settlement are varied so as to add as beneficiaries any of the people in (i) to (vi) above who was not previously a beneficiary, or

(IV) a person in (i) to (vi) above enjoys any benefit from the settlement.

The occurrence of one of these events will bring the entire assets of the settlement within these new rules, not merely the additional assets or the assets from which the settlor or one of the relatives listed above can benefit. Therefore great care needs to be taken before doing anything with a pre-19 March 1991 trust.

Trusts where the settlor is non-UK domiciled

A trust is not within the above rules which impose a tax charge on the settlor if he (or any of the settlors if there are more than one) is not domiciled in the UK at any time in the year in which the capital gain arises. (The trust also does not fall within the rules if the settlor is neither resident nor ordinarily resident in the UK throughout that year, as in such circumstances deeming the gains to be realised by the settlor would be ineffective as he would not himself be liable to UK capital gains tax).

A trust is not within the rules set out below which impose a tax charge on a beneficiary if the settlor is not domiciled in the UK both

(1)   at the time he created the trust, and

(2)   throughout the year in which the capital gain arises.

If a settlor is domiciled in the UK when he creates his trust but becomes non-UK domiciled before the gain arises, the gain will not be taxable on the settlor even if he (or one of the close relatives listed earlier) has an interest in the settlement. It will, however, be taxable on the beneficiaries (including the settlor if he is resident or ordinarily resident in the UK when he receives a benefit from the trust) under the rules considered below.

Where a person is not UK domiciled and will not become so, an overseas settlement can take assets out of the scope of UK capital gains tax entirely. This applies even to UK assets (with some exceptions) and even if the settlor is a beneficiary and brings the funds into the UK.

Other trusts

If a trust is neither one in which the capital gains are taxable on the settlor as he (or one of the close relatives listed earlier) has an interest in the settlement, nor one the gains of which are outside the scope of capital gains tax entirely because the settlor is non-UK domiciled, an overseas trust can at least defer capital gains tax — and, in the same way as with income, the deferral can be turned into a saving if the assets are distributed to a beneficiary in a year in which he is neither resident nor ordinarily resident in the UK.

If the trust (or a company owned by the trust) realises a capital gain, no UK tax charge arises while the gain remains in the trust. This applies even if the settlor and his spouse are beneficiaries; indeed, even if the settlor is the primary beneficiary. A capital gains tax charge will, however, arise on a beneficiary when he receives a distribution or any benefit from the trust — except, of course, to the extent that the distribution or benefit has already given rise to an income tax charge.

This tax charge on the beneficiary will apply to most trusts created before 19 March 1991 and to those created later either in which the settlor does not have an interest or where he has died in a year of assessment prior to that in which the gain arises.

Where a capital gain is distributed to a beneficiary after 5 April 1992 he can also be liable to a surcharge on the tax. Broadly speaking, this surcharge is:

20%	if the gain is distributed in the second tax year after that in which it arose (e.g. if a 1991/92 gain is distributed in 1993/94),
30%	if the gain is distributed in the third year after that in which it arose (e.g. if a 1991/92 gain is distributed in 1994/95),
40%	if the gain is distributed in the fourth year after that in which it arose,

50%   if the gain is distributed in the fifth year after that in which it arose,

60%   if the gain is distributed in a later year (e.g. if a 1991/92 gain is distributed in 1997/98 or a later year).

This tax surcharge is, in effect, equivalent to interest at 10% p.a. for the period that the gain remains within the settlement — but there is no surcharge if it is distributed in the year after that in which it is realised, and the surcharge does not increase further if the gain is retained in the settlement for more than six years. This surcharge is, in most cases, likely to be an acceptable price to pay to defer payment of the tax.

Change of residence of a settlement

If a UK resident settlement becomes non-UK resident after 18 March 1991 it is treated as disposing of all its assets at their market value at the time of its emigration and re-acquiring them. This creates a capital gains tax charge within the settlement while it is still within the scope of UK tax. This migration charge applies even if the settlor is non-UK domiciled.

A settlement will become non-UK resident if the English trustees resign and are replaced by non-UK residents. It could well also become non-UK resident if a majority of the trustees cease to be resident in the UK. Accordingly, if you are a trustee you need to consider whether your ceasing to be UK resident could also cause the trust to cease to be UK resident — thus triggering a capital gains tax charge.

Clearly the Revenue need a mechanism to enforce the payment of the tax on the deemed disposal. To achieve this, every person who was a trustee at any time within the twelve months prior to the trust's emigration is made personally liable for the tax if it is not paid by the trustees within six months of the date on which it becomes payable. There is an exemption for a person who was not a trustee immediately prior to the emigration, having resigned earlier, but only if he can show that at the time he ceased to be a trustee there was no proposal that the trust might cease to be UK resident. There is also an exception for a person who ceased to be a trustee before 19 March 1991.

If the residence of an overseas settlement is changed to the UK, as could happen if you are a trustee at the time that you come back to resume UK residence, it will remain within the scope of the tax charge on beneficiaries in relation to capital gains that arose before the change of residence. The capital gains tax base cost of assets that it holds at the time of its immigration will remain their original cost. In some cases, particularly if the settlor is not UK domiciled so that the tax charge on beneficiaries does not apply, it may be advisable to sell and reacquire the assets in the tax year prior to that in which the trust becomes UK resident.

Using an offshore trust in connection with emigration

As indicated earlier, a person who wishes to emigrate from the UK faces two major problems in conserving his assets for the benefit of his family; escaping the UK tax net and avoiding tax in his new home country. Most countries tax their residents on worldwide income and gains. By creating a trust in a tax haven between leaving the UK and becoming resident in his adopted country the emigrant can often obtain the best of both worlds. He can take his assets with him when he leaves the UK, thus avoiding the capital gains tax that he would have had to pay if he had put them into a settlement while still resident or ordinarily resident in the UK, but arrive into the tax system of his new country without them, so avoiding bringing them into that country's tax net. As a trust is a separate legal entity the assets of which are —nominally at least — not under his control, there would normally be no obligation to even declare the trust's income or capital gains to the tax authorities of the new country. As in many cases a distribution from the trust would not create a tax liability, it is normally possible for a person to 'park' the bulk of his free funds into the offshore trust, leaving the capital to accumulate for the benefit of himself and his family but with the ability (subject to the agreement of the trustees) to obtain as much of the income as is needed to maintain his desired life style, and to obtain use of the capital if so required.

If you intend to emigrate at some time in the future you could consider putting cash now into an overseas trust and using this to purchase assets instead of doing so personally. Although you will obtain no advantage while you remain UK resident, when you leave you will already have separated those assets in the trust from yourself. This will avoid the inconvenience of possibly having to spend some time in a third country between emigrating from the UK and moving to your adopted country. It also guards against the risk of a future government introducing a capital gains tax charge when an individual emigrates.

Existing UK companies

It is not possible to change the country of residence of a company that is incorporated in the UK. Accordingly, your emigration will not take out of the UK tax net assets within an existing UK company that you own. Nor will transferring the shares to overseas trustees. You will need to consider what action, if any, might be available to mitigate the tax. It may even be worth paying some tax now in order to take the future growth in value of the assets, and the future income they will produce, out of the scope of UK tax.

Chapter 12

National insurance and social security

Liability for contributions

Although you can escape from the UK tax net the day you go abroad if you are taking up full time employment overseas which stretches over a complete tax year, the same does not necessarily hold true for national insurance. You will continue to be liable to pay full national insurance contributions for the first 52 weeks that you are abroad if

(*a*) you are under 65 (60 for a woman),

(*b*) your employer has a place of business in the UK,

(*c*) you are 'ordinarily resident' in the UK, and

(*d*) you were resident in the UK before you took the job.

The Contributions Agency (which is now responsible for the collection of national insurance) tends to ignore the interpretation of ordinary residence that has been given by the courts for tax purposes and has instead formulated its own tests. It seems doubtful whether these will be upheld by the courts if a dispute arises. The tax definition attempts to interpret the words on the basis of ordinary language, not in the context of the tax legislation as such. It is, accordingly, probably a general definition that is equally applicable to national insurance. Nevertheless, as the national insurance appeals procedure is very cumbersome, the best advice is to put up with the Contributions Agency's definition. If you intend to return to live in the UK within five years they regard you as remaining ordinarily resident here. If you do not, they still regard you as ordinarily resident here unless, normally, you have severed all connections with the UK. If you are going abroad for more than five years and do not want to pay contributions, they expect you to write to them at their Overseas Branch telling them how long you will be away, if you are keeping somewhere to live in the UK, and what you have done with your furniture and belongings while you are away. They will then tell you if they consider that you will remain ordinarily resident here.

There are five different types of national insurance contributions, each with its own set of rules. If you are an employee or a director you will pay Class 1 contributions (and if you have a company car your employer may pay Class 1A contributions as well). Class 1 contributions consist of primary contributions (which you pay) and secondary ones (which your employer pays). The self-employed pay two sets of contribution — Class 2 contribution which is a fixed weekly amount (paid either by stamping a contribution card or, more often, by monthly direct debit) and Class 4 contributions, which are earnings related and collected by the Inland Revenue with the income tax on the earnings. Class 3 contributions are voluntary. They can be paid by someone who is not working, or otherwise not liable to pay national insurance, in order to preserve one's entitlement to claim national insurance benefits.

If your employer does not have a place of business in the UK there is no obligation to pay UK national insurance. If you are sent by your company to work for an overseas subsidiary you need to identify who your employer is. Has your UK employer seconded you to the overseas company, in which case you will remain liable to national insurance for the first 52 weeks, or has your contract of employment been terminated and you have entered into a fresh contract with the overseas company? Take care before you say that, of course, it is the latter. If so you may have forfeited your rights to redundancy pay if you are later made redundant, to compensation if you are dismissed, and to remain in the company pension scheme.

If you are self-employed you have an obligation to continue paying Class 2 contributions (the weekly stamp) while you are ordinarily resident in the UK. This appears to mean for up to five years if you are intending to return to the UK in that period. You only have an obligation to pay Class 4 (earnings related) contributions if your profits remain liable to UK tax, i.e. you remain resident in the UK for tax purposes.

Voluntary contributions

If there is no obligation to pay contributions you cannot voluntarily pay Class 1 (employee's) contributions in order to maintain your contributions record. You can, however, volunteer to pay Class 2 or 3 contributions if you meet the following qualifying conditions.

Class 2 (the self-employed weekly fixed rate contribution)

(*a*) You lived in the UK for a continuous period of three years (at any time in your life),

(*b*) you are working abroad, and

(*c*) you were either an employee or self-employed immediately before you went abroad (or you were unemployed but would normally be employed or self-employed).

Class 3 (voluntary contributions)

You lived in the UK for a continuous period of three years (at any time in your life).

You may wonder why any one should volunteer to pay national insurance. After all, most people going to work overseas hope to escape from the UK tax net. The reason is that UK social security benefits depend on your contributions record during your working life. Class 3 contributions count towards your contributions record for retirement pension, widow's payment, widowed mother's allowance and widow's pension. Class 2 contributions count not only for these benefits, but also for maternity allowance, invalidity benefit and sickness benefit.

Procedure

If you wish to make voluntary payments you should obtain a form CF83 from any office of the Department of Social Security, complete it and send it to their Overseas Branch. It is best to do this before you go overseas in case the DSS have any queries about your form. If you apply before you go overseas you must pay the contributions by direct debit on a monthly basis or by cheque or bank transfer at the end of the year.

Alternatively, you could delay completing the form until you return to the UK and pay the contributions in arrears. However, unless you are going to be abroad for a short period only this is not advisable. Late payment will affect your right to some benefits such as sickness, unemployment or maternity benefits. Furthermore, if Class 2 contributions are paid more than twelve months after the end of the year to which they relate, they must be paid at the highest rate ruling at any time between the year to which they relate and the year of payment. Class 3 contributions must similarly be paid at the highest rate in force in the period if they are paid more than 24 months after the end of the year to which they relate. Voluntary contributions cannot be paid more than six years after the end of the year to which they relate.

Working in the European Community

If you work in another EC country you will normally pay social security contributions in that country and will not need to pay contributions to the UK scheme. This does not apply if you are sent to work overseas by a UK employer and your period overseas is not expected to exceed twelve months (unless you are replacing another employee sent from the UK who has completed his term of posting). In such circumstances, you remain liable to pay UK contributions and need not contribute to the social security scheme of the country in which you work. You need to produce to the tax authority a certificate from the DSS, form E101, which your employer needs to apply for.

The DSS take the view that they can issue a form E101 only if either

(*a*) a person has been sent to another EC country in continuation of his UK employment (i.e. he has been sent abroad by the person for whom he normally works in the UK), or

(*b*) a person has been recruited in the UK with a view to immediate employment elsewhere within the EC by a UK employer who normally carries out activities in the UK which are comparable with those which the person sent abroad will be employed to carry out, and there is a direct relationship between the UK employer and the person concerned during his employment overseas (if the services of that person are hired to another undertaking in another EC country which in turn makes them available to another undertaking this breaks the necessary direct relationship).

It is understood that the first time that an employer applies for a form E101 will prompt a visit by the DSS to make sure that the company is complying with all the DSS regulations. Presumably the Government feel that it is so unreasonable for a person to want to lay claim to his rights under EC law that any employer who makes such a claim deserves to be suspected of evasion in other areas!

If the period actually worked overseas unexpectedly exceeds twelve months 'owing to unforeseeable circumstances' your employer can complete another form, E102, applying for permission for you to continue to contribute to the UK scheme. This must be done before the end of the first twelve months. The UK will then seek permission from the tax authorities in the country in which you are working to extend the period for paying UK contributions. However, the extension cannot be for more than a further twelve months.

If you are self-employed and expect to work in the other country for not more than twelve months you can similarly complete the form E101 (and, if necessary, the E102) and remain in the UK scheme. As social security contribution levels on the continent are generally significantly greater than in the UK it is generally better to remain in the UK scheme as long as you can.

If you pay social security contributions in another EC country, after you return to the UK these contributions count towards UK social security sickness benefit, unemployment benefit and maternity allowance contribution requirements provided that

(i)   you were sent to work in that other country by your UK employer,

(ii) you remained ordinarily resident in the UK while you were working overseas, and

(iii) you are not entitled to draw the corresponding benefits in the other country.

It is worth reading the DSS leaflets NI 38 (Social Security Abroad) and SA 29 (your Social Security, health care and pension rights in the EC) to check the up-to-date position. These can be obtained free from your local DSS office.

To retain your contributions record for other UK benefits you will need to make voluntary contributions to the UK scheme.

For social security purposes the EC covers:

Belgium
Denmark   (other than the Faroe Islands)
France   (including Corsica, Guadeloupe, Martinique, Reunion and French Guiana, but not Monaco)
Germany
Greece   (including Crete and the Greek Islands)
Irish Republic
Italy   (including Sicily, Sardinia and Elba, but not Vatican City or San Marino)

Luxembourg
Netherlands (other than the Netherlands Antilles)
Portugal (including Madeira and the Azores)
Spain (including the Balearic Islands, the Canary Islands, and Ceuta and Melilla in North Africa)
UK (including Gibraltar)

Bilateral agreements

The UK has also entered into bilateral social security agreements with a number of other countries. These are generally along the lines of the EC agreement. You will pay contributions in the UK for the first twelve months if you are sent to the other country by your UK employer and will be exempt from social security contributions in the other country, provided that you obtain a certificate from the DSS confirming that you are continuing to pay UK contributions. In any other case, you will pay social security in the other country and be exempted from UK contributions. The DSS has published explanatory leaflets which should be consulted if you are going to one of the countries in question to ascertain the precise position for the country to which you are going. These are:

Australia (*see DSS leaflet SA5*)
Austria (*see DSS leaflet SA25*)
Barbados (*leaflet not yet published*)
Bermuda (*see DSS leaflet SA23*)
Canada (*see DSS leaflet SA20*)
Cyprus (*see DSS leaflet SA12*)
Finland (*see DSS leaflet SA19*)
Iceland (*see DSS leaflet SA24*)
Israel (*see DSS leaflet SA14*)
Jamaica (*see DSS leaflet SA27*)
Jersey & Guernsey (*see DSS leaflet SA4*)

Malta (*see DSS leaflet SA11*)
Mauritius (*see DSS leaflet SA38*)
New Zealand (*see DSS leaflet SA8*)
Norway (*see DSS leaflet SA16*)
Philippines (*see DSS leaflet SA42*)
Sweden (*see DSS leaflet SA9*)
Switzerland (*see DSS leaflet SA6*)
Turkey (*see DSS leaflet SA22*)
USA (*see DSS leaflet SA33*)
Yugoslavia (*see DSS leaflet SA17*)

Social security benefits

National insurance benefits depend on your contributions record. Apart from pension benefits it is the contributions record in the two complete tax years before the calendar year in which you are claiming the benefit that matters. In other words, to claim benefit in 1993 you need to have met the contribution requirement in the tax years 1990/91 and 1991/92. For sickness benefit you must have paid or been credited with an amount equal to 50 contributions at the Class 1 (employed) lower earnings limit (or 50 Class 2 — self-employed — contributions) in each of those years, and at least half of those contributions must actually have been paid (not merely credited) in one of those years. The same conditions apply to unemployment benefit with the exception that only Class 1 contributions qualify. To qualify for statutory maternity pay, you must have worked for your employer for six months or more in any EC country. If you do not meet the test you can claim Maternity Allowance if you have paid at least 26 Class 1 or 2 contributions in the 52 weeks ending in the 15th week before the baby is due. None of these benefits are normally payable whilst you are outside the UK.

Sickness benefit and maternity allowance can be claimed if either

(*a*) you have gone abroad temporarily for the specific purpose of receiving treatment for incapacity that began before you left the UK, or

(*b*) you were continuously incapable of work for at least six months up to the date you left the UK and have only gone abroad temporarily.

In no circumstances will unemployment benefit be paid abroad.

If you work abroad for more than twelve months and remained liable to pay UK national insurance for the first twelve months, you will be credited with contributions for the time you were overseas after the first twelve months, provided you remain ordinarily resident in the UK.

The rules on retirement pension are considered in Chapter 7. The contribution record for widowed mother's allowance and widow's pension is the same as for the retirement pension but, of course, based on the late husband's contributions.

Child benefit

Child benefit is payable for the first eight weeks of a temporary absence abroad. You need to complete a claim form. Obtain leaflet CH6 (Child Benefit for Persons leaving Britain) which explains the rules in more detail. This has a claim form in the back of it.

If you are going abroad permanently, you must return your order book to the DSS. If you are going to another EC country and continue to pay UK national insurance as an employee (but not as a self-employed person) you will remain entitled to child benefit whilst you continue to pay Class 1 national insurance contributions. If you or your spouse become liable to pay social security in the country where you are living you will become entitled to that country's child allowance and your entitlement to child benefit in the UK will cease.

If your spouse remains in the UK and is employed or self-employed, entitlement to child benefit will continue whilst she is here but only if the child stays here also.

The DSS will not pay child benefit into an overseas bank account. It must either be paid into your UK account or you must authorise someone in the UK to draw it in cash.

Other benefits

If you are in receipt of *attendance allowance* or *mobility allowance* you can continue to draw this for up to six months if your absence abroad is temporary. The six-month period can be extended if you go abroad specifically for treatment of an illness or disabling condition that began while you were in the UK. If you are in receipt of *family credit* this will continue to be paid for the balance of the 26-week award period but a new claim cannot be entertained. *Guardian's allowance* is tied to child benefit; you can continue to draw this as long as you draw the child benefit. *Industrial injuries* disablement pension will continue, even if you go overseas permanently. However, the constant attendance allowance will normally be paid only for the first six months of a temporary absence abroad and the reduced earnings allowance and unemployability supplement for the first three months. If you are in receipt of invalid care allowance this will continue if your absence abroad is temporary. Severe disablement allowance and income support will not normally continue but may do so if you are going abroad for a short visit only.

If you are in receipt of any of these benefits it is advisable to check with your local social security benefit office well in advance of going abroad to ascertain exactly how you will be affected. Even if the benefit will not continue, you need to know that fact to plan your finances properly.

Chapter 13

Your new home

Buying a house

If you intend to buy a house or other property in your new country you obviously need to use a lawyer in that country to look after your interests. However, you need to realise that the function of the lawyer in that country is not necessarily the same as that of a solicitor in England.

In this country solicitors act in an adversarial capacity, i.e. your solicitor is protecting your interests in opposition to the other side's solicitor who is protecting his client's interests. There are rules of the game about disclosure, and it is in your interest not to actually cheat the other side, but your solicitor is not concerned to spell out problems to the other side that they may have overlooked. A solicitor cannot normally act for both sides, and where he can both must have agreed to it. This separation of roles does not apply in some countries. For example, the role of the notary in Spain is simply to draw up the documents and ensure that they comply with the law. He acts for both parties because he is not concerned with the negotiation of the terms of the deal. You need to engage a Spanish lawyer (known as an *abogado*) in addition to the notary to protect your interests — and you need to specifically check that he is not acting for the other side as well.

In non-English speaking countries many professionals, such as lawyers, speak English fairly well. However, as it is not their native language they often do not appreciate some of the nuances of the English language and may not be able to explain problems to you sufficiently well for you to appreciate their significance. Also, as English property law is very complex they may well not understand English legal concepts that you take for granted and are mentally applying to the foreign interest you are acquiring. Although it adds an extra cost, it is often sensible to involve an English solicitor as well. If he is experienced in property purchases in your new country he will be aware of the potential problems and thus knows what to look out for when dealing with his foreign counterpart. He may well also be in a better position than you to select a lawyer in the overseas country, either because he will know people there or will know other people in England on whose recommendation he relies.

You also need to give thought to who should own your house. In some countries, particularly in Europe, it is common for houses to be owned by a limited company as taxes on transfers of property are far higher than taxes on transfers of shares. If the house is owned by a company, when you want to sell it you sell the shares of the company instead, but the tax implications of a company owning the property need to be thought through. If the company is incorporated in your new country it will probably attract taxes there. It will certainly attract tax if it is incorporated in the UK — although the best of both worlds might sometimes be achieved if the company holds the property simply as a nominee for you. If the company is incorporated in a tax haven it will probably not attract tax there, but the country where the property is situated may impose special taxes on property held by tax haven companies. Both France and Spain do this, for example.

If you intend to return to the UK, the company may become UK resident when you return as the Inland Revenue may be able to show that you control and manage it. The location of the company may also affect its marketability when you come to sell. Most people who buy property in Spain use either a Gibraltarian or Channel Islands company. If you use, say, a Turks and Caicos Islands company the tax effect may be the same, but a prospective purchaser may be reluctant to buy a company incorporated in an unusual jurisdiction. There is no ideal solution that can be used whichever country you are going to and whatever your circumstances. All that we can do is to point out the factors you need to consider. The solution you adopt will depend on the country concerned, on whether you intend to spend the remainder of your life there, and, if not, your future intentions.

Mortgages

If you intend to buy an overseas property the next question to consider is likely to be raising a mortgage. Should you do this in your new country or in the UK? If you need to use UK assets, such as your existing house, as security, it may be easier to raise the mortgage in the UK — although it has to be admitted that most UK lenders are not interested in lending money to buy overseas property. You will probably have better luck with one of the international banks based in the Channel Islands or the Isle of Man. They are used to lending on the security of UK property and generally have offices in the UK which will be able to deal with enforcement of the security if this becomes necessary. Their international outlook also tends to make property elsewhere more acceptable as security to them than to UK-based lenders. If you do not need to use a UK property as security it is probably easier to borrow in the country where the property is located.

If you are buying through a company and you, and the company, will become UK resident again at some stage, you should normally try to borrow in the UK as interest payable to an overseas lender is not always allowable for UK corporation tax purposes and is also likely to attract withholding tax. In most cases you should try to arrange things so that your company will not become UK resident when you return. If you are buying as an individual this does not matter, as interest will not be allowable for UK tax purposes irrespective of where the borrowing is arranged. Incidentally, this is a point you need to bear in mind if you are likely to return to the UK and intend to let your overseas property when you return. You will be taxable in the UK on the rents from the property less running costs and similar expenses but with no relief for interest payments. Make sure that the letting will be viable on this basis!

Should your borrowing be in sterling or in the currency of your new country? This depends on how you intend to repay the loan. As a general rule, if you are going to repay it by selling the foreign property it should be in the foreign currency. If you are going to repay it by selling UK assets, a sterling borrowing is probably preferable. This is because it is unwise to get involved in the risk of currency price movements. If the money to repay the loan will arise in a foreign currency it is less risky for the loan to be in the same currency.

Another consideration is interest rates. If a UK lender is reluctant to take a foreign property as security he is likely to give tangible expression to that reluctance by charging a higher rate of interest than normal. This particularly applies to foreign currency loans. It is likely to be more expensive to borrow francs in the UK than it is to borrow them in France. The interest rate on a foreign currency borrowing may be significantly lower than on a sterling borrowing. The difference reflects the exchange risk. But if you can repay the borrowing out of funds that arise in the same currency, such as your overseas salary or the proceeds of sale of the house, you do not have an exchange risk so there is no point in paying a substantially higher rate to borrow in sterling or in foreign currency in the UK.

The terms on which you can borrow may also affect where you make the borrowing. If you want to acquire a property in Canada you may well be able to borrow in the UK on the basis of a 25-year mortgage, either at a fixed interest rate or with a rate that moves gradually in line with base rate changes. If you borrow in Canada it is normal for the interest rate to be fixed in three - or five-year steps, i.e. you will borrow at a fixed rate for three years, at the end of which a new rate will be fixed for the next three years, and so on. You can therefore be faced periodically with large, unplanned for, increases in your mortgage repayments.

Removal

Even in the EC you cannot simply pack all your furniture into a self-drive van and take it with you, unless you want to spend a great deal of time arguing with the Customs authorities in your new country. Various documents will need to be completed to show that the goods are being imported from the UK, perhaps to demonstrate that you are an EC or a UK resident, perhaps to show that you own the furniture, perhaps to show that you have a house in your new country, perhaps to show that you have been granted, or at least applied for, a residence permit in your new country if this is needed, and almost certainly listing the items and their approximate values. In some countries there will also be import duties to pay.

Fragile goods are going to need more care in packing if they are going to be taken in a container by rail to a UK port, the container lifted by crane onto a freighter, and then transported on the deck of the ship across the Atlantic, than if they are simply to be loaded onto a van and driven from London to Southend.

There is not a lot of point in packing your fridge and your washing machine, waiting two months for them to arrive at your new home — or alternatively paying an enormous sum in air freight — only to find that they will not function in your new home without an adaptor and that you could have replaced the items locally at a price that compares favourably with the transport costs that you have incurred. This seems to apply especially to video recorders. A different system is used in most overseas countries and the cost of an adaptor is likely to be almost as much as the cost of a new machine. If you intend to buy a new video recorder in the UK before you leave because prices are cheaper here, most major retailers can sell you one which will be compatible with the system in your intended new home, but you need to tell the shop the country in which you intend to use it.

Do-it-yourself international removals are not to be recommended. Find a removal firm with a good reputation and experience of international removals. Do this well in advance of your move. When they come round to give you an estimate do not be afraid to ask whether it is sensible to move things that you have doubts about, listen to the advice they proffer as to what you ought to consider abandoning, and follow it unless you have a good reason not to. Check that they have comprehensive insurance cover in case of damage to your furniture. Then leave everything to them and do not begrudge the cost.

Remember also that international removals are expensive and the costs could well be less if you leave behind things that will not fit into your new house, things that you haven't used for years and are unlikely ever to use again, mechanical and electronic items that are getting old and for which replacement parts are unlikely to be available in your new country, and things that are unlikely to be called for in your new country — such as cases of winter clothes if you are moving to a location near the equator. Of course, the same applies to moves in the UK, but most of us tend to take everything that can be moved 'just in case' we might need it at some future time. 'Just in case' is an expensive luxury if you are moving abroad.

If you are not taking your furniture with you, perhaps because you will let out your UK home and therefore will leave the furniture in place and buy new items for your new home, air freight is worth considering for your clothing and other personal effects. It is even cheaper to send such goods as luggage in advance — you take it to the airport a few days before you fly out and deliver it to the airline — although you then have to check your goods through customs at the other end and get them from the airport to your new home (with air freight you pay a forwarding company to take care of these chores). Sending even personal effects by air is not cheap but it is quick and the cost may be an acceptable price to avoid having to live for a few weeks with the bulk of your possessions in transit.

If you want to take cuttings from your garden, or the home-made jam that someone gave you two years ago, remember that many countries have import restrictions on plants and foodstuffs. Check that they will be allowed in before you pack them.

Before engaging the removals firm check what will happen at the other end. Will they hand over to a local firm once the goods reach your new country and wash their hands of any problems that arise after that? Will they themselves deliver your furniture to your new home, or will they hand over to a local associate but take responsibility for its work? You ideally want to be able to deal with only one person, whoever does the actual work. There is a lot to be said for having someone with local knowledge to help you settle in — but moving is sufficiently traumatic in itself that you can do without trying to explain to someone who doesn't understand English what you want put where in your new home.

Do not underestimate the time scale of an international move. You may be able to leave your UK house after breakfast and be at your villa on the Costa del Sol the following evening. Your furniture could well need four weeks (no, that's not a misprint for days) to make the same journey. This is one of the things you need to clarify with the removal firm. Unless you want to pile sleeping bags and camping equipment into your car and sleep in a bare house for a few weeks, you are going to have to stay somewhere else for a period — either with friends in England before you leave or in your new country while you await the arrival of the furniture.

If you have bought a villa or apartment on a new development make sure that the removers know precisely where it is. There may be hundreds of similar apartments and the roads are often not clearly marked. If possible, drive there yourself a few days in advance and draw them a detailed map starting from the nearest well-signposted town or village. If you have bulky pieces of furniture, consider whether there are likely to be difficulties in getting them into your property, and, if so, whether the extra cost that will be involved is likely to be worthwhile. Also make sure that you discuss any potential problems with the removers well in advance. They may not be real problems to an expert. On the other hand, if they are going to need a crane to get your antique chest of drawers into your bedroom, and will need to remove the windows to do that, it is likely to spend the first few days not in the bedroom but in the garden if this need is not identified until the van arrives at your new home.

Remember also to make the necessary arrangements to have the utilities connected at the other end. You may well need to give significantly more notice than in this country. If the telephone company wants six months' notice, enquire locally if there are ways that this can be expedited. There often are!

Like any move within the UK you also need to make arrangements for the electricity, gas and other utilities to be disconnected at your present home. If you forget to do this it is rather more difficult to remedy the omission if you are living in, say, Spain than if you have simply moved to a different UK location. Remember also that if you have equipment that is plumbed in you may need to arrange for a plumber to disconnect it — and for one to reconnect it at the other end. The removal firm will not normally attempt this.

If you are buying new furniture or other items for your new home it is generally best to do this in your new country. If the items are not available in your new country you can avoid UK VAT on new purchases in the UK under the personal export scheme provided that you are not going to another EC country and are going abroad for at least a year. However, the procedure is complex and is normally not likely to be worthwhile. In particular, the goods must be delivered direct to a ship or aircraft, which means that they cannot be packed with your other possessions. The supplier may also want you to pay the tax and reclaim it from him when you can produce proof of export — which you need to obtain yourself from a Customs officer at the airport or port of embarkation.

Pets

If you are taking a pet with you, you will probably need an import licence. You will almost certainly need vaccination certificates. Which vaccinations are needed will depend on where you are going. Check if there are quarantine requirements and exactly what they involve.

Hard as it may seem, the best advice is normally not to take your pet with you. A dog or cat often cannot acclimatise to the new country as readily as you can and it can be cruel to expect an elderly dog or other pet to adapt to a completely different regime. You may think that your dog will enjoy the freedom of the Spanish sand dunes that stretch for miles from your villa after having spent the last ten years knowing only your house, your back garden, a local park and the various stretches of pavement along which you are accustomed to taking it for walks. The odds are that you will be wrong; it will pine for the old environment and may have a hard time surviving the sand dunes, particularly if it has to overcome territorial disputes with local dogs.

It is essential that you consult your vet, both about the advisability of taking the pet abroad and whether it is healthy enough to survive the trip. The advice will often be to find a new home for it in the UK, or even to have it put down. If so, the kindest thing is to accept that advice.

You also need to consult your local Animal Health Office or Divisional Veterinary Officer to check the regulations in force in both the UK and your new country at the time of your removal. If you do not know where to find it, your vet should be able to tell you.

Taking your car abroad

You can purchase a car in the UK, take it overseas and avoid paying the UK VAT on the car. However, you should check whether or not you have to pay VAT or its equivalent in your new country. Car security can be a problem in many countries, so consider having a good alarm system fitted. Sun roofs and air-conditioning can be very useful in hot countries. People moving to Spain, for instance, often choose diesel powered vehicles as diesel is half the price of petrol and easily available. Before buying the car, check that there are facilities for having it serviced in your new country. Also bear in mind that it is sensible to use a left hand drive car in countries where one drives on the right hand side of the road.

(*a*) *New purchase*

> To make a tax-free export you have to comply with the VAT export scheme. You have to buy the car from the manufacturer or sole UK selling agent. The car can be a British or foreign make.

The manufacturer or UK selling agent will give you a form, VAT 411, to complete and you must:

(i) undertake to go abroad for at least twelve months (although you can bring the car back for temporary visits);

(ii) take the car abroad within six months of purchasing it (you may use it within the UK up to then);

(iii) keep the car for your use for twelve months abroad before selling it or allowing someone else to use it.

Remember, the car can be seized by Customs and Excise *and never returned* if you break any of these rules. Even if the car is stolen and is in the UK when it should be abroad, Customs can seize and keep it. After twelve months abroad, you can re-import the car to the UK and not pay VAT. You should insure it for its full value (i.e. including VAT) until the twelve months abroad have ended.

(*b*) *Existing car*

You cannot obtain a VAT refund if you have purchased the car second-hand or have owned it for more than six months.

Leaflet V526, available from local Vehicle Licensing Offices, is very useful if you plan to take your existing car abroad. Complete section 2 on the back of the Vehicle Registration Document, entering the proposed date of export, and send it to your local Vehicle Licensing Office well in advance of your departure. They will then issue a Certificate of Export (V561). The rules for Northern Ireland or Isle of Man are slightly different.

You will need to declare the car to Customs on entering your new country. If you are going to another EC country you will have to pay VAT on importation if you obtained a refund in the UK. There may also be Customs duties to pay. The car may also need to be re-registered in your new country: the aggravation caused by the bureaucracy involved may well outweigh the VAT saving.

You need to check the position locally in relation to your driving licence. The period for which you can drive on your UK licence varies. In some countries you can, in practice, do this indefinitely whereas others insist on your exchanging your UK licence for a local one virtually as soon as you become resident there. You can, and should, obtain an international driving licence from the AA (you do not have to be a member to get this). This is valid for a year but you must obtain it in the UK. You will need to provide two passport photographs when you apply for the licence.

Insurance is another thing you need to check. You probably need to pay an additional premium. It may be that your insurance company will be reluctant to cover you at all after the first few months and that you will need to reinsure locally.

Before deciding to take your car abroad, look at the sort of cars that the locals drive. If they are all rugged four-wheel drive vehicles, ask yourself why. The local roads may not be up to the standard you are used to. If the roads require a different standard of suspension, for example, you are likely to find your UK car uncomfortable to drive.

Car hire

The major international car hire firms are represented in most major countries. For example, the Avis International Directory lists 144 different territories in which they are represented. This covers most of the world, the major exceptions being China, India, Iraq, Iran, Afghanistan, Bolivia, Paraguay and much of North and Central Africa. Hertz in London could not provide us with a list of countries where they are represented but we imagine that their spread is similar. If you use one of these major companies you can make the necessary arrangements from the UK. As in the UK, the normal method of payment in most countries is by credit card, and you will need to produce your UK driving licence. In some countries an International Drivers Permit (or International driving licence) is also needed, and not all credit cards are accepted everywhere. It is advisable to check in advance exactly what you need. Avis offers a special discount rate in most countries for long term hire, i.e. two to eleven months. However, it is probably sensible to wait until you arrive in your new country before committing to long term hire. A local hire company is likely to be much cheaper than the major international ones — and, if you are going to stay in one town, can probably give you the facilities you need.

Banking

It is advisable to open a local bank account even if you are going to be living in a country for only a few months. Local stores and tradesmen will be reluctant to accept UK cheques — and probably even Eurocheques. You are likely to have to show your passport as proof of identity. As in the UK, choose a bank for its convenience. Is there a branch near where you will live and does the bank have a strong branch network? There is generally no point in choosing a branch of your UK bank. However, if you are only living temporarily in a country you are likely to keep your main funds elsewhere, probably in the UK, the Channel Islands or the Isle of Man, so you do not want problems in topping up funds in your local account. It is therefore advisable to choose a bank with a branch in London or one with a strong branch network that is likely to be tied in to the UK clearing system. Your UK bank can probably tell you which bank it has an association with in your new country and it might be worth considering choosing that bank. Even if you are emigrating to a country you may want to maintain the bulk of your funds elsewhere, bringing in money only as and when you need it.

Many countries operate exchange controls. You need to ascertain what the rules are when you open your account. Exchange controls normally restrict payment out of the account to another country. They may also prevent you holding sterling in your new country. They are unlikely to restrict transfer of funds into your account. Where exchange controls operate, concessions often apply on 'non-resident accounts' (these are often called 'convertible accounts'). An immigrant can often maintain a non-resident account for some years after coming into the country. If you can do this it is generally a sensible option. If you are purchasing a property in Spain, for example, you will need to import the currency for this purpose into a 'convertible' Peseta account. This account will then receive the sale proceeds of the property if and when you dispose of it, and allow you to 'convert' the funds received back to your original currency.

In many countries cheques take a lot longer to clear than in the UK so the balance shown on your bank statement can be deceptive. Check the local banking rules; they may be very different from in the UK. For example, in France you will experience difficulties if you want to pay into your account a cheque made out in favour of someone else. Furthermore, if one of your cheques bounces you could find that your bank will close your account and report the fact to the Bank of France — which will blacklist you so that no other bank will open an account for you. In Spain a bounced cheque can result in a visit from the local police, which is not a pleasant experience.

Remember that rates of exchange can fluctuate enormously. In 1990 the exchange rate for the £ against the dollar went from $1.5 to virtually $2 to the pound in the space of six months. If your main account (e.g. in the Channel Islands) is in a different currency to your local account, careful timing of transfers can save you a great deal of money. Do not keep your local balance so low that you risk having to transfer funds over when the rate is particularly unfavourable. Keep an eye on the exchange rate and bring more money into your new country at times when the rate is especially attractive.

Your UK bank will tell you that their travellers cheques are acceptable all over the world. However, the degree of acceptability varies. In some countries they can only be cashed in banks — or even in specific banks — and in others they will be widely accepted in shops. Outside Europe, dollar denominated travellers cheques are likely to be more widely accepted than sterling ones.

Credit cards

The same qualifications apply for credit cards as for travellers cheques. American Express, Diners Club, Mastercard (Access) and Visa are all acceptable in most countries throughout the world. But in some countries one or other of these cards cannot be used at all or can only be used in major cities. If you are going to rely on the use of your credit cards ask your card company for a directory of local merchants who will accept your card in the country to which you are going, and make sure that there is a reasonable spread of them near the place you will be living. Incidentally, if you visit the UK and the Inland Revenue suspect that your account of your movements is not wholly accurate, they may well look at your credit card purchases to check where you were on a particular day. If your credit card is a UK card they have power to obtain this information from the credit card company.

This may be a reason for getting a local credit card. As against that, overseas bills take longer to be charged to your credit card account than local ones so you can increase your credit period by using a UK registered credit card in your new country. On the other hand, this may be easier said than done. A friend who had a well paid job in Chicago had great difficulty obtaining US credit cards — almost universally required as a form of identity in the United States. The reason was that she did not have a credit rating in the United States which the card companies could consult to check her creditworthiness. Eventually, she was forced to negotiate a bank loan that she did not need simply to establish a credit record and thus obtain her credit cards. If you are tempted to retain your UK cards to avoid such problems you may find that the card company wants to withdraw the card as they do not like to send statements to overseas addresses. You may have to agree to a direct debit arrangement on your UK bank account as a condition of continuing with the card. An alternative is for the credit card company to be instructed to send the monthly statements to your bank and the bank to be authorised to settle them. Another option is to notify the credit card company that you have changed your address to that of a friend (or ask the post office to redirect your mail to the friend's address) and leave the friend to forward the statements to you.

If you choose to bank in, say, Luxembourg, you would be able to obtain a credit card (normally Visa) which is neither available for scrutiny by the Inland Revenue nor by the tax authority of your new country. If you are particularly concerned about secrecy this could be an advantage.

Communications with the UK

Telephone

Although International Direct Dialling (IDD) is available in most countries, the international phone lines can be limited, so do not assume that you will be able to telephone friends and colleagues in the UK without trouble. In some countries public telex and telegram facilities are available only in large towns. Postal efficiency also varies from place to place. Airmail post to the UK is generally reasonably quick — at least if you post it in a large town — but other post can sometimes take a long time to reach the UK. This is not necessarily because of distance. In some countries parcels take a lot longer than letters.

Newspapers

The quality of newspapers varies, even in major countries. For example, in North America most of the newspapers concentrate on local news and, apart from a few papers such as the Wall Street Journal and New York Times, are sparse on international news. This is compensated for to a large degree by extensive television world news coverage. Where the local language is not English but there is a local English language paper, this is more likely to carry English news. In many countries English newspapers are available as imports in cities and major towns, albeit often two or three days out of date. You can, of course, also have daily papers and most magazines sent airmail to you from England on subscription — but remember that such a subscription could be looked on by the Inland Revenue as another indication of UK domicile.

Radio

The BBC World Service and its US equivalent, Voice of America, can be received on the radio in most countries. Wavelengths vary. In some countries they broadcast mainly on short wave, so you need to have a short wave receiver. Most modern radios can receive only VHF and long wave. Even if the radio can receive short wave, reception can be poor unless you have a good quality radio. It also needs to be realised that these stations are unlikely to broadcast continuously. You need to ascertain which part of the day — or night — you can tune in to the BBC in your particular country.

Mail order

Many UK mail order companies will not send goods abroad. Those that will include Freemans, Littlewoods, Harrods and Fortnum and Mason. If you want to send presents to UK friends or relatives, any UK mail order firm is likely to oblige provided that you will pay through one of the major credit cards. The Good Book Guide specialise in international mail order of books and can send you any book in print, including paperbacks. As English language books, particularly children's books, are very hard to find in many countries it is advisable to put your name on their mailing list before you go.

You can, of course, use Interflora for flowers.

Residence permits, etc.

You may well need a residence permit to live in your new country. This applies even to EC countries. The grant of the permit is automatic in such cases but the bureaucracy may nevertheless take some time. For example, if you are going to live in France it still takes about six weeks to get a long stay visa which you then show to the authorities in your local department, which will issue you with a residence permit (*carte de séjour*). In some districts this can be short-circuited as the local *préfet* has discretion to issue a *carte de séjour* without production of the visa, but there is no published list of who will do this. In most countries if you need a residence permit you will either need to obtain this in the UK or will need to obtain a long stay entry visa in the UK to be eligible to apply locally for the residence permit. You are advised to make enquiries from the embassy of the country you are going to as to what is required well before you intend to leave the UK.

If you are intending to stay indefinitely in a country you may wish to consider becoming a citizen of that country so as to be able to vote there and exercise other rights of citizenship. If so, you need to check locally what is required. You are likely to need a minimum length of residence in a country before you can apply for naturalisation. You may also have to renounce your British citizenship, although some countries permit dual citizenship. Becoming a citizen of your adopted country, particularly if you renounce your British citizenship at the same time, is likely to result in your becoming domiciled there for UK tax purposes. Check if this has any disadvantages; for example, naturalisation may render your children liable for national service in your adopted country.

British Embassy

If you are going to work in a country that is politically unstable, it is wise to let the British Embassy know that you are there.

Health

You need to be vaccinated against contagious diseases if you are entering certain countries. Even if a vaccination certificate is not mandatory it is advisable if you are going to a country where one of such diseases is endemic. Diseases commonly vaccinated against are Yellow Fever, Cholera, Typhoid Fever, Tetanus, Poliomyelitis, Hepatitis A and Malaria.

The Department of Health publish a leaflet, the Traveller's Guide to Health (T1), which sets out compulsory and advisory vaccination requirements for various non-EC countries. It is worth obtaining an up to date copy of this from the Department of Health — it is also available from some public libraries. Many doctors do, however, believe that the leaflet is over-enthusiastic at recommending vaccinations.

It is also advisable to have a check-up from your family doctor before you leave. You should tell him that you are going abroad and where, so that he can warn you of any special problems you may face. For example, your abnormal blood pressure may not be a problem in England but you need to know if going to a country with a hot climate might aggravate the condition and lead to serious ill-health.

If you suffer from a condition that is controlled by drugs, e.g. diabetes or asthma, the treatment that you are taking may not be available in the country you are going to. If so, it is likely to be better for your doctor to try you on a different medication if, as is often the case, there is an acceptable alternative, while you are in England, rather than you having to change your medication when you go abroad and your body having to cope with that change simultaneously with the change of climate. Even where the drugs you use are available in your new country they may well go under a different trade name and your doctor will need to tell you this or the generic name. You should also ask him for a prescription that you can carry with you. It is advisable to also ask for a written report of your medical history that you can pass to a doctor in your new country. If, as will often be the case, you are not entitled to free medical treatment in your new country, you also need to obtain an idea of the cost of your regular medication so that you can work this into your budget.

It is also advisable to have a dental check up and an eye-test while you are still able to claim benefits under the National Health Service. If you wear glasses, it is advisable to take a spare pair with you. You should, in any event, ask your optician for a note of your prescription.

You need to discover how the medical system works in your new country immediately on arrival. Don't wait until you fall ill before finding out if you need to register with a doctor, whether you need health insurance, etc. Ask for recommendations from neighbours for a good, preferably English speaking, local doctor and go to see him. Give him the medical record and prescriptions that you have brought with you and authorise him to contact your UK general practitioner to clarify any problems. Tell your GP in advance that you are going to do this.

If you are going to a warm climate give yourself time to adapt. Don't spend too much time in the sun for the first few weeks, adopt a stricter standard of hygiene than you used in the UK, check with local people how safe it is to drink the water (in most towns there is unlikely to be a problem) and what sorts of food have potential for illness. Don't immerse yourself in the culture of your new country by going out every night during the first few weeks you are there and sampling all the local delicacies. Your body will need time to get used to a radical change of diet in the same way as it needs time to become accustomed to a different climate.

Free or subsidised medical treatment

The UK has reciprocal health care arrangements with a number of countries. The following offer free or subsidised treatment, but only in an emergency and only to visitors, not to permanent residents:

Australia*
British Dependent Territories* (Anguilla, British Virgin Islands, Falkland Islands, Hong Kong, Montserrat, St Helens, Turks and Caicos Islands)
Bulgaria*
Channel Islands*
Czechoslovakia
Finland
Hungary
Iceland*
Malta
New Zealand
Norway
Poland*
Romania*
Sweden*
Russia

* If you are going to one of these countries you should take with you your NHS medical card as you will need to produce this. In the other countries your passport will normally be sufficient.

Austria will allow such treatment in an emergency if you have a British passport, even if you have become resident there. Yugoslavia used to do so but the current position is doubtful.

You can also get emergency treatment in the European Community provided that you take with you a certificate of entitlement, form E111. However, if you are living or working in the country you will normally have to qualify under the country's own rules instead.

If you are in receipt of a UK pension or widow's benefit you will normally be entitled to free or cheap medical treatment in the same way as a pensioner of your adopted country. In any other case, you are entitled to such treatment whilst you continue to pay UK national insurance contributions or during a period that you would have been entitled to sickness benefit had you remained in the UK. The paperwork that you will need to produce varies, so you need to check the exact position with the DSS before you leave the UK.

NHS medical treatment

In no circumstances will the NHS reimburse you if you pay for medical treatment abroad, even if you are in one of the countries with which the UK has an arrangement under which you could have been treated free.

If you are living abroad and return to the UK for medical treatment, you will not be able to get this free under the NHS.

Private health insurance

Even where you may be eligible to benefit from one of the reciprocal agreements entered into by the UK and referred to above, you are strongly advised to take out medical insurance whilst you are overseas. If you are a member of BUPA, PPP or a similar private health scheme, you are unlikely to be covered by your present policy. However, both of these organisations operate expatriate medical schemes, Private Patients' Plan International Health Plan and BUPA International Lifeline. Other UK expatriate medical insurers to consider are Europea-IMG Ltd, Expatriate Health Care and Exeter Hospital Aid Society. As the different policies vary widely both in price and in the cover they provide, it is worth asking all of these for their brochures and choosing the policy which best suits you. These are, of course, not the only companies providing medical insurance. Your insurance broker may be able to suggest other names.

Remember that private medical insurance is an annual policy — the insurers can refuse to renew your contract or can charge a very high premium if claims prove to be very high. The insurers are also likely to exclude from cover anything arising from an existing condition — which means that if it worsens suddenly you may find yourself facing heavy medical bills. It is normally also the insurers' practice to fix these premiums on the basis of age bands. The cost of cover can increase dramatically with advancing years. Most companies also have a limit on the age at which they will accept new members, so do not leave aside medical insurance until you become infirm. It will probably be too late by then.

Personal accident insurance

If you will continue to work while you are overseas it is worth considering both personal accident insurance and permanent health insurance. If you are sent overseas by your employer these may well already be included in your remuneration package.

Permanent accident insurance provides cover against accident or sickness, the benefits being in the form of either a lump sum or an income. The payments are made following death, loss of sight or a limb, or on permanent total disability. Unfortunately the contract is of an annual nature and subject to your state of health at the beginning of each year and can, therefore, be cancelled by the insurance company. Any lump sum paid is usually free of tax but income benefits are treated similarly to those from permanent health insurance policies, i.e. they are tax free until they have been received for one complete tax year.

Because these policies can be cancelled, they are not as good as permanent health insurance but they should be considered.

Permanent health insurance (PHI)

Male workers are seven times more likely to be away from work for more than six months than they are to die. The insurance which can soften the blow of long-term illness or disability is misleadingly called *permanent health insurance*. It offers nothing of the sort, but once you sign up the insurance company is bound to keep you on the books, however sickly you become and however repetitive your condition.

PHI provides a replacement income up to pension age to substitute income lost through prolonged sickness or disability — which is often defined as 'unable to perform any part of normal duties'. Payments start after a deferred period of a minimum of four weeks but this is more likely to be at least 13 weeks. The premiums are reduced if the deferred period is extended. The premiums depend on occupation, the age of entry, whether you are male or female and the deferment period, and are fixed once the contract is in force. The maximum benefit payable is normally 75% of salary (less a single person's basic National Insurance Invalidity Pension). Benefits are tax free up to the end of the first complete tax year; thereafter they are classed as unearned income. This should not be confused with sickness and accident insurance where the benefits are paid out after eight days, are tax free, only last for 104 weeks, and where premiums may be increased each year, although renewal can be refused if disability has occurred.

The contract cannot be cancelled by the insurance company, neither can it refuse to renew the contract if your health deteriorates. Note that different companies can have different definitions of disability — some are harsh, while others take a more lenient approach. Policies are usually written to the age of 60 or 65 and benefits will cease at that age even if the disability continues. The level of insured benefits can either remain constant or increase in line with the retail prices index or by a fixed percentage.

If your employer does not include you in a scheme or pay the premiums, consider taking out cover yourself. A policy usually guarantees a continuation of your income in the unfortunate event of long-term disability and is suitable for those working abroad. Cover and benefits vary but the protection is a must for the working expatriate.

Old age

Last year *The Times* ran an article on growing old in Spain. It contrasted the reality with the fiction of the BBC soap opera, Eldorado. It points out that thousands of expatriate Britons 'find growing older and poorer difficult in a relatively underdeveloped country where care of the old and infirm is regarded as a family responsibility and not one for the state'. None of us like to think of old age. If you are retiring overseas you are unlikely to consider yourself old even though you are in your sixties. It is, however, important to consider how you are going to cope, and whether you are likely to have the ability to do so, if you grow infirm far from your friends and relations, before you make up your mind to emigrate.

The dream of a couple spending the rest of their lives in their villa in Spain, Italy, Portugal, France or wherever, when both are active and both love that country in which they have spent many a happy holiday, may seem idyllic. It may well be idyllic. But will it stay that way? The article in *The Times* quotes a private district nurse in Spain on the reality when one partner dies and the other falls ill: 'They often have a lovely house in the mountains, maid and gardener, do not speak Spanish, have no transport or telephone, and no chance of getting one. I ask about relatives at home, but either they have none or feel they do not want to bother them . . . I have also arranged to take people back to England when their money has gone and they are infirm. They simply have to go back and be cared for by the State system in England.'

Could this describe you in ten years time? In a Spanish hospital the patient's family will see to his food, cleanliness and laundry. They will descend on the hospital and look after their relative's needs. The English expatriate may have no one to fill this role, particularly if he has kept himself to himself and not mixed much with the local community.

That is not to say do not retire abroad. Many people have done so and had a satisfying and fulfilling retirement. I have a friend in his late seventies who is widowed but who is very much enjoying his retirement in Italy. He comes frequently to England to stay with his children and they go to Italy virtually every year to visit him. With good medical insurance and adequate financial backing the medical and nursing aid that you will need abroad is almost always there to be bought. If you make an effort to learn the language, you will make friends in the local community who are likely to help tend for you in case of need. However, the time to consider what would happen if things go wrong is before you irrevocably commit yourself to your new country. If finances are tight, you want to buy a property in a fairly remote place (or that is all you can afford), and you think that living in Spain or Italy you will be able to eke out your budget more readily than in England, think hard. Emigration may well be a mistake.

Death

Most of us try not to think too much about death either. Our parents' generation thought about setting aside funds to pay for the funeral to avoid the horror of a pauper's grave, and in some parts of the country people still do. But death itself is not something we like to think too much about. It is also not something that we can do much to plan for. However, in the context of financial planning, there are two things that ought to be considered in advance; what is to happen to your assets and what is to happen to your body? Both need to be considered in the context of making a will. This is dealt with in Chapter 10 as far as the disposition of the assets is concerned.

This disposition of the body really comes down to whether you want to be buried in your adopted country, or whether you want your body flown back to England for burial or cremation (or ashes flown back to be scattered in England), or don't you care one way or the other? If you want your body returned to England you should specify this in your will. It is not a difficult task, most undertakers can cope with it, but it will obviously be more costly than being buried where you die. Bear in mind, though, that a wish to be buried in England or for your ashes to be scattered in this country is likely to be taken as strong evidence of an intention to remain domiciled in the UK. Even the Inland Revenue are unlikely to suspect that someone has deliberately died to save tax. But do not assume that death puts an end to tax planning! Burial in the UK may bring your worldwide assets into the embrace of UK inheritance tax. You may be able to thwart this final demand of the taxman as a wish to be buried next to your parents, or your wife, rather than as a wish to be buried in England!

Remember also that it is the custom in most Mediterranean countries to hold the funeral within 24 hours of death, so your wishes must be known by someone locally who can take swift action if required.

Chapter 14

Think of the family

The practical problems of re-establishing the family in the new country will normally affect the spouse more than the expatriate worker. To avoid constant and potentially confusing reference to 'the husband or wife who is working', or the use of the somewhat stilted phrase 'the working spouse', it is assumed below that the working spouse will be the husband, but the same considerations obviously apply if it is the wife. If the husband is sent by his employers to a foreign branch, they are likely to make an effort to help him to settle into his new job. They are also likely to help him, at least on a temporary basis, to find accommodation. How much help is given beyond that varies. It is, however, unlikely to extend to helping his wife to find a job or to helping her make friends. She is likely to be on her own.

If the husband is sent not to a foreign branch but is required to set up an office in the new country, the employer is unlikely to be able to assist (other than financially) with any of the practical problems of relocation. Furthermore, in such a case he is likely to need to devote a considerable amount of time, outside normal office hours, to working or developing business contacts to establish the firm. This means both that the wife has a lot of time on her hands when she is on her own, or when she and the children are on their own, and that she will have to solve the day-to-day problems of relocation without much help from her husband.

Remember the spouse

The first question that needs to be considered if the overseas posting is relatively short term is whether it is right for the family to relocate to the overseas country with the husband. This probably sounds like a silly question as most families naturally wish to stay together. However, if the wife is unlikely to be happy in the new country, the separation is not going to be for too long a period, and the husband's job will permit fairly frequent visits back to the UK for long weekends, it can be a sensible solution, particularly where the children are at a critical point in their education.

If the wife remaining in the UK is felt to be a possible, although unattractive, option or if it is ruled out completely, the next question is whether it might be sensible for the husband to go abroad a few months ahead of the wife. This has a number of merits. The husband does not have to cope simultaneously with the pressures of settling into a new job and the worry of how easily his family are settling into their new life. It enables the wife to visit the husband in the new location, first at weekends when he is at home and perhaps then for a week or two so she can, to some extent, sample life in the new location with him at work — although remembering that a week in a strange town does not provide a great deal of guidance as to how easily one is likely to be able to survive there for a couple of years. It also gives the husband the opportunity to garner local knowledge from his new colleagues. After he has worked with them for a few weeks and got to know them he is likely to obtain honest and helpful advice which will enhance the family's enjoyment. Things such as the part of the town in which the family are likely to most comfortably fit, the best schools, the difficulties of living in a particular spot without a car, the places to shop, social customs, etc. cannot be gleaned from guide books which rarely cover such things in depth and, in any event, because such things change rapidly, could well be out of date even before they are published. The husband can also spend some time house or flat hunting so that when the family join him they can immediately set up home again, not spend the first few weeks living in a hotel, which is really not conducive to family life.

Of course, to some extent, this sort of information can be obtained by a visit, or several visits, to the new location before the employee takes up his job. However, even if the husband's future colleagues try to help they are unlikely to be as forthcoming at that stage as after they have got to know him, and it is improbable that either he or they will be able to identify all of the questions that he ought to ask. In particular, house hunting over a long weekend is unlikely to result in the ideal home unless the family are blessed with a great deal of luck.

If the wife intends to seek employment in the new location she is likely to achieve this more rapidly if the husband has done a bit of groundwork for her such as trying to identify the type of jobs that are likely to be available, where it is best to look for them and whether the wife's UK qualifications will be accepted in the new location if qualifications are required for the type of job that the wife currently does. This point is particularly important. If she needs to pass supplementary examinations to be able to practice in her chosen career she may be able to start the necessary study before leaving the UK.

It is also vital in some countries that the wife develops an understanding of local customs — particularly dress code — before she arrives in the host country. Such things are taken very much more seriously in some countries than in the UK. A few hours incarcerated in a local police station, or, worse, a few days in a local jail, is not the ideal way to begin life in the new country. Revealing clothing that may either be acceptable or may be tolerated, albeit flouting social conventions, in the UK can be breaking the law in some Middle East countries.

Children

Young children usually look on a stay overseas as an adventure and need little persuasion to go. They will need extra attention for a time when they begin to miss their school friends, and encouragement to make friends in the new country. You may also have to be fairly ruthless over which toys go with you and which stay behind.

Older children can be more of a problem, particularly if they are in their teens and building a degree of independence and spending increasing time with friends. Ties with friends are closer and more important, and the removal overseas is likely to curb the level of freedom that they have achieved as no parent will be happy letting a teenage child roam around on his or her own in a strange country. The older child may also be concerned about the risk that the move may damage his schooling. The topic of education is considered separately in Chapter 15. A teenage child will have his own views on what he wants to do and is entitled to have them taken into account.

If a 15- or 16-year old child is strongly opposed to going overseas and the job in the foreign country is only for a year or two, very careful thought needs to be given to the problem. It may be better to leave him at home with a friend or relative to keep an eye on him and provision for frequent visits to the family, than to force him to go with the family. If he goes overseas reluctantly and either his education or his friendships were to suffer badly as a result, this may well alienate him from the family.

Some older children will welcome the chance to live abroad. If your teenager falls into this category you may have a different problem. Having obtained his school leaving qualifications overseas he may well want to complete his university education overseas and it may be difficult to persuade him to return to the UK with the family.

Some practical matters

When going overseas most people think of the big things: tax, housing, children's education, investment of savings, and insurance, but it is easy to overlook some of the little things. It may therefore be helpful to mention a few.

(*a*)   A favourite British pastime is to complain about the inefficiencies of British Rail and London Transport or one's local transport authority. In comparison with some countries most of the UK has a fairly frequent, fairly fast, fairly comprehensive and fairly reliable public transport system. Do not assume that similar facilities will exist in your new country. In particular, whilst most countries have efficient public transport in the centre of big towns, in many cases public transport in the suburbs is wholly by bus and transport between towns can be poor. In some cases, for example the USA and Canada, the main public transport between towns is either by air, which involves getting to the airport, the usual waiting around that all flights entail and getting from the airport at the other end, or by long distance bus, which is slow.

(*b*)   The British also like to complain about the weather. It is not actually that bad. We tend not to have extremes of anything; no extreme heat for days but no extreme cold either and no long rainy season or long dry season. Although most of us, particularly the young, profess to yearn for continuous sunshine the reality may be different. When my six-year old nephew went to Singapore he found the continual heat very oppressive for several months.

(*c*)   If both spouses cannot drive, or you have teenage children who are too young to drive in your new country, check out the public transport before choosing a house. For example, there are some beautiful houses in Connecticut with the nearest neighbour a quarter of a mile away and the nearest employment 50 miles distant. It is a lovely place to live if you like solitude and have a car. It will probably be hell if you don't drive.

(*d*) Foodstuffs, even well-known brands that you imagine are internationally available, are frequently not on sale in other countries. If there is something that you — or the children — are particularly fond of, take a supply. Don't worry about the funny looks the man at Customs might give you. A friend of mine returned to the UK seven years ago after living for about six years in Chicago. Whenever I or any other of his friends visit the USA we take a shopping list of breakfast cereals and other American food that his young children still hanker after.

(*e*) The same goes for children's books, particularly for very young children, and particularly if you would like them to learn English rather than American.

(*f*) Your electrical gadgets, including shaver, hairdryer, and food processor will probably not work in your new country without an adaptor. Nor will your television and video, even with an adaptor, in many cases.

(*g*) In some countries certain consumer goods such as televisions, computers, hi-fi systems and children's toys can be very cheap by comparison with prices in England. Resist the temptation to bring too much back home with you when you return. You wouldn't be the first person to discover that your UK house in which you lived comfortably before you went abroad has shrunk to such an extent when you fill it with your newly imported possessions that you need to move somewhere larger.

(*h*) Some years ago I had a friend whose husband was sent by his firm to Tanganyika. I think they were both in their late twenties at the time. She regaled us with the fact that, like all expatriates there at the time, she had two domestic servants. This left her with lots of free time, some of which she used to develop a liaison with a fellow expatriate which led to the break up of her marriage. When she returned to England she found life without any domestic help so difficult that she could not settle down here again.

(*i*) Many people look on a friend relocating overseas as potential for a cheap holiday. While you may be delighted to see your close friends again, and be happy to put them up for a few days and show them around town, you probably don't want to do this for someone different every couple of weeks. And you are probably less eager to welcome casual acquaintances, particularly if they are not able or willing to fend for themselves and expect your family to provide free accommodation, meals, maid services and a tourist guide merely because your child was at the same school as theirs. When my brother-in-law's employer sent him to Singapore my sister was surprised to find how many friends she seemed to have made in the three years or so she was living in Hampshire. She even had a family she had never met before sleeping on her living room floor for a couple of nights; they turned up late at night and told her that a mutual friend had assured them that she would extend them a welcome!

Chapter 15

Children's education

The key decision that needs to be made in respect of children is obviously the effect on their education. There are basically three choices: to leave the child at school in England, to send him to an 'English' school in the host country or, if it does not have one, a neighbouring country, or to send him to a local school. Which option to adopt depends primarily on the age of the child, his adaptability and financial considerations.

It also needs to be borne in mind that qualifications, particularly university degrees, are increasingly being required before one can enter a profession and a qualification obtained in one country will not necessarily be regarded as an acceptable substitute for that of another. For example, my own professional body, the Institute of Chartered Accountants in England and Wales, has two methods of entry: as a university graduate who then does a three-year training programme, or an A level GCE entrant who must take a four-year course — and will find it virtually impossible to enter into a training contract with an international firm as they generally only recruit graduates. I was surprised to discover recently that the Institute declines to treat degrees from most foreign universities as equivalent to an English degree as a matter of course, although it will regard them as meeting A level standards and is sometimes prepared on an individual basis, to accept them as a degree level qualification.

Leaving aside the extraordinary degree of chauvinism that this displays in what ought to be an international profession, a 14-year old who goes abroad with his parents and completes his education in, say, the USA, returning with them to the UK six or seven years later with a US degree, will find himself at a serious disadvantage if he wishes to become a chartered accountant. I doubt that my professional body is unique in this respect. Accordingly, if the child's career is likely to be in the UK the acceptability in the UK of the qualifications that he will obtain needs to be investigated before putting him into an overseas educational system. This is unlikely to be a serious problem with young children but, with increasing competition for some university places, could be relevant if it is likely that the child, having obtained a foreign school-leaving level qualification, will take a university course in this country. However, universities and other academic institutions are normally willing to accept foreign school qualifications.

Another problem that needs to be appreciated is the effect on the child of switching to a different system of education in mid stream. A seven- or eight-year old is unlikely to experience difficulties. For a 15-year old a switch could be disastrous. He will not only have to overcome the trauma of switching schools but is likely to find that some of what he has learned is not relevant to the qualification in his home country or is unsuitable for it (e.g. where the UK places emphasis on teacher assessment in a subject but the host country qualifications rely wholly on passing exams). He will also inevitably find that in some subjects his knowledge is behind that of the rest of the class and in others he is so far ahead that he becomes bored.

A UK school

In pure educational terms leaving the child at school in England is probably best for most children, at least in theory. It is unfortunately impractical in many cases and forces upon the family a separation which they might well not otherwise have chosen. It could also well have a damaging effect on the child who may feel that he is being sent to boarding school or to stay with relatives because he is in the way, and is likely to resent being denied the opportunity of the adventure of living for a time in a foreign country.

Staying at school in the UK generally requires having someone in the UK willing to take responsibility for the child. This will normally mean either enlisting a relative or family friend, or the wife herself remaining in the UK. If the child is to continue at a day school this places a heavy burden on the relative or friend — who effectively has to take the child into his home as one of his family. If he goes to a boarding school and will join the family abroad during the vacation periods the responsibility is far less onerous. Most boarding schools now expect the child to be accommodated elsewhere for half term and want a guardian available in England to take responsibility for decisions, e.g. choice of subject to be taken, or the provision of pocket money, on which parents are normally consulted. It is also sensible to have someone in England whom the child knows, to whom he can turn for help with problems.

Although all schools train pupils for GCSE and all must follow the national curriculum, it must be remembered that there are two distinct school systems in the UK, public schools and state schools, and it is difficult to move from one to the other beyond infant school level. This is because the private school system consists of preparatory schools which take the child from 7 to 13, preparing him for the common entrance examination and senior schools which the child joins at 13 or 14 (although there is increasingly provision to take a child at 11), whereas in the state system the child moves from primary school to secondary school at the age of 11, normally without having taken an exam. The types of learning are therefore different. The preparatory school, having the child for an extra two years, ought to be able to educate him to a greater depth than the primary school. The senior school, having him for two years less, needs to impose more intense learning methods than the secondary school.

In the private system most preparatory schools are day schools although there are some boarding schools. Virtually all the senior schools are boarding schools — many of which take day pupils. In the state system virtually all the schools at both primary and secondary level are day schools. There are a few state boarding schools — which charge fees for board but provide the education for free and are thus far cheaper than public schools. There are, however, only about 50 of them altogether. They are usually in rural areas and although they take children of parents whose UK home is in other parts of the country they generally give priority to those living in their own catchment area. In the past they have also been subject to the control of the local education authority in whose area they are based. With the advent of the Grant Maintained School — which is self-governing and not dependent on the LEA (many of whose decisions seem to be influenced by political as much as by educational ideologies) — some of these boarding schools are now grant maintained and it is likely that more will follow. One such school is The Woodroffe School in Lyme Regis. It is worth checking with the Grant Maintained Schools Foundation what others exist at the time you intend to go abroad. It is also worth checking with your own LEA (which is normally your local authority) if there is a state boarding school in your area. Application for a place at a state boarding school is made direct to the school.

As there are few state boarding schools, if you opt for a boarding education in the UK this is normally likely to mean a private school. For a first class school it is also likely to mean the child passing the common entrance exam and passing an interview with the school of your choice. If your job abroad is a posting that is thrust on you by your firm at a few months' notice when your child is 12 or 13, he may find difficulty with both these hurdles. The common entrance examination has papers in English, French and mathematics, all of which must be passed, and history, geography, science and religious knowledge, where a failure is not necessarily fatal, plus an optional choice of Latin, Greek and additional mathematics. Children from state schools tend to find especial difficulty with French and mathematics. If you are aware that you will get an overseas posting at some stage, or the nature of your job entails a series of overseas postings — and your finances will permit it — it may be sensible to enter your child in a preparatory school to prepare him for a private senior school.

Help in finding a private school can be sought free of charge from Gabbitas, Truman and Thring, an educational charity, who will discuss the options with you, help you decide whether a UK boarding school is a sensible choice and suggest two or three possible schools to approach. The Independent Schools Information Service (ISIS) publishes a number of leaflets and an annual paper-back guide 'Choosing Your Independent School'. Their associated company ISIS International provides, at a fee, a placement and consultancy service and operates a clearing list of schools prepared to offer places to children of expatriates.

The standard advice to parents contemplating sending a child to boarding school is to visit several schools first, not only to look at their educational standards but also the location and the state of the buildings and to try to form a judgement on the relationship between staff and pupils. After all, the school will in effect become your child's home and the staff his parents for the greater part of the next few years, so the standard of education he is likely to receive is not the only, and indeed probably not the most important, consideration. Whilst this may be difficult for parents given only a few weeks' or a few months' notice of a move, it is essential. Indeed, if the child is to be sent to a boarding school and has previously attended a day school it is advisable for the mother to remain in the UK for a period to help settle the child in the school.

Some employers will provide help with school fees when an employee is posted overseas. If this help is not available, the cost of the child's schooling needs to be taken into account in considering the financial merits of working overseas. Even where the employer pays, remember that the child's schooling may well outlast the job, or at least the overseas posting. The employer is unlikely to be prepared to pay the school fees after the employee returns to the UK — and even if it does the cost is a benefit in kind of the father for tax purposes and will attract a substantial tax charge. Accordingly, before sending your child into the independent system you need to be reasonably confident that when you are abroad you will accumulate sufficient savings to be able to fund the school fees on your return. Most public school children find a move to the state system difficult — although the development of sixth-form colleges makes such a transition easier at the age of 16. Local education authorities do have power to assist parents with school fees but, in practice, are unlikely to do so, particularly where the parents themselves are not contributing to local taxation.

Parents with young children at boarding schools also need to consider how the child gets from the school to their overseas home for holidays. The airline will look after the child at the airport and on the plane and the parent will meet him at the foreign airport. However, some arrangement needs to be made to look after the child from school to the UK airport (which may well involve an overnight stay) and back again. It is best to allot this task to a relative or friend in the UK. If none is available, commercial child escort services are provided by Universal Aunts Ltd, Welmet and Education Guardian Advisory Services Ltd. The Women's Corona Society provides a similar service to its own members.

Overseas 'English-type' schools

Overseas 'English-type' schools can again be day schools or boarding schools. In most cases if the parents opt for a boarding education it is safest to choose a UK based school rather than an overseas one. If a child will not be living with his parent it is difficult in most cases to see much merit in his boarding overseas. There are, however, exceptions. Some schools board pupils with local families, which can be a valuable and rewarding cultural experience for the child. If the parent will live a great distance from the UK a boarding school in a country nearer to that to which the parents have been moved may facilitate visits to the parents, or by the parents to the school.

Overseas English schools vary in quality. They also tend to be found only in major cities. Fees tend to be high. In the European Community there is a supervisory body, COBISEC (Council of British Independent Schools in the European Community), which has entered into an arrangement with the Department of Education for HM Inspectors to inspect member schools to ensure that their educational standards at least are equivalent to UK ones. Most overseas English schools take pupils from a wide range of nationalities. Where an English school is not available in a particular place, many International schools will provide a curriculum suitable for GCSE levels. These are usually American schools geared towards the US college system. Most also offer the International Baccalaureate which is becoming increasingly accepted by UK universities and other establishments of higher or further education.

A directory of British and International Schools, 'The International Schools Directory' is available (price £17) from the European Council of International Schools. Many such schools have a waiting list for admissions.

Local national schools

For those who either cannot afford school fees or want their children to mix with local children, which can be a valuable experience, particularly for younger children, the other option is a local national school. Clearly, there are a number of problems, the most obvious of which is that teaching will be in the local language, so if this is not English the child will have to learn the language before he can start his education. The pattern of education is different. For example, in most of Europe and Australia, formal education starts at the age of six as compared with five in the UK. In third world countries education may often be fairly rudimentary as far as UK needs are concerned, and expatriates will be firmly discouraged from consuming the scarce educational resources devoted to bright local children. Discipline in many overseas countries is much harsher than children are used to in the UK.

Nevertheless, studying at a local school, particularly at primary level, can be very rewarding for the child and can also speed the integration of the family into the local community. My six-year old nephew blossomed when he went to his mainly Chinese (although English speaking) local school in Singapore and I have no doubt that when he returns to the UK he will be far more educationally advanced and a far more rounded person than if he had stayed in his UK school.

Home teaching

A final possibility if you cannot find a suitable local school is to teach the child yourself. This obviously demands a great commitment from the parents, but may be the most practical solution for the child who is unsuited to boarding education, particularly if the father's job entails frequent changes of location. Home teaching is obviously a daunting task without help. Fortunately this is available. An educational charity, Parents' National Education Union, provides a service, World-Wide Education Service (WES), aimed at children from three to eleven under which the parent teaches the child under the guidance of WES, with a London-based tutor available to provide support and to assess the work of the child. For secondary school age children, home study courses for GCSE and A level courses are available from Mercers College and the National Extension College. However, it is not easy for teenagers to reach GCSE or A level standards by correspondence courses, particularly where the parents are not themselves proficient in the subject being studied.

School fees planning

Unless a good local school is available most expatriates are likely to end up sending their children to a fee-paying school either in the UK or overseas. An overseas employment frequently carries with it either a significantly higher salary than one being earned in the UK or a package of benefits including the payment of school fees. Accordingly, funding school fees for the duration of the employment is not normally too difficult. However, finding the continuing fees after the return to the UK is another matter.

There is no easy, highly tax efficient, way to provide for school fees.

There are three main sources for funding school fees:

From capital — i.e. a lump sum.

From income.

Other sources.

From capital

You pay a lump sum to an insurance company, a broker or a school, and the money is invested in a variety of ways. Some schemes have some tax advantages (in particular the school fees composition schemes and educational trusts). The three main types of capital schemes are as follows.

(*a*) School fees composition schemes.

(*b*) Educational trusts.

(*c*) Fixed interest schemes.

School fees composition schemes

You pay a lump sum to a school as school fees paid in advance. The school then invests the money, usually in an annuity which starts paying out when the child goes to school. The amounts you must invest will vary from school to school depending on the fee levels and the discounts they might give you for paying in advance.

These schemes are essentially deferred annuity contracts. Because the school usually enjoys charitable status, its income is free of tax. The school pays the lump sum over to an insurance company in return for an annuity. The annuity, in the hands of the school, is tax free. The scheme is thus particularly attractive to a person who will be a higher rate taxpayer when he returns to the UK or a person who is taxable on his investment income in the country in which he is working, since he will not be liable to either income tax or capital gains tax arising from the investment of the lump sum by the school. If, instead, he purchased the annuity, there would be income tax to pay.

The size of the discount which the school is able to offer will depend largely on the length of the period before the fees become due and the level of interest rates at the time the lump sum is paid.

Children's education

Advice should be taken on the inheritance tax position of the parent or any other relative who makes the lump sum payment.

One of the main advantages of the school fees composition schemes is that they are reasonably simple to formulate and convenient to operate. However, they can be very inflexible. For example, if the child is currently of primary school age and does not attend the senior school you have chosen, for any reason — perhaps because he fails the common entrance exam — a repayment might be made, but usually on very unattractive terms. Schemes vary as to what happens if the child leaves the school or dies before his education has been completed. A parent should also clarify with the school what will happen if the tax advantages relating to educational charities are abolished in the future. You need to be sure that both this risk, and the risk that increases in the level of fees chargeable by the school might not keep pace with those on which the school calculated the lump sum payment, are undertaken by the school not by you.

Educational trusts

Educational trusts are designed to overcome some of the disadvantages of the school fees composition schemes, since they are independent versions of the composition fees schemes created by the schools themselves. You can usually switch funds from the benefit of one child to the benefit of another (which may not be the case with school fees composition schemes) and you do not have to nominate the school to which the fees are to be paid until shortly before the child starts school. If the child should die before the end of the plan, the amount paid into the plan, less any school fees payment already made from the plan, is usually guaranteed to be repaid under the trust deed. A disadvantage is that the capital cannot normally be repaid in any other circumstances (as such a power would nullify the tax benefit) so you are committed to sending your child, or at least one of your children, to a fee-paying school.

The tax advantages of the deferred annuity contract being paid to an educational trust are the same as for the school fees composition scheme, therefore from this point of view the scheme is attractive.

Fixed interest schemes

The lump sum is applied to purchase suitable fixed interest investments such as British Government stocks, local authority bonds and national savings certificates. It may also be possible to make use of existing investments owned by the payer. The scheme is tailored so that the investments will mature, as far as possible, shortly before the necessary funds are required to pay the school fees.

These schemes are more flexible in that the investments are not restricted to educational purposes — the money can be used for anything if circumstances change. However, it can take some time to work out an appropriate scheme and identify suitable investments. The income produced by the investments is taxable on the parent (or whoever takes out the scheme) although most of the return arises from capital growth and the investments selected will be ones that attract exemption from capital gains tax.

From income

There are a number of different ways in which these schemes can be set up. Most involve saving regularly by taking out investment-type life insurance policies, maturing year by year as the fees become due. Thus, the payments are spread over a longer period than the period of education. The amount of monthly savings required is obviously less if you start these policies sooner rather than later. The scheme should also include some insurance should the income provider die early, become disabled or be made redundant.

There are three main methods of school fees planning out of income.

(*a*) Life assurance schemes.

(*b*) Unit trust regular savings plan.

(*c*) Deferred annuities through an educational trust.

Life assurance schemes

These are essentially endowment policies. An ordinary term life assurance pays your estate a lump sum on death but pays nothing if you survive the agreed period. An endowment policy not only pays a lump sum on death but can pay you a tax-free lump sum at the end of the term. In other words, you are bound to get your money back (either dead or alive!). The lump sum can be guaranteed, so you know exactly how much you, or your estate, will receive. An endowment is a way of saving, but you must save for at least seven and a half years (and possibly longer) to avoid extra tax charges. You can pay monthly, and if a series of such policies is taken out to mature in successive years, the lump sums received on maturity can be used to fund the school fees. Such plans can be very effective.

Many financial advisers are able to provide a detailed schedule of estimated costs. The plan may also include a series of automatic policy loans to ensure that fees are available when due.

Unit trust regular savings plan

These can either be straightforward unit-linked savings plans or they can represent direct investments into unit trusts on a regular (usually monthly) basis. In this latter case, no life cover is provided and consideration should be given to this separately. A unit trust savings plan provides greater flexibility than unit-linked savings plans since it may be terminated at any time without penalty. Capital gains tax on realisations and income tax on income would be payable.

Deferred annuities through an educational trust

These are similar to a lump sum investment in an educational trust, except that rather than paying a lump sum to an educational trust, premiums are paid monthly. Each premium purchases a guaranteed level of fees provided by way of a deferral annuity arranged through an educational trust.

Children's education

If you are working in a country that does not levy an income tax, or levies it at a very low rate, you may well be able to obtain a better return by investing the money yourself outside the UK. These products are largely aimed at the UK residents and because the funds are invested in the UK the income generally suffers UK tax at either the 25% basic rate or, sometimes, the 33% corporation tax rate. If you are likely to be abroad for a year or two only it is probably worth accepting this tax to get the scheme going and to protect the position after your return. This problem can, in theory, be eliminated by using an offshore insurance company or unit trust group but if you do this you may find that you fall foul of tax anti-avoidance rules after you return to the UK.

Other sources

Apart from meeting the costs of school fees from your own capital or income, the following are other ways which may be open to parents:

(a) Borrowing — you may be able to arrange a loan based on the security of your home or other investments, or based on investment-type life insurance policies.

(b) If the parent is a partner in a UK trading partnership, it may be possible to arrange for a lump sum to be withdrawn from the partnership and have it replenished with a bank loan. Tax relief might be obtained on such a loan.

(c) A loan could be made against your pension funds.

(d) Setting up an accumulation and maintenance trust fund with grandparents', not the parents', money has tax advantages.

(e) As a last resort, capital might be released by moving to a cheaper house.

Local authority grants for university/polytechnic

Grants may sometimes be available from your local authority towards your child's higher education in the UK, even though you are residing outside the UK, but the rules are complex. You should always consult your own local authority to ascertain whether your child is eligible for a grant.

There are two key points which the expatriate parents must establish.

(a) Your residence abroad is intended to be a temporary one and that you intend to return to the UK.

(b) Your child is intent on pursuing a full-time education course in the UK.

As you can see, intention to return is important.

It can sometimes be difficult to work out to which local authority you can apply for a grant. The rules are as follows:

(i) You apply to the local authority where the child is 'ordinarily' resident on 30 June prior to the commencement of any course in the autumn term (or 31 October or 28 February if the course starts in spring or summer).

(ii) If he is not then ordinarily resident in the UK it is the local authority for the area where the student was ordinarily resident at any time in the two years before 30 June (or 31 October or 28 February for spring or summer terms).

(iii) If he was not ordinarily resident in the UK in that period it is the local authority for the area where the student was physically resident before 30 June (or 31 October or 28 February). This would usually be in the area in which the student's school is located.

(iv) If he was not physically resident in the UK at that time it is the local authority for the area where the university or polytechnic is located.

There are two kinds of courses:

Designated courses

These include courses at most universities, polytechnics and teacher training colleges. They are 'designated' by the Secretary of State for Education and Science. They are usually a minimum of three year's duration. Grants are mandatory awards, i.e. the local authority must pay the grant if your child is accepted on the course. (In fact, 90% of the grant is paid by central government.) Mandatory awards include fees for tuition, registration, admission, matriculation, examination and graduation. College fees are also covered at the Universities of Cambridge, Oxford, Durham, Kent, York and Lancaster.

Discretionary courses

These might include one-year secretarial courses, foundation art courses, nursery nursing courses and Ordinary National Diploma courses. The local authority does not have to pay a grant and usually only pays for those students who have done well in the exams.

You should apply for grants as early as possible: don't wait for your child to be accepted. When you apply, include with your application form a letter setting out your personal circumstances in detail, including the following.

Reason for living outside the UK.
How long you intend to be abroad.
How long you have been abroad.
The courses for which your child is applying.
Child's age and school performance.
Where school holidays have been spent.
Where school holidays might be spent.
Whether or not you have a UK home.
Why you think your child is eligible for a grant.

Remember that you need to demonstrate that your intention is to return to the UK soon, and emphasise the temporary nature of your period overseas.

Usually, there are three forms which need to be completed.

Application form — Includes exam results, career goals of child and headteacher's assessment.

Children's education

Income form — Includes your full income and addresses for third party confirmation (e.g. accountants, employer). If divorced or separated, the parent with whom the child lives should complete the form.
College acceptance form — Completed by the college.

The local authority mandatory or discretionary award only covers the course fees. It does not include residence costs (e.g. board and lodging), deposit money, materials or equipment. Maintenance grants are available for these costs, but they are means tested and most expatriates earn too much to qualify for them.

Chapter 16

Investment

Why invest?

Or to put it another way, why save? Investment is simply finding a home for your savings. This probably sounds a somewhat stupid question. After all, we've all been brought up to believe that saving is 'a good thing'. Nevertheless, stop a minute and give it a bit of thought. It is doubtful if saving, of itself, is a good thing. It takes money out of the economy, and as the song says it's 'money that makes the world go round'. If we all save everything we earn (after, of course, providing for our bare necessities) it will create a depression and massive unemployment. Also, if saving is of itself a good thing why should the Government penalise it by taking in inheritance tax (assuming that you die domiciled in the UK) 40% of your savings — of course, they don't touch the first £150,000 but that is not much more than the price of a decent suburban house, so, leaving aside your house which most of us don't mentally categorise as savings, the Government want 40% of everything that you've managed to save.

So why save? It is an important question to which everyone will have different answers. Some possible answers are as follows.

(*a*) To generate income in retirement.

(*b*) To generate some capital at retirement to enable me to do the things that I didn't have time or money to do when I was younger.

(*c*) To supplement my income in retirement.

(*d*) To provide a cushion against inflation after retirement.

(*e*) So that I can give my children a better start in life than I had.

(*f*) So that I can leave something for my children.

(*g*) The ability to save is a reflection of my success.

(*h*) I have no immediate needs that I can think of to spend my money on.

(*i*) I want to be able to give my children a public school education.

(*j*) I don't want my children to have to struggle to educate my grandchildren; I feel that I should finance this.

(*k*) I don't want to risk being a burden on my children.

(*l*) I want to make sure that my spouse has the resources to maintain her standard of living after I die — when my pension will cease and even if my widow is entitled to a pension it will be at a lower rate.

Investment

(*m*) To buy a bigger house.

(*n*) To buy a boat or a Rolls-Royce or whatever else you have always dreamed of owning.

Get a piece of paper and write down any additions to this list you can think of. Cross off any of the above items that don't apply to you. Now put your list into order of importance. Perhaps it wasn't such a stupid question after all. You cannot start to consider how you should invest your savings until you have identified what you want to achieve from them.

Before we look at the limitations that your objectives place on your investment strategy you ought to take another look at your list and ask yourself some more questions. If you are retiring abroad these questions are: 'Are my savings sufficient to meet all my objectives? If not, should I eliminate some of my objectives, or should I try to satisfy them all to a limited extent? For example, should I say I can't afford to pay the grandchildren's school fees — probably £10,000-£15,000 per child per annum — and have the standard of living I aspire to, so shall I forget the school fees, or reduce my own expectations for my retirement, or give my children a contribution towards school fees and accept a lower standard of living than I would have liked and still live comfortably?'

If you are going abroad to work the additional questions are: 'How long is it before you will need the money? Two years? Five? Twenty? Thirty? Fifty? Is your job abroad your one chance to get some money behind you or will you have further opportunities to save significant amounts in the future? Even if you think there will be other opportunities are you willing to take the risk that they may not materialise? To what extent do you think that your objectives will be met from other sources, such as by inheritance from your parents?'

Now take another look at your list of objectives. You may want to revise it. You are now ready to consider investment.

Investment strategy

You are not, however, ready to start looking at where to put your funds. Before you can do this you need to work out your investment strategy, i.e. how to direct your funds so as to secure the most advantageous position to meet your objectives. We can't develop your investment strategy for you because we don't know what is on your list of objectives, and it is this list that will determine your strategy, but we can give you some general guidance.

(*a*) To the extent that you need the money within the next five to ten years it would be a bit stupid to put it into a pension fund that you can't touch for twenty years, an endowment policy that matures in twenty or even ten years' time, or a similar long term investment.

(*b*) If you see a need for extra income in a few years' time, invest for capital growth for the time being, so that you maximise the capital available to generate that income.

(*c*) If you are reliant on generating income from your savings remember that the more attractive an investment appears the riskier it is likely to be and you can't afford to take risks. If your bank is only prepared to pay you 6% interest and someone else promises 14% is it because the bank is greedy? That may be part of the reason but the banks have to compete hard for savings nowadays so it is probably not the main reason. Is it because your bankers are ignorant and do not know how to generate the best return? That is unlikely. Is it because the 14% is based on optimistic assumptions, or requires you to lock your money up longer than you want to? Is it because the promoter is going to speculate with your money and although the big return could be there it is equally possible that you could lose your money? Is the big return capable of being achieved? It is unlikely that people who put their savings with Barlow Clowes or BCCI or any of the other financial organisations that have collapsed in recent years asked themselves these questions. If you are prepared to put your money wherever you can get the best return for the time being without investigating why, you are not motivated by your investment objective; you are motivated by greed.

(*d*) The capital growth you can generate will also depend on the degree of risk you are prepared to take.

(*e*) If you will need your capital at different times, work out how much you will need and when. You can then choose your investments to, hopefully, produce the right amounts at the right time.

(*f*) Even if you are prepared to take risks it is unwise to do this with the whole of your savings. Put some into something fairly risk-free, some into something riskier and a fairly small proportion into the very risky things that could make you a lot of money or could lose you the lot. As a rule of thumb if you want to get into commodities, or precious stones, or stamps, or rare books or similar speculative investments, restrict yourself to a maximum of 5% of your savings.

(*g*) Do you know that even Stock Exchange investments are graded? The big, safe (one hopes) companies are Alpha stocks. The smaller but still relatively safe ones Beta stocks, and the small companies Gamma and Delta stocks. Although it is probably very unfair to a number of good companies a sensible investment maxim is small = high risk = better growth potential.

(*h*) Keep some funds liquid in case of emergency, i.e. keep £10,000 — £20,000 in a bank or building society deposit so that you can get your hands on it quickly if a gale blows off the roof of your villa.

(*i*) If you plan to return to the UK, investments that will mature after your return need to be approached in the light of UK tax. If you want to take advantage of your ability to save without attracting such tax consider short term investments that you can realise at the time you come back and start your real investment strategy at that stage.

(*j*) Remember that needs and intentions change. You may think now that you won't need your funds for 30 years, but it will be unfortunate if in 20 years' time you find that everyone retires at 50 and you cannot supplement your income from your savings until you reach 60.

(*k*) If you think that you will need extra income at some stage you can meet this need either by generating income or using capital to supplement income, so you do not necessarily need to invest to produce income.

(*l*) To what extent is history a mirror of the future? The FTSE-100, the leading UK stock exchange index, rose from 1140.3 in September 1984 to 2366 by September 1987, an increase of 27% p.a. It then crashed to 1749.8 at the end of October 1987, still an increase of 15% p.a. From October 1987 to October 1991 it rose from 1749.8 to 2624.6, an increase of 11% p.a. If the Government gets inflation under control will these rises still happen or will they be a thing of the past? In devising your investment strategy you are going to have to take a view on questions like that.

(*m*) Spread your risk. Of course, this also means spreading your opportunities but it is better to trade off a bit of growth potential for a significant increase in security. If you have saved £100,000 and after careful consideration you feel that the investment scheme you've come across offering a 24% yield is safe, we still would not recommend you to put the whole £100,000 into it. We probably would not put more than £15,000 into it, but then we may be more averse to risk than you are.

(*n*) If the value of your investment depends on share or property prices, leave yourself some leeway on maturity. If you have decided that you want £100,000 of your savings to mature when you reach 60 it is usually safer to go for something that you can realise at any time between, say, age 59 and 62. It would be somewhat unfortunate if there is another stock exchange crash, or property slump a few days before your 60th birthday. If this happens you want the ability to defer realising your investment until prices recover a bit. You also do not want to be sitting around at 59 predicting another stock exchange crash and praying that it does not happen until after you reach 60 and are able to realise your investment.

Choosing an investment adviser

You now need to find yourself an investment adviser. If the amount which you have available for investment is less than about £50,000 this may be easier said than done.

Why use an investment adviser? After all, you have already developed your investment strategy, which is the key thing; you are reasonably intelligent; a dab hand with a pair of scissors; and if you take all the quality Sunday papers for a month you will end up with a pile of coupons from a wide selection of investment houses covering a number of different investment mediums. Well, yes, you could do it that way — in the same way as you could buy your house overseas by walking round town for a couple of hours looking for estate agents signs and buying the one that looks prettiest from outside. You would have to be pretty silly to do that. You will have restricted your choice to those properties that you happen to have seen advertised, will have done no research on what else might be available, will have made your choice on insufficient information (you will not have seen inside the house or asked a professional to do a structural survey) and will have no idea if the price you are paying is realistic. No one in his right mind would do that if he were going to spend £150,000 on a house; so why do it when you are going to spend £150,000 on an investment portfolio?

No one wants to spend money for the sake of it. If you are going to use an investment adviser what are you getting for the fee he will charge — or the commission that he will earn, which amounts to the same thing as, at the end of the day, it comes out of your pocket? What you ought to be aiming to get is:

(*a*) The benefit of his experience.

(*b*) His knowledge of what is available in the market place.

(*c*) His knowledge of which companies use conservative projections and which may be over optimistic.

(*d*) His knowledge of which investment managers have performed well in the past and his assessment of whether they may have had internal changes which makes it less likely that they will continue to do so in the future.

(*e*) His ability to take your investment strategy and determine if it is really what you ought to be looking for or if there are snags in it that he can discuss with you.

(*f*) The ability to select from the different types of investments that can satisfy your strategy those that are most appropriate to your needs.

(*g*) A willingness to keep your investments under review and make or advise changes where appropriate.

(*h*) An individual who will take responsibility over a period of years for your investments, not a company with a rapid staff turnover so that you are dealing with someone new every time you phone.

(*i*) Someone who is reasonably accessible — and, if you will be living in a significantly different time zone, who will provide you with a phone number where you can contact him during your daytime rather than his.

(*j*) Someone who operates through established local offices in the place where you live, even if he is based in the UK. This indicates a commitment to service clients in that country.

(*k*) Sound administrative back-up.

(*l*) A person who will get in touch with you on a regular basis, not wait for you to get back to him when you feel that your investment strategy may need to be reviewed.

(*m*) Someone with enough knowledge of tax to realise that what is an appropriate investment for a UK based investor is not necessarily the most appropriate for you as your tax position will be different.

(*n*) Someone whose choice of investment is motivated by your needs, not the commission that he can earn by putting you into a particular product.

(*o*) Someone who is not going to run off with your money.

Before considering how you find an adviser you need to decide where you should look for him. Should this be in the UK before you go, or in your new country when you get there? To an extent this depends on where you are going and for how long. If you will only be away for a few years it is normally best to choose a UK based adviser as you will not want to change advisers when you return. If you are retiring overseas or expect to work overseas for ten or twenty years, look at what advice is available in your new country and how closely investment advisers are regulated there by the authorities. It makes most sense to have your investment adviser in the country in which you live, other things being equal, because he can get to know you better — and thus better appreciate your real needs — than the UK based adviser, and he is more aware of changing circumstances in your new country that are likely to influence your needs. However, you ideally want someone that you can easily communicate with. This may be difficult to find in non-English speaking countries, and you are unlikely to find a satisfactory adviser if you have to select from a handful of English speaking people. You also want someone who is honest and reliable. Whilst this is to an extent a matter of luck, you are less likely to engage a crook in a jurisdiction which regulates financial advisers than in one that does not. In some countries such as Spain and Portugal where there are a lot of British expatriate retirees, UK advisers have set up branch offices or send staff over on frequent visits to meet clients. Such an arrangement can sometimes provide the best of both worlds.

Having decided where your adviser will be based, how do you actually find him? The best way is by recommendation. Mention to friends that you are looking for an investment adviser, particularly if you know that the friend uses one, and see what response you get. If you have decided that your adviser should be in the UK it is best to speak to UK friends rather than people in the expatriate community that you are joining. You know them better and for longer so can trust their advice more, and you should be more interested in the potential adviser's general investment skills than his knowledge of the particular problems and opportunities of expatriates. If he has proved helpful and reliable to your UK friends he almost certainly has the ability to adapt to your special investment needs as an expatriate.

If you do not have any friends who are likely to know an investment adviser ask your bank, solicitor or accountant or another professional adviser for recommendations. They are all likely to know someone. Your bank will probably recommend itself or its associated financial services company. By all means include them on your shortlist. But explain to the bank manager that although you will talk to the bank's financial service's staff you need to compare their service with that of other advisers and ask for another recommendation as well. If you do not know anyone you can approach ask the regulatory authority for some names or keep your eye open for advertisements. In the UK the regulatory authority for independent advisers is FIMBRA (Financial Intermediaries Managers and Brokers Regulatory Association). FIMBRA produces a booklet called 'How to Spot the Investment Cowboys' and they will send you a copy on request. They will also send you a list of independent advisers. The magazine 'Money Management' will send, on request, a list of those advisers who charge fees rather than take commission on what they sell you. Provided you know what commission is being paid, it is not necessarily a bad thing for the adviser to earn commission: this can frequently work out cheaper for you than a fee.

If you have been given recommendations make a shortlist of three and make appointments to go and see them. If you do not have anyone to recommend people and are relying on a list from a regulatory authority, or a trawl through the Yellow Pages, or advertisement in the newspaper or journals such as *Expat Investor* or *Resident Abroad*, it would be advisable to start with a longer list — say six names.

When you turn up for an appointment tell the firm how much money you have available to invest, explain that you are going overseas to retire, or to work for approximately X years, as the case may be, that you are seeking an investment adviser, the firm has been recommended to you, and that you are going to talk to two other firms that have also been recommended. Then let them ask you questions. A good firm will ask questions aimed at discovering your investment strategy (don't let them know that you've already thought about that yourself), the degree of risk you are prepared to take, whether you are more comfortable with UK based investments and those based in the UK's offshore islands (the Channel Islands and the Isle of Man) or whether you would be equally happy with US or European based ones, and ought to give you a rough idea of the sort of investments they would consider for you.

If they seem to be talking sense you can then ask them some questions. Try for a start: Who will you be dealing with? How experienced is he? Can he be contacted outside normal business hours? What fees will the firm charge you or are they remunerated by a commission on what they sell you? If they charge you a fee what will happen to the commission? Will they pocket this as well, will they take it and credit it to you, or will the investment manager that they use invest a larger sum on your behalf to reflect that he is not paying a commission?

Investment advisers in the UK are divided into three categories: an insurance and unit trust company's direct sales force; tied agents, which are advisers who can only sell the range of products produced by one company; and independent ones who must survey the whole marketplace and select what they feel is most appropriate for your needs. It is unlikely that a single company will have developed all of the best products. Accordingly, you ought to have a better chance of ending up with a good spread of investments if you choose an independent adviser. Remember also the maxim of 'spread your risk'; you cannot do this if you put all of your money into the product of one company. An independent financial adviser will almost certainly be a member of FIMBRA, so add to your list of questions, 'Is the company a member of FIMBRA?'.

You also need to decide whether to give your financial adviser discretion to manage your investments or whether you want him to consult you first. If your knowledge of investments is very limited, consulting you is unlikely to achieve very much. If you are always going to accept his recommendations it is better to give him discretion to act, provided that he immediately informs you of what he has done. This is particularly important in relation to sales. If your adviser thinks that the value of your investments is going to slump wouldn't you prefer him to convert them into cash immediately, rather than to spend a couple of days trying to contact you, by which time the slump may have already occurred?

Your tax position

Having chosen your financial adviser do not expect him to know your tax position. This will vary from country to country and will also depend on whether you hold, and intend to retain, your investments personally or whether you decide to put some or all of them into an offshore trust or company. Offshore trusts are considered in Chapter 11. If your investment funds are more than about £100,000 you ought to consider whether it might be appropriate to put some of your funds into such a trust.

In many countries you are not taxable on income that does not belong to you, even though you may be able to benefit from it at some stage. Depending on where it is located, an offshore trust may well not be taxable on its income and will almost certainly not be taxable on capital gains. This means that your funds can grow at a faster rate than if you hold the investments personally and can only reinvest the after-tax income and gains.

In some countries you will not be taxable on investment income arising elsewhere if you are only living in the country for two or three years. If you are in this position you need to let your investment adviser know as you will yourself, in effect, constitute a tax free fund.

You do not yourself need to understand how much tax is paid on your income before it gets to you, but your financial adviser does, as this will reflect where the investment should be based. If you are going to invest in US securities it is likely to be better to do this through the Channel Islands than through the UK. However, this tax benefit needs to be weighed against the investment expertise available for a similar product in the different countries. Even if you are not taxed on the income in your adopted country, saving tax should not be your real objective; what you want to do is to maximise the growth of, and yield from, your investment. In this context getting the best investment management expertise is more important than saving tax along the way.

What currency do you want?

You may need to make one further investment decision before considering specific types of investment. If you receive the funds in a currency other than sterling you need to decide in which currency you want to invest them. If you intend to return to the UK eventually you will probably want your savings in sterling at that stage. If you need to save to buy a house you will probably want them in the currency of the country where the house will be. Choosing the right time to convert currency is difficult even for the professionals. Unless you have a specific need for foreign currency you ought to avoid currency speculation. Convert your savings to sterling as soon as you have identified that the amount is surplus to your living requirements in your new country. During some months you will obtain a favourable exchange rate; some months you will lose out. Overall, though, you will have converted the savings to sterling at an average rate. Of course, you will lose out if the value of your currency rises as compared to sterling, but you will not have lost money — only the opportunity to reap a windfall profit — whereas if you leave the funds in foreign currency and the value of that currency against sterling falls you may see your savings evaporate.

Of course, if your investment strategy calls for an international spread of investments you will need to invest in overseas currencies, but in such circumstances the exchange risk is a factor that you will have taken into account in deciding where to invest.

Unless you are either a currency expert, or a gambler by temperament, you should avoid keeping free money on bank deposit in foreign currencies even if the interest rate looks very attractive. Fluctuations in exchange rates can be both sudden and violent. This is very much a risk investment.

The main types of investment

If you decide to do it yourself and not engage an investment adviser you will have to pick your own investments. However, you need to know what sort of investment vehicles are available. If you use a financial adviser it is helpful to understand the implications of what he is investing in. It might therefore be useful briefly to describe the main options.

Direct Stock Exchange investments

Investing on the Stock Exchange requires not only skill but also good research, staying closely in touch with the market, and a fair degree of luck. If you have a minimum of £250,000 to invest in stocks and shares, find a stockbroker to manage it for you — or ask your investment adviser to find you a stockbroker (if he is not one himself). If you are an avid reader of the *Financial Times* and the *Investors Chronicle* and like playing the market, by all means continue to do so — preferably with not more than about 20% of your savings, leaving the other 80% to your investment adviser to deal with. Otherwise forget stocks and shares.

Last year one of the major UK banks ran an extraordinary series of television advertisements. Extraordinary because they gave the impression that experience is irrelevant in investment. In one of them a young woman, who looks around 25, explains that she joined the bank five years earlier, worked in the machine room, took time off to have a baby — and is now the branch's mortgage adviser. As the child looks about three she could not have had very much experience in that role — which suggests that the bank doesn't take mortgages very seriously even though in most cases the purchase of a house is by far the biggest investment decision the customer has made to date. Another such advert is concerned with touch screen stock exchange dealing. The script goes 'You tap in the details and if you like the price you take it . . . It appeals to all sorts of people . . . It's not surprising . . . It's as easy as . . . Exactly (video of a child riding a bicycle)'. The bank may not find it surprising that all sorts of people like to buy and sell shares instantly without advice on the prospects of the company or whether the price looks sensible. I find it incredible!

Unit trusts

The safest way to invest in stock exchange securities is through a unit trust. A unit trust is a sort of investment consortium. The management company takes in several million pounds from investors in small blocks of £500, £1,000, £10,000 etc. and invests the whole pot together. Accordingly, for your £500 you get a tiny share in a fairly large number of investments. There is no capital gains tax within the unit trust. The dividends suffer tax in theory, but in most cases tax is withheld by the company that pays the dividend and this is likely to cover the unit trust's tax liability on the income. If you are living in a country that does not have a capital gains tax, or, like the UK, exempts the first slice of gains, unit trusts can be attractive.

The main snag is that unit trusts normally invest in a particular sector of the market. Accordingly, if you want to spread your investment over different market sectors and into different countries, which you ought to do, you need a range of unit trusts. You then really need someone to manage these, i.e. to decide when to go out of one fund into another, whether to switch from one company's Japanese fund to a different company's Japanese fund etc. A unit trust has what is called a 'bid offer spread'. This is the difference between the price at which the unit trust manager will buy units and the price at which he will sell them. It is normally around 5%. Therefore, any time you switch into a different unit trust you lose 5% of your capital and the growth in value of your investment in the new fund has to make good this loss before you see any benefit from the switch.

Investment bonds

An investment bond is a single premium life insurance policy issued by an assurance company. It offers a simple way to enjoy a return from a spread of investments, as the assets of the bond can be invested in a range of investment funds investing in equities around the world, government bonds, cash or a mixture of different types of investment. The investment management is carried out by investment experts of the company which issues the bond, who take the difficult investment decisions on behalf of the investor.

The cost of switching investments is far less than for unit trusts, but there is obviously a management charge within the fund. If the insurance company is in the UK it pays tax on the income and capital gains. However, a number of leading offshore insurance companies based in countries such as Guernsey and the Isle of Man issue offshore investment bonds offering a choice of underlying funds which are ideal for expatriates. The choice available includes speciality funds so that the investor can direct his investment into, say, the Japanese or UK stock exchange. Others offer a mixture of equity markets, or equity and bond investments, thus offering the investors a balanced portfolio of investments. For example, one market leader offers the choice of four managed funds each invested to reflect a different degree of risk and reward.

The investor can choose to channel his investment into one or several of these underlying funds. Normally he can also switch between the funds without cost. It can therefore be seen that this type of insurance bond offers a great deal of investment choice and the investor is able to redirect his investments within a bond to take account of differing market opportunities, normally without charge. There is no tax consequence or cost on the switching of investment between funds within a bond.

The investment bond issued from offshore centres is an extremely tax efficient investment vehicle. A bond issued by an insurance company on, say, the Isle of Man under Isle of Man legislation bears no tax on the investment profits. All income and gains earned under the bond would accumulate tax free. The bond, being a policy issued from the Isle of Man, remains an IOM asset and, therefore, your place of residence — whether it be Spain, the UK or elsewhere — does not normally affect this tax efficiency. It is easy to appreciate the positive effect on investment returns that this tax efficiency will have.

Bonds also offer access to the capital invested. The investor can take a regular income from his or her bond. Thus, the offshore investment bond offers a straightforward method of converting a lump sum investment into a regular income. This can normally be taken on a monthly, quarterly, half-yearly, or even on an annual basis. The proceeds of the bond are paid without the deduction of any tax and there is no notification of this to any Revenue authority. The taxation of income taken from the bond will, of course, depend on the rules of your adopted country. Responsibility for the declaration of income to the appropriate Revenue authorities rests entirely with the investor.

Because of the UK's tax anti-avoidance rules it may be undesirable to retain offshore bonds on return to the UK so this is unlikely to be a sensible investment for the expatriate who will be away for only two or three years. A longer term investor who intends to return to the UK at some stage needs to review the advisability of retaining his bond on his return; he may be advised to surrender it and reinvest in a UK based one.

Personal/private portfolio bonds

A number of insurance companies issue a variant of the investment bond which are known as 'personal' or 'private' portfolio bonds. These offer all the fiscal advantages of an offshore investment bond but with complete investment freedom. The assets of the bond will be invested in the investor's own private and personally selected portfolio of holdings. The investor can invest in any marketable security quoted on any recognised stock exchange and it will normally be possible to transfer the investor's existing investment holdings into the bond. Furthermore, there is no requirement to disturb chosen investment preferences, or any existing investment management arrangements between the investor and his advisers. The bond 'wrapped around' the investor's own portfolio converts potentially taxable investments to a tax exempt status, and the insurance company takes over the administration, thus removing the paperwork headache from the investor. Offshore personal portfolio bonds normally look for a minimum initial investment of at least £25,000 but offer an excellent solution to most investors.

A personal portfolio bond can be 'tailor made' to meet your individual investment objectives and the level of security you require. A bond may hold a selection of international equities for the seasoned investor looking for all out growth . . . BUT equally, a bond can be designed for absolute security to hold a series of exempt gilts to provide for high and regular income with the potential for capital growth dependent on currency exchange and interest rate movements. Quarterly valuations are provided to keep you in touch with your investment performance. The appointment of your own independent investment adviser also provides that important personal relationship which is so necessary when you are living outside the UK.

Your selection of adviser must be carefully made. You can provide maximum certainty over your adviser's credentials by only appointing a firm who is a member of a UK recognised regulatory authority e.g. the Stock Exchange or FIMBRA. These regulatory authorities enforce rigorous membership standards to ensure that you receive advice appropriate to your circumstances. Their members generally carry professional indemnity insurance to protect you if they are negligent — but do check this out first. You may be aware that FIMBRA members and members of the other regulatory bodies have to contribute to a compensation fund. If so, do not put too much reliance on this. These funds do not normally pay compensation to non-UK residents.

The different tax treatment of investment bonds as compared with unit trusts is not necessarily the most important distinction. Dividend income received by the insurance company generally suffers tax at source and rental income is normally taxed in the source country, so the tax saving on income invested via an offshore life office is limited to tax on interest, and, for the wealthy investor, the difference between the rate of tax suffered at source and higher rate tax. To my mind, of far greater importance than the tax saving is the ability to switch investments within a bond more cheaply and more quickly than with a portfolio of unit trusts.

If written in trust, an investment bond also has inheritance tax advantages, and the very real benefit that the money can be passed quickly to the beneficiaries on the holder's death without having to wait for what is often many months for probate to be obtained. Furthermore, the non-UK domiciled investor who wishes to invest in UK shares needs to do this via some sort of offshore vehicle to keep his funds outside the scope of UK inheritance tax and the offshore investment bond has the advantage of providing such a vehicle, normally at no cost. The normal ability to take a 5% p.a. withdrawal from a bond tax-free (or to be precise, while deferring any UK tax thereon) can also be a useful facility for an investor who, although not ordinarily resident in the UK, is likely to visit the UK for one or two years for a sufficient period to make him resident here. Far more importantly, in most jurisdictions an investment bond also avoids bringing the income into the scope of tax in the country of which the expatriate has become a resident.

The offshore personal portfolio bond has the added advantage over other offshore bonds of giving the bond-holder a large degree of control over the investment of his funds and the flexibility to partake of investment opportunities that may not be available to the insurance company itself or where the investment required is on a smaller scale than the managers of the insurance company's own funds would contemplate. It also preserves for the non-UK resident and non-ordinarily resident investor his UK capital gains tax exemption.

The UK Inland Revenue has recently started to attack such bonds under an anti-avoidance provision, section 739 of the Income and Corporation Taxes Act 1988, but this has no effect whatsoever on holders who are not ordinarily resident in, or are not domiciled in, the UK. Even where a holder becomes UK resident at a later date it has no effect on income arising during the period of non-residence. This is not to say that the bond necessarily remains an attractive investment to the returning expatriate after he becomes UK resident, but rather that the time to review its suitability is, like any other investment, during the year of assessment prior to that in which he plans to return to the UK.

The notes to the UK 1992/93 tax return specifically state 'If you can show that the purpose of the transfer (and any operations associated with it) was not to avoid tax, these provisions will not apply'. The courts have interpreted 'tax' to mean any UK tax but it is generally accepted not to extend to overseas taxes. Even the Revenue's note stops short. The legislation goes on to say that the incidental avoidance of UK tax does not matter if the acquisition of the bond was a bona fide commercial transaction not designed for the purpose of avoiding liability to taxation [ICTA 1988, s 741(b)]. In the vast majority of cases the non-UK resident investor will not have in mind avoidance of UK tax when he takes out his bond as, with the exception of inheritance tax, he is not liable for such tax and thus has no need to seek to avoid it. As a subsequent decision to return to the UK can hardly itself be in order to avoid UK tax, once it is shown that the avoidance of UK tax was not one of the purposes of taking out the bond, subsequent return to the UK would not bring it within the scope of section 739.

Accordingly, virtually the only category of returning expatriate who need feel concern is the person who left the UK for just long enough to cease to be ordinarily resident to seek to avoid tax on a capital gain and whose sojourn abroad was comparatively temporary.

Because an investment bond can convert past capital gains into taxable income (although the UK tax legislation does contain broad rules to prevent this in many cases) it is not necessarily sensible for the returning expatriate simply to retain his bond when he comes to the UK — in the same way as it is not necessarily sensible for him to retain a portfolio of investments which have increased in value without taking steps to wash out the inherent gain. It may be better to convert it into a bond with a UK office of the insurance company. He may be advised to surrender it completely.

Roll up funds

To the extent that you decide to keep your savings in cash, consider an offshore roll up fund. These are basically cash deposits. However, technically what you own are redeemable shares in the offshore company. These shares do not pay dividends. However, the price at which the company will redeem them is their original cost plus the interest that the company has generated from investment of the funds while it has held them. The effect is therefore to have converted the income into a capital gain. If the country where you are living does not tax capital gains this could take the 'income' out of charge to tax. It will, in any event, normally defer crystallising a tax liability until the shares are redeemed. In the meantime the value is growing in a tax free environment.

The UK has introduced anti-avoidance rules. These tax the profit on redemption of the shares as income but still permit the funds to accumulate without tax in the interim. You obviously need to check that your new country does not have similar rules.

If you are planning now to retire abroad in a few years' time, an offshore roll up fund can be an attractive home for your savings in the interim. The 'interest' earned will not attract tax as it arises, and you need not redeem the shares until you have ceased to be UK resident so the anti-avoidance rules will not apply at that stage. However, you may need to consider the capital gains tax position in your new country.

If you plan to return to the UK at some stage, you need to cash in the investment in the roll up fund before you become UK resident again. If you do not, you will have succeeded in bringing all of the income that accumulated while you were overseas into the UK tax net!

Chapter 17

Returning to the UK

Tax aspects

Returning for short periods

Once you have established permanent residence abroad there is no objection to your returning to the UK for brief visits. You obviously need to ensure that your visits are not of sufficient duration to label you as a UK resident. For most people this means keeping visits below three months a year on average and below six months in any one year. It is dangerous to plan to return for 80 to 90 days regularly every year as the 90-day rule is not a statutory one. The rules on residence are considered in Chapter 2. Even if your visits make you UK resident in a particular year this may not matter. You will only be taxable in the UK in that year on UK income (on which you are normally taxable here in any event) and on overseas income which you bring into this country during that year. Accordingly, with a little planning you can be UK resident in one year without incurring a UK tax liability. You must, however, ensure that you do not become ordinarily resident here. That would bring your worldwide income into the UK tax net.

It is inadvisable to return to the UK at all between the date you emigrate and the following 5 April as the Revenue might then contend that you remain UK resident until the last time you leave the UK in the tax year. Visits in the following tax year ought to be kept to a minimum also. If you delay filing the form P15 it is the visits in that year which will largely determine what provisional ruling the Revenue make as to your residence status.

If you are seeking to establish non-UK domicile, every visit that you make to the UK is likely to make it harder to demonstrate that you have severed your connections with this country.

Returning permanently

If you have been working abroad and will return to the UK after completing your tour of duty, or you retired abroad but have changed your mind and decided to return, you need to plan ahead for your return. From the date that you arrive you will again become resident and probably also ordinarily resident in the UK and thus fully liable to UK tax on your worldwide income. Remember also that, although by concession the Revenue will only regard you as becoming UK resident from the date of your return, they could treat your residence as starting from the previous 6 April. Accordingly, if large amounts of tax are at risk, it is safer to plan on the assumption that you will become UK resident again on that date.

If you are unsure whether you will remain indefinitely in the UK but may be here only for a period before going overseas again, the rules on ordinary residence for immigrants are slightly different to those on emigration.

(*a*) You will be treated as ordinarily resident here from the date you return to the UK if it is clear that you intend to live here for at least three tax years.

(*b*) You will also be treated as ordinarily resident from the date of your arrival if either

  (i) you already own accommodation in the UK,
  (ii) you buy such accommodation during the tax year of your arrival, or
  (iii) you rent accommodation under a lease of three years or more during that year.

(*c*) If you do not have such accommodation but either buy or rent in a subsequent year you will be treated as ordinarily resident in the UK from the start of that tax year. The Revenue Booklet IR 20 talks of a year 'in which such accommodation becomes available'. It is not clear what this means in the case of rented property. It almost certainly means you take a lease of three or more years. They say elsewhere that in considering whether accommodation is available for one's use they ignore a property rented furnished for less than two years or unfurnished for less than one year, which is inconsistent with this.

(*d*) If you did not originally intend to stay for at least three years but form such an intention subsequently, you will be treated as ordinarily resident from the beginning of the tax year in which you form that intention (or from the date of your arrival if it is during the first year).

(*e*) In any event, you would be treated as ordinarily resident in the UK from the beginning of the tax year after the third anniversary of coming to the UK if you are not already ordinarily resident here.

(*f*) If you are treated as ordinarily resident here solely because you buy or rent a house here (i.e. you had not formed an intention to stay here for three years), and you dispose of that property and leave the UK within three years of your arrival, you can be treated as not having become ordinarily resident here.

(*g*) If you come to the UK as a student for a period of study and education, you will not become ordinarily resident until you have been here for four years instead of the normal three unless you own accommodation (or take a lease of over three years) or intend to make regular visits to the UK averaging over 90 days after completing your course of study (paras 3.8 – 3.13, Booklet IR 20).

Income tax planning

You need to bear in mind the following tax traps.

(*a*) Most overseas income is taxable in the UK on a preceding year basis. This means that the quantum of a person's taxable income for the tax year 1993/94 is not the income generated in that year, but the income that arose in the year to 5 April 1993 (1992/93). It is irrelevant that you may have been non-UK resident in 1992/93. The Revenue are not, in theory at least, taxing the income of that year; they are simply pretending that the income earned in 1993/94 when you are UK resident was equal to that of the previous year. To avoid this, consider ceasing the source of income in the year in which you become UK resident, e.g. close your overseas bank deposit account or sell your overseas investments. It can work both ways, of course. If you open a new source of income two years before you become UK resident again (you must have at least one complete tax year of income from the source) and try to achieve a low income figure in the year before you return, this low figure will form the measure of the taxable income from that source in the year of your return.

(*b*) This principle also applies to self-employment. If you intend to carry on a business in the UK as a self-employed person, can you start up in a small way before you come so as to have a low preceding year's income when you come to the UK?

(*c*) If you have money in an offshore roll up fund, cash it in during the year before you become UK resident again. If you don't, you will be taxable in the UK on the rolled up income that accrued while you were abroad.

(*d*) Consider surrendering investment bonds, too. Although there are provisions to exclude from UK tax the income that accrued while you were overseas, they do not work very well and it is generally best to surrender the bond and start again. However, this does not necessarily apply if it has not increased in value.

(*e*) If, after you become UK resident, you will still spend a significant amount of time working overseas and think that you may be able to benefit from the 365-day rule for overseas earnings (see Chapter 5), time that you spent overseas during your period of non-UK residence cannot be brought into account. In some cases it might be sensible to bring yourself into the UK tax net earlier than you otherwise might have done.

(*f*) If you are a beneficiary of an offshore settlement, a distribution of all of the accumulated income to you before you become UK resident is likely to be sensible. If capital gains have been realised in the settlement, it would be sensible to distribute those as well whilst you are still non-UK resident.

(*g*) If you have become non-UK domiciled and will return to your new country after you return to the UK, there is especial scope for planning. A non-UK domiciled individual is taxable on overseas investment income and on overseas earnings from a job which has no UK functions on a remittance basis. This means that the income will not attract UK tax unless and until it is brought into the UK. If all of the income of such a person arises outside the UK, he can become UK resident without becoming liable to UK tax if he can continue not to remit any of the income. This can normally be done, at least for a period, by segregating income from capital overseas and remitting only capital. This is a complex area. It requires at least two overseas bank accounts — one to contain capital (which will include income arising before the person became non-UK resident) and the other to contain income. Under no circumstances should income pass through the capital account even if it is immediately transferred out to the income account. The capital account will be used to meet UK needs and the income account to meet overseas bills. If substantial capital gains are likely, more than two bank accounts may be needed. This is a very complex area and specific advice needs to be taken.

The form P86

The Inland Revenue have produced a form, P86, for completion by people who come to the UK from overseas. This is a non-statutory form. It is difficult to see any advantage in volunteering to complete it — although if you are entitled to a tax repayment you may, in practice, need to complete it if you want the repayment promptly.

Although the form states 'I need certain information in order to decide your residence status for UK tax purposes', not one of the questions appears to have any relevance to your residence from the time you come to the UK. They appear to be designed to enable the Revenue to see if there is any chance of contending that you became resident in the UK earlier than you think. They can also affect the decision on your domicile — although, as stated in Chapter 9, if they are prepared to discuss your domicile status with you, which they will not do unless you can show that this will affect the tax you have to pay, they will want you to complete a different form in any case.

Inland Revenue
Income Tax

Reference
/

District date stamp

Arrival in the United Kingdom

As you have come to the United Kingdom for the first time, or after a period of absence, I need certain information in order to decide your residence status for United Kingdom tax purposes and to give you the correct income tax allowances.

Will you please therefore answer all the questions below then sign the form and send it back to me.

1. What is your nationality?

2.a. On what grounds do you claim this nationality?

b. where were you born?

3.a. In which country do you usually live?

b. Have you retained a residence in that country?

4.a. When did you arrive in the United Kingdom?

b. If you know it please enter your National Insurance number, (unless it is already shown on this form).

5.a. Where did you work and who for during the five years before your arrival in the United Kingdom?

b. When did each employment begin and end?

Attach a separate sheet if necessary

c. Was any part of these employments carried out in the United Kingdom?

If 'Yes' please give details on a separate sheet

P86 (1991)

Please turn over

5.d.Has the most recent of these employments continued (on leave or otherwise) since you arrived in the United Kingdom?

   e.If 'Yes' when is it likely to end?

   f.If you visited the United Kingdom during the five years before the date entered at 4a. overleaf, please give the dates each visit started and finished

6.a.Did you or your husband or wife (if you are married) have any accommodation for your use in the United Kingdom at any time during the five years before you arrived?

   b.Have you or your husband or wife (if you are married) held any accommodation for your use in the United Kingdom since you arrived?

   c.If 'Yes' to either a or b

    1. what type of accommodation is it?

    2. what is its address?

    3. if it is owned, when was it bought?

    4. if it is rented

      a. is it rented furnished or unfurnished?

      b. what is the period of the tenancy agreement?

      If you have held accommodation at more than one address, please give the details for each, on a separate sheet

7.a.Do you intend to stay permanently in the United Kingdom?

   b.If 'No'

    1. how long do you expect to stay? (for example, for 2, 3 or 10 years, or indefinitely)

    2. if known, on what date do you expect to leave?

Signature _____ Date _____ 199 ___

A2068 2466L Dd FAL0100967 550M 11 91 TP Gp649 ♺ Recycled paper

It may be helpful to consider the questions on the form.

1 & 2   Nationality is irrelevant in tax matters with one exception which applies only to non-UK residents. As you are being given the form because you are becoming resident, the only rationale we can see for these questions is to possibly hold the answers against you in the event of a future claim to be non-UK domiciled.

3   The answer will normally be the UK. If you want to contend that you are not becoming ordinarily resident in the UK, inserting 'the UK' here will effectively destroy that contention; you must insert the country where you intend to continue to normally live.

4   This will determine the tax year in which you will become UK resident.

5   The objective of these questions seems to be to determine if you owe any tax for past years — if you worked in the UK during the five-year period, expect a request for the name and tax district of your last UK employer to enable your file to be traced. If you answer 'Yes' to 5(c) expect further enquiries. You are liable to UK tax on the earnings for such work, although in many cases this liability may be overridden by a double taxation agreement. Question 5(d) and (e) are important in the context of ordinary residence. If the answer to (d) is 'yes' and (e) is 'within three years' you could well not become ordinarily resident in the UK provided that your answer to question 7(b) is that you intend to leave when the employment ceases. Question 5(f) seems designed solely to enable the Revenue to determine whether they can establish that you became UK resident earlier than you think. It is odd that it is slipped in at the end of 5, a question dealing with employment.

6   Question (a) is obviously directed at whether you were really non-UK resident in the last five years. If you answer 'Yes' here and also at 5(c) you are probably in trouble. 6(c) 1–3 do not appear to be relevant to anything. If the answers to 6(c) 4 are 'furnished' and 'under three years' you are on the way to being non-ordinarily resident.

7   (a) If you answer 'Yes' here you have just acquired a UK domicile if you did not previously have one.

    (b) If you answer 'indefinitely' you are also volunteering to be UK domiciled. If you put ten years, you are well on the way to being regarded as UK domiciled in year 11. It is safest either to put 'not yet decided', which is neutral, or, better, to tie your stay to an event, e.g. until the children's schooling is complete or 'while my career pattern demands it'. Even then, if you are still here after that event has arrived you may have a problem.

Capital gains tax planning

If you hold assets which have increased in value since their acquisition you need to consider uplifting their capital gains tax base cost. If you do nothing, when you eventually sell the asset, the base cost for capital gains tax purposes is calculated by reference to your original acquisition (it will normally be the actual cost unless the asset was acquired before 1 April 1982), not the market value at the time you become UK resident. If you do not wish to retain the asset you need simply to sell it in that year. If a sale and reacquisition is impracticable, an alternative is to put the asset into a trust for your benefit. Again, the trust's capital gains tax base cost will be the value of the asset at the time it is put into the trust.

Conversely, if you have assets which have decreased in value, delay selling them until after you return to the UK. Losses which you realise while you are non-UK resident cannot be carried forward and set against gains arising after you again become resident in the UK.

You obviously need to consider your capital gains tax position in your adopted country. It may be necessary to spend a few weeks somewhere else between leaving your own country and arriving in the UK, and to realise your capital gains in that period when you are a resident of neither country.

If you have retired and let out your UK house and have decided that it is no longer suitable for you, consider the capital gains tax position. If you have been working outside the UK and want your time overseas to count as a period when you are deemed to have occupied the property as your principal residence (so attracting exemption from capital gains tax) you need to reoccupy it for a period after you return to the UK.

Alternatively, you can sell the house while you are still non-UK resident.

Inheritance tax planning

If, as will almost always be the case, you remain UK domiciled during the time that you spent overseas, there is no special scope for inheritance tax planning as all of your assets will have remained within the scope of that tax. If you did cease to be domiciled in the UK you need to consider whether your return to the UK is likely to result in your becoming UK domiciled again. This will not always be the case. For example, if a UK expatriate, working for a US multinational company, who had acquired a New York domicile is sent by his US employer to work in its London office, he is likely to retain his New York domicile on his return to the UK provided that he retains an intention to go back to New York at some stage. If you will become UK domiciled, consider putting all of your non-UK assets into an offshore trust while you are still non-UK domiciled. This will take them out of the scope of UK inheritance tax. If you will not become UK domiciled, consider putting all of your UK assets into an overseas company so that they will, in effect, be transformed into a non-UK asset, i.e. the shares, and thus kept out of the scope of inheritance tax.

Other points

If you control a non-UK company, will your return to the UK result in the company becoming managed and controlled from the UK? If so, it will be treated as a UK resident company on your return. Consider liquidating it before you come back. Alternatively, can you take steps, e.g. by strengthening the board of directors, to ensure that management and control will remain overseas?

The same applies to trusts. If you are a trustee and the settlor was UK domiciled or resident when he created the settlement (or at a time when he added further assets to it) your migration to the UK will make the settlement UK resident for income tax purposes. If the settlor was, or becomes, domiciled in the UK and you effectively manage and control the settlement it will also become UK resident for capital gains tax purposes. The safest thing is for you to resign as a trustee before you return to the UK.

National insurance

Coming back to the UK will, in general, render you liable to national insurance again from the time of your return if you take up employment or self-employment here. If you are sent to the UK by your overseas employer on a temporary basis you may be able to escape national insurance for at least the first year if you continue to pay social security in your adopted country and your stay in the UK is not expected to exceed twelve months. This is not a general relief. It applies only if your adopted country is an EC country or one with which the UK has a double taxation agreement. The rules are, of course, the same as those that apply where a UK resident is sent overseas, which are considered in Chapter 12. If you do not become ordinarily resident in Great Britain you are also statutorily not liable to national insurance for your first fifty-two weeks in this country if you are not ordinarily employed in the UK, your employment is with an employer who does not have his place of business in the UK and the duties of your employment are normally performed overseas. Place of business for this purpose implies a centre of management; not every UK office will constitute a place of business.

VAT

You can bring back your personal possessions free of both import duty and VAT, provided that you can demonstrate that they have been both owned and used for at least six months prior to coming to the UK. Therefore, if you are going to buy goods to bring back with you, you need to buy them early enough — and preserve the receipts. You must have been living in your adopted country for at least twelve months to qualify for this relief. The relief must be claimed, normally within twelve months of the goods being imported. In practice, it is normally claimed on importation. If this is not done (or you cannot produce the evidence to substantiate your claim), you will have to pay the import duty and VAT on importation and reclaim it when you produce the evidence that you are entitled to the relief. Personal possessions for this purpose include household effects, provisions, pets, animals for riding, cycles, cars, caravans, pleasure boats and private planes, provided that they are not being imported for business use. You may need to demonstrate that the articles have suffered customs duty or VAT in the country of purchase (not been exempted as exports) as the relief is intended to avoid double taxation. You must also retain the goods for twelve months after your return to the UK — although it is unlikely that Customs will go through your dustbin or attend your local jumble sale to check that you are not in breach of this condition.

If you are coming from an EC country, the period for which you must have owned the goods is reduced from six to three months, other than for cars, caravans, boats and planes.

House hunting

As a house is very much a matter of personal taste it is not sensible to leave it to someone else to identify a suitable property if you intend to buy. You should come to the UK and look at potential properties yourself. Even then, it is important you find a good solicitor and make sure that he can readily contact you if you are not going to stay here long enough to complete the purchase. Paying a deposit in the UK does not generally commit either buyer or seller to the sale. It is not until the contract is signed that the vendor is committed to sell to you. Accordingly, if you are not readily available to make all necessary decisions between identifying the house and the contract being signed, you may well find that your purchase falls through. In particular, if, before the contract is signed, the vendor receives a higher offer from someone else he is likely either to accept it and return your deposit or give you the opportunity to match or top it within a very short time scale.

Therefore, even if you intend to buy, it will normally be sensible to rent a property for a short period when you first return to the UK to give yourself time to identify the one you intend to buy. Although in the past there has been a dearth of properties to rent in the UK, this is no longer the case — except, sometimes, in rural areas.

The safest way to identify a property, apart from coming over and finding one yourself, is to ask a friend or relative to do this for you. If you feel that this is too much of an imposition, get a friend to send you the names and addresses of a handful of estate agents in the area in which you want to live that deal in rented properties and contact them direct. If you have no friends in the UK, the Yellow Pages telephone directories are a useful source of names. You are likely to find these in major libraries. Alternatively, your local British embassy or British Chamber of Commerce will probably have them. Most estate agents are happy to deal with non-residents. There are some that tend to specialise in non-residents but, as you are coming to live in the UK permanently and understand the basics of buying and selling property in the UK, you are likely to be better off looking for a good local estate agent rather than for someone who is used to dealing with foreigners.

You can also, of course, ask people on your list of agents to send you details of properties that might suit you to purchase in the longer term. You can then identify in advance those you want to view — although if you ask for the list too long in advance you risk the property no longer being on the market. Although an estate agent will prefer to sell you something where he has been retained by the vendor, if you do not like anything on his books and he knows of something suitable in the hands of another agent, he is likely to bring it to your attention — although he may expect you to pay him a finder's fee if he cannot persuade the other agent to share the selling commission.

Removals

The advice on returning to the UK is no different to that on leaving. Find a removal company that is used to handling international removals and leave it to them; consider carefully what you really want to bring back and dispose of the rest before you start; and don't expect the move to happen overnight. Even from Europe it can easily take two or three weeks for the goods to clear Customs.

If you have been living in a country where insects are a problem, think especially hard about what you bring home. As a friend who came back from America said to me, 'You don't want to ship back the cockroaches — you don't even need a breeding pair to infest your new home; you only need one in infested furniture'.

If you have pets remember that the UK has strict quarantine regulations. You will have to leave the animal in a quarantine kennel, at your cost, for six months. If you do not think that your pet can survive the separation, it may be kinder to donate it to a friend in your current country or have it put down. It is a criminal offence to seek to bring animals into the UK in breach of the quarantine rules. These are very strictly enforced.

Useful addresses

Government departments

Bank of England
Threadneedle Street
London EC2
tel: 071 601 5545

Department of Social Security
Overseas Branch
Benton Park Road
Newcastle-upon-Tyne
NE98 1YX
tel: 091 285 7111
(for enquiries)

Department of Social Security
Leaflet Unit
Block 4, Government Buildings
Honeypot Lane
Stanmore
Middlesex
(for leaflets)

Department of Health
International Relations (Health) A
Hannibal House
Elephant & Castle
London SE1 6TE
tel: 071 972 2000

Inland Revenue
Claims Branch — Foreign Division
St John's House
Merton Road
Bootle
Merseyside L69 9BB
tel: 051 922 6363
(Rules on residence and domicile
and itself deals with the tax
affairs of some non-residents)

Inland Revenue
Inspector of Foreign Dividends
Lynwood Road
Thames Ditton
Surrey KT7 0PD
tel: 081 398 4242

Inland Revenue
Public Enquiry Room
West Wing
Somerset House
London WC2R 1LB
tel: 071 438 6420
(leaflets can generally be obtained
from any local HM Inspector of Taxes
office).

Education

Council of British Independent Schools
in the European Communities (COBISEC)
c/o The British School of Brussels
Chaussee de Leuvain
Tervuren B3080
Belgium
tel: Brussels 767 4700

Education and Guardian Advisory
    Services Ltd
11 Seaton Avenue
Mutley
Plymouth PL4 6QJ
tel: 0752 261229

Useful addresses

European Council of International
   Schools (ECIS)
21B Lavant Street
Petersfield
Hants GU32 2EL
tel: 0730 2682446

Gabbitas Truman & Thring
   Education Trust
Broughton House
5, 6 & 8 Sackville Street
London W1X 2BR
tel: 071 734 0161

Grant Maintained Schools Trust
239 Vauxhall Bridge Road
London SW1
tel: 071 828 9855

Independent Schools Information
   Service
56 Buckingham Gate
London SW1E 6AG
tel: 071 630 8793/4
(ISS International tel: 071 630 8790)

Mercers College
Ware
Herts SG12 9BU
tel: 0920 465926

National Extension College
18 Brooklands Avenue
Cambridge CB2 2HN
tel: 0223 63465

Open University
Student Enquiry Service
PO Box 71
Milton Keynes
MK7 6AB
tel: 0908 653 231

Universal Aunts Limited
PO Box 304
London SW4 0NN
tel: 071 738 8937

Welmet Ltd
84 Richmond Road
London SW20 0PD
tel: 081 947 8702

Women's Corona Society
Commonwealth House
18 Northumberland Avenue
London WC2N 5BJ
tel: 071 235 1230

Woodroffe School
Lyme Regis
Dorset DT7 3LS
tel: 0297 442232

Worldwide Education Services
10 Barley Mew Passage
Chiswick
London W4 4PM
tel: 081 994 3622

Trade associations

British Association of Removers
3 Churchill Court
58 Station Road
North Harrow
Middlesex HA2 7SA
tel: 081 861 3331
(it is advisable to use a remover who is a
member of their Overseas Group)

Financial Intermediary Manager, and
   Brokers Regulatory Association
   (FIMBRA)
Heartsmere House
Marsh Wall
London E14 9RV
tel: 071 538 8860

Institute of Chartered Accountants
   In England & Wales
PO Box 433
Chartered Accountant's Hall
Moorgate Place
London EC2P 2BJ
tel: 071 628 7060

London Society of Chartered
   Accountants
Friendly House
52 Tabernacle Street
London EC2A 4PL
tel: 071 490 4390

Law Society
50 Chancery Lane
London WC2A 1SX
tel: 071 242 1222

Royal Institute of Chartered Surveyors
12 Gt George Street
London SW1P 3AE
tel: 071 222 7000

Health, etc.

British Airways Travel Clinics
156 Regents Street
London W1
(vaccinations)
tel: 071 439 9584

Exeter Hospital Aid Society
5 & 7 Palace Gate
Exeter EX1 1EU
tel: 0392 75361

British Medical Association
BMA House
Tavistock Square
London WC1H 9JP
tel: 071 387 4499

Private Patients Plan
Phillips House
Crescent Road
Tunbridge Wells
Kent TN1 2PL
tel: 0892 512345

BUPA International
Prudent House
Essex Street
London WC2R 3AX
tel: 071 353 5212

Thomas Cook Vaccination Centre
45 Berkeley Square
London W1
tel: 071 499 4000

Europea-IMG Limited
Provender Mill
Mill Bay Lane
Horsham
West Sussex RH12 1SS
tel: 0403 51884

Other

The Visa Shop
Charing Cross Station
Shopping Arcade
London WC2
tel: 071 379 0376
(will get visas from embassies
for a fee and will advise
which vaccinations are required
for various countries)

Expat Investor
Tolley Publishing Co Ltd
Tolley House
2 Addiscombe Road
Croydon, Surrey
CR9 5AF
tel: 081 686 9141
(journal for expatriates)

Resident Abroad
102-108 Clerkenwell Road
London EC1M 5SA
tel: 071 251 9321
(journal for expatriates)

DHL International (UK) Ltd
Orbital Park
178-188 Gt South West Road
Hounslow
Middlesex TW4 6JS
Tel: 081 890 9393
(international couriers)

The Expatriate
25 Brighton Road
South Croydon
CR2 6EA
(journal for expatriates)

Useful addresses

Good Book Guide
91 Great Russell Street
London WC1B 3PS
tel: 071 580 8466
(mail order books sent overseas)

Harrods
Knightsbridge
London SW1
tel: 071 581 0927

Fortnum & Mason
181 Piccadilly
London W1A 1ER
tel: 071 734 8040

The Weekly Telegraph
PO Box 14
Harold Hill
Romford
Essex RM3 8EQ
tel: 4023 81000
(weekly airmail newspaper
drawn from Daily and Sunday
Telegraph)

Avis Rent-a-Car Ltd
Hayes Gate House
Uxbridge Road
Hayes
Middlesex UB4 0JN
tel: 081 848 8733

Hertz Rent-a-Car Ltd
Radnor House
1272 London Road
London SW16 4XW
tel: 081 679 1777

Automobile Association
Fanum House
Basingstoke
Hampshire RG21 2EA
tel: 0256 20123

Eurodollar Rent-a-Car Ltd
Swan National House
3 Warwick Place
Uxbridge
Middlesex
tel: 0895 56565

The Diners Club Ltd
Diners Club House
Kingsmead
Farnborough
Hampshire
tel: 0252 516261

Access
National Westminster Bank plc
Card Services Department
Southend-on-Sea
SS99 9BR
tel: 0702 352255
(lost/stolen cards — tel: 0532 778899)

Barclaycard
Customer Services
PO Box 28
Liverpool L32 8UY
tel: 051 473 2500
(lost/stolen cards — tel: 0604 230230)

American Express Europe Ltd
Customer Services
PO Box 70
Edward Street
Brighton BN2 1YP
tel: 0273 696933
(lost/stolen cards — tel: 0273 696933)

Some additional reading suggestions

Free booklets

DSS Leaflets	NI 38	Social Security Abroad
	SA 29	Your Social Security & health care and pension rights in the EC
	DSS	Country leaflets (listed in Chapter 12)
	CH6	Child Benefit for persons leaving Britain
Vehicle Licensing Office	V526	Taking your car abroad?
Department of Health	T1	Traveller's Guide to Health
Inland Revenue	IR1	Extra-statutory concessions
	IR6	Double taxation relief
	IR20	Residents and non-residents liability to tax in the UK
	CGT4	Capital gains tax: owner-occupier houses
	CGT6	Capital gains tax: retirement relief on disposal of a business

Other books

(This is no more than a selection of the books available. The inclusion of a book on this list is not intended as a recommendation and its omission is not intended as a criticism.)

Daily Telegraph Guide to Working Abroad
Godfrey Golzen
Kogan Page

Working Abroad
Harry Brown
Northcote House
(NB latest edition was in 1986)

Daily Telegraph Guide to Living & Retiring Abroad
Michael Furnell
Kogan Page

Some additional reading suggestions

Retiring Abroad
Harry Brown
Northcote House
(NB latest edition was in 1987)

Travellers Health
Dr Richard Dawood
Oxford University Press

Preservation of Personal Health in Warm Climates
Ross Institute of Tropical Hygiene
Keppel Street, Gower Street, London WC1E 7HT
tel: 071 636 8636

Notes for Newcomers
(Information leaflets on 100 individual countries)
Women's Corona Society
Commonwealth House,
18 Northumberland Avenue,
London WC2N 5BJ
tel: 071 839 7908

Daily Telegraph Guide to Buying a Property in France
Philip Jones
Kogan Page

Buying and Selling your Home in France
Henry Dyson
Longman (Allied Dunbar Library)

Your Home in Italy
Flavia Maxwell
Longman (Allied Dunbar Library)

Your Home in Portugal
Rosemary de Pougemont
Longman (Allied Dunbar Library)

Blackstone Franks Guide to Living in Portugal
David Franks
Kogan Page

Blackstone Franks Guide to Living in Spain
Blackstone Franks
Kogan Page

Your Home in Spain
Per Svenson
Longman (Allied Dunbar Library)

Expatriate Tax Manual
Colin Cretton
Butterworths

World Travel Guide
Colombus Press
(This book is produced for the travel trade and contains much useful information about individual countries. Many public libraries subscribe to it).

Choosing your Independent School
ISIS (see useful addresses)
(UK schools only)

The International Schools Directory
ECIS (see useful addresses)

Embassies

British embassies and high commissions overseas and foreign embassies and high commissions in London

Country	*Local British Embassy*	*London Embassy*
Afghanistan	British Embassy Karte Parwan Kabul Afghanistan	31 Princes Gate London SW7 071 589 8891
Algeria	British Embassy Résidence Cassiopée Bâtiment B 7 chemin des Glycines Alger-Gare 16000 Algeria	6 Hyde Park Gate London SW7 071 221 7800
Andorra	British Consulate in Barcelona Edificio Torre de Barcelona Diagonal 477-13 Apartado de Correos 12111 08036 Barcelona Spain	Sindicat d'Initiativa de las Valls d'Andorra 63 Westover Road London SW18 081 874 4806
Angola	British Embassy Rua Diogo Cao 4 Luanda	87 Jermyn Street London SW1Y 6JD 071 930 5762
Antigua & Barbuda	British High Commissioner's Office 38 St Mary's Street St John's Antigua	Antigua House 15 Thayer Street London W1M 071 486 7073
Argentina	British Embassy Dr Luis Agote 2412/52 1425 Buenos Aires Argentina	53 Hans Place London SW1X 071 584 6494

Country	Local British Embassy	London Embassy
Australia	British High Commission Commonwealth Avenue Yarralumla Canberra Australia	Australia House The Strand London WC2B 071 379 4334
Austria	British Embassy Jaurèsgasse 12 Austria	18 Belgrave Mews West London SW1X 071 235 3731
Bahamas	British High Commission BITCO Building 3rd Floor East Street Nassau Bahamas	10 Chesterfield Street London W1X 071 408 4488
Bahrain	British Embassy 21 Government Avenue Manama 306 Bahrain	98 Gloucester Road London SW7 071 370 5132
Bangladesh	British High Commission Abu Bakr House Plot 7 Road 84 Gulshan Model Town Dhaka 12 Bangladesh	28 Queen's Gate London SW7 071 584 0081
Barbados	British High Commission (PO Box 675) Lower Collymore Rock Bridgetown Barbados	1 Great Russell Street London WC1B 071 631 4975
Belgium	British Embassy Britannia House 28 rue Joseph II B-1040 Brussels Belgium	103 Eaton Square London SW1W 071 235 5422
Belize	British High Commission (PO Box 91) Embassy Square Belmopan Belize	10 Harcourt House 19a Cavendish Square London W1M 071 499 9728

Embassies

Country	Local British Embassy	London Embassy
Bermuda	Honorary British Trade Correspondent (PO Box HM 655) c/o Visitors' Service Bureau Front Street Hamilton HM CX Bermuda	None
Bolivia	British Embassy Avenida Acre 2732-2754 La Paz Bolivia	106 Eaton Square London SW1W 071 235 4248
Botswana	British High Commission Private Bag 0023 Gaborone Botswana	6 Stratford Place London W1N 071 499 0031
Brazil	British Embassy (Caixa Postal 07-0586) Setor de Embaixadas Sul Quadra 801 Conjunto K 70.408 Brasília DF Brazil	32 Green Street London W1Y 071 493 8587
Brunei	British High Commission (PO Box 2197) Hong Kong Chambers 3rd Floor Jalan Pemancha Bandar Seri Begawan Brunei	49 Cromwell Road London SW7 071 581 0521
Bulgaria	British Embassy Sofia Boulevard Marshal Tolbukhin 65/67 Bulgaria	186-188 Queen's Gate London SW7 5HL 071 584 9400
Burkina Faso (Upper Volta)	The British Embassy Immeuble Les Harmonies Third Floor angle boulevard Carde et avenue Dr Jamot Plâteau Abidjan 01 Côte d'Ivoire	5 Cinnamon Row Plantation Wharf London SW11 071 738 2820

Country	Local British Embassy	London Embassy
Burma	British Embassy (PO Box 638) 80 Strand Road Rangoon Burma	19A Charles Street London W1X 071 629 6966
Burundi	British Consulate (BP 1344) 43 Avenue Bubanza Bujumbura Burundi	None
Cameroon	British Embassy (BP 547) Avenue Winston Churchill Yaoundé Cameroon	84 Holland Park London W11 071 727 0071
Canada	British High Commission 80 Elgin Street Ottawa K1P 5K7 Canada	McDonald House 1 Grosvenor Square London W1 071 629 9492
Central African Republic	British Consulate c/o SOCACIG BP 728 Bangui Central African Republic	None
Chad	British Consulate Avenue Charles de Gaulle (opposite Air Chad office) BP 877 Ndjamena Chad	None
Chile	British Embassy La Concepción 177	33 Regent Street London SW1Y 071 734 0803
China (People's Republic of)	British Embassy 11 Guang Hua Lu Jian Guo Men Wai Beijing People's Republic of China	49 Portland Place London W1N 071 636 5726

Embassies

Country	Local British Embassy	London Embassy
Colombia	British Embassy (Apdo Aéreo 4508) Torre Propaganda Sancho Calle 98 No 9-03 Piso 4 Bogotá Colombia	3 Hans Crescent London SW1X 071 589 9177
Costa Rica	British Embassy Apartado 815 Centro Colón 1007 San José Costa Rica	Flat 1 14 Lancaster Gate London W2 071 723 9630
Côte d'Ivoire	British Embassy Immeuble Les Harmonies Third Floor angle boulevard Carde et avenue Dr Jamot Plâteau Abidjan 01 Côte d'Ivoire	2 Upper Belgrave Street London SW1X 071 235 6991
Cuba	British Embassy Carcel 101-103 Edificio Bolivar e Morro y Prado Apdo 1069 Havana Cuba	167 High Holborn London WC1 071 240 2488
Cyprus	British High Commission (PO Box 1978) Alexander Pallis Street Nicosia Cyprus	93 Park Street London W1Y 071 629 1984
Czechoslovakia	British Embassy Thunovská 14 125 50 Prague 1 Czechoslovakia	25/30 Kensington Palace Gardens London W8 071 229 1255
Denmark (and Greenland)	British Embassy 36/38/40 Kastelsvej DL 2100 Copenhagen Ø Denmark	55 Sloane Street London SW1X 071 235 1255
Djibouti	British Consulate Gellatly Hankey et Cie BP 81 Djibouti	None

Country	*Local British Embassy*	*London Embassy*
Dominica (Commonwealth of)	British High Commission (PO Box 675) Lower Collymore Rock Bridgetown Barbados	1 Collingham Gardens London SW5 071 370 5194
Dominican Republic	British Consulate Saint George School Abraham Lincoln 552 Santo Domingo (PO Box 818) Dominican Republic	2/103 Lexham Gardens London W8 071 370 3231
Ecuador	British Embassy (Casilla 314) Calle González Suárez 111 y 197 Quito Ecuador	3 Hans Crescent London SW1X 071 584 1367
Egypt	British Embassy Sharia Ahmed Raghab Garden City Cairo Egypt	75 South Audley Street London W1Y 071 499 2401
El Salvador	British Embassy The Inter Inversión Building Paseo General Escalón 4828 (PO Box 1591) San Salvador El Salvador	1st Floor 5 Great James Street London WC1N 071 430 2141
Equatorial Guinea	British Consulate Director Cocoa Rehabilitation Centre c/o Ministrerio de Agricultura Granaderia y Desarrollo Rural Apdo 504 Malabo Equatorial Guinea	None
Ethiopia	British Embassy (PO Box 858) Fikre Mariam Abatechan Street Addis Ababa Ethiopia	17 Princes Gate London SW7 071 589 7212

Embassies

Country	Local British Embassy	London Embassy
Fiji	British Embassy (PO Box 1355) Victoria House 47 Gladstone Road Suva Fiji	34 Hyde Park Gate London SW7 071 584 3661
Finland	British Embassy 16–20 Uudenmaankatu 00120 Helsinki Finland	22 Grosvenor Gardens London SW1W 071 235 9531
France	British Embassy 35 rue du Faubourg St Honoré Cedex 08 75383 Paris France	58 Knightsbridge London SW1X 071 235 8080
Gabon	British Embassy (PO Box 476) Immeuble CK2 boulevard de l'Indépendence Libreville Gabon	27 Elveston Place London SW7 071 823 9986
The Gambia	British High Commission (PO Box 507) 48 Atlantic Road Fajara Banjul The Gambia	57 Kensington Court London W8 5DG 071 937 6316
Federal Republic of Germany	British Embassy W-5300 Bonn 1 Friedrich-Ebert-Allee 77 Federal Republic of Germany	23 Belgrave Square London SW1X 071 235 5033
Ghana	British High Commission (PO Box 296) Osu Link off Gamel Abdul Nasser Avenue Accra Ghana	13 Belgrave Square London SW1X 071 245 9314
Greece	British Embassy 1 Ploutarchou Street 106 75 Athens Greece	1A Holland Park London W11 3TP 071 727 8040

Country	Local British Embassy	London Embassy
Grenada	British High Commission 14 Church Street St George's Grenada	1 Collingham Gardens London SW5 071 373 7808
Guatemala	British Embassy Edificio Centro Financerio (7th Floor) Tower Two 7a Avenida 5–10 Zona 4 Guatemala City Guatemala	13 Fawcett Street London SW10 071 351 3042
Guinea Republic	British Consulate Magus Ltd BP 158 Conakry Guinea Republic	None
Guinea-Bissau	British Consulate Mavegro Int CP 100 Bissau Guinea-Bissau	None
Guyana	British High Commission (PO Box 10849) 44 Main Street Georgetown Guyana	3 Palace Court London W2 071 229 7684
Haiti	British Consulate 21 avenue Marie-Jeanne Cité de l'Exposition Port-au-Prince Haiti	None
Honduras	British Embassy (PO Box 290) Tegucigalpa Edificio Palmira 3er Piso Tegucigalpa DC Honduras CA	115 Gloucester Place London W14 071 486 4880
Hong Kong	British Trade Commission (PO Box 528) Bank of America Tower 12 Harcourt Road Hong Kong	6 Grafton Street London W1X 071 499 9821

Embassies

Country	Local British Embassy	London Embassy
Hungary	British Embassy 1051 Budapest Harmincad Utca 6 Hungary	46 Eaton Place London SW1X 071 235 8767
Iceland	British Embassy (PO Box 460) Laufásvegur 49 101 Reykjavík Iceland	1 Eaton Square London SW1W 071 730 5131
India	British High Commission Shanti Path Chanakyapuri New Delhi 110021 India	India House Aldwych London WC2B 071 836 8484
Indonesia	British Embassy Jalan MH Thamrin 75 Jakarta 10310, Indonesia	38 Grosvenor Square London W1X 071 499 7661
Iran	British Embassy 143 Ferdowsi Avenue Tehran 11344 Iran	27 Princes Gate London SW7 071 584 8101
Iraq	British Embassy Zukaq 12 Mahala 218 Hay al-Khelood Baghdad Iraq	22 Queen's Gate London SW7 071 584 7141
Ireland (Republic of)	British Embassy 31-33 Merrion Road Dublin 4 Ireland	17 Grosvenor Place London SW1X 071 235 2171
Israel	British Embassy 192 and 198 Hayarkon Street Tel Aviv 63405 Israel	2 Palace Green London W8 071 937 8050
Italy	British Embassy Via XX Settembre 80A 00187 Roma Italy	38 Eaton Place London SW1X 071 235 9371

Country	Local British Embassy	London Embassy
Jamaica	British High Commission (PO Box 575) Trafalgar Road Kingston 10 Jamaica	1/2 Prince Consort Road London SW7 071 823 9911
Japan	British Embassy No. 1 Ichiban-cho Chiyoda-ku Tokyo 102 Japan	101–104 Piccadilly London W1V 071 465 6500
Jordan	British Embassy (PO Box 87) Abdoun Amman Jordan	6 Upper Phillimore Gardens London W8 071 937 3685
Kenya	British High Commission (PO Box 30465) Bruce House Standard Street Nairobi Kenya	45 Portland Place London W1N 071 636 2371
Kiribati	British High Commission (PO Box 69) Bairiki Tarawa Kiribati	None
Republic of Korea (South)	British Embassy 4 Chung-dong Chung-ku Seoul 100 Republic of Korea	Korea Trade Centre Vincent House Vincent Square London SW1P 071 834 5082
Kuwait	British Embassy (PO Box 2) 13001 Safat Arabian Gulf Street Kuwait City Kuwait	45/56 Queen's Gate London SW7 071 589 4533
Laos	British Embassy Wireless Road Bangkok 10330 Thailand	None

Embassies

Country	Local British Embassy	London Embassy
Lebanon	British Embassy Middle East Airlines Building Tripoli Autostrade Jal ed-Dib East Beirut Lebanon	90 Piccadilly London W1V 071 409 2031
Lesotho	British High Commission (PO Box 521) Maseru 100 Lesotho	10 Collingham Road London SW5 071 373 8581
Liberia	British Embassy (PO Box 120) Mamba Point Monrovia Liberia	2 Pembridge Place London W2 071 221 1036
Libya	British Interests Section Embassy of the Italian Republic (PO Box 4206) Sharia Uahran Tripoli Libya	Libyan Interests Section Royal Embassy of Saudi Arabia 119 Harley Street London W1 071 486 8387
Liechtenstein	British Embassy Thunstrasse 50 3005 Bern Switzerland	Represented by Switzerland
Luxembourg	British Embassy 14 boulevard Roosevelt 2018 Luxembourg-Ville Luxembourg	27 Wilton Crescent London SW1X 071 235 6961
Macau	British Trade Commission (PO Box 528) Bank of America Tower 12 Harcourt Road Hong Kong	Represented by Portugal
Madagascar	British Embassy Première Etage Immeuble 'Ny Havana' Cité de 67 Ha 101 Antananarivo Madagascar	16 Lanark Mansions Pennard Road London W12 081 746 0133
Malawi	British High Commission (PO Box 30042) Lilongwe 3 Malawi	33 Grosvenor Street London W1X 071 491 4172

Country	Local British Embassy	London Embassy
Malaysia	British High Commission (PO Box 11030) 185 Jalan Ampang 50732 Kuala Lumpur Malaysia	45/46 Belgrave Square London SW1X 071 235 8033
Mali	British Embassy 20 Rue du Docteur Guillet Dakar Senegal	None
Malta	British High Commission (PO Box 506) 7 St Anne Street Floriana Valletta Malta	16 Kensington Square London W8 071 938 1712
Mauritania	British Embassy 20 rue du Docteur Guillet Dakar Senegal	None
Mauritius	British High Commission (PO Box 186 Curepipe) Severn Lodge King George V Avenue Floréal Mauritius	32 Elvaston Place London SW7 071 581 0294
Mexico	British Embassy (Apartado 96 Bis) Lerma 71 Col. Cuauhtémoc 06500 México DF México	8 Halkin Street London SW1X 071 235 6393
Monaco	The British Consul-General in Marseille deals with enquiries relating to Monaco	4 Audley Square London W1Y 071 629 0734
Mongolia	British Embassy (PO Box 703) 30 Enkh Taivny Gudamj Ulan Bator Mongolia	7 Kensington Court London W8 071 937 5238

Embassies

Country	Local British Embassy	London Embassy
Morocco	British Embassy 17 boulevard de la Tour Hassan Rabat Morocco	49 Queen's Gate Gardens London SW7 071 581 5001
Mozambique	British Embassy (Caixa Postal 55) Avenida Vladimir I Lénine 310 Maputo Mozambique	21 Fitzroy Square London W1P 071 383 3800
Nauru	British Embassy in Fiji (PO Box 1355) Victoria House 47 Gladstone Road Suva Fiji	3 Chesham Street London SW1X 071 235 6911
Nepal	British Embassy (PO Box 106) Lainchaur Kathmandu Nepal	12A Kensington Palace Gardens London W8 071 229 1594
Netherlands	British Embassy Lange Voorhout 10 2514 ED The Hague The Netherlands	38 Hyde Park Gate London SW7 071 584 5040
New Zealand	British High Commission (PO Box 1812) 9th Floor Reserve Bank of New Zealand Building 2 The Terrace Wellington New Zealand	New Zealand House Haymarket London SW1Y 071 930 8422
Nicaragua	British Embassy El Reparto 'Los Robles' Primera Etapa Entrada principal de la Carretera de Masaya 4a Casa al Mano Derecha Managua Nicaragua	8 Gloucester Road London SW7 071 584 3231

Country	Local British Embassy	London Embassy
Nigeria	British High Commission (Private Mail Bag 12136) 11 Eleke Crescent Victoria Island Lagos Nigeria	Nigeria House 9 Northumberland Avenue London WC2N 071 839 1244
Norway	British Embassy Thomas Heftyesgate 8 0244 Oslo 2 Norway	39 Eccleston Street London SW1W 071 730 9900
Oman	British Embassy (PO Box 300) Muscat Oman	44a/13 Montpelier Square London SW7 071 584 6782
Pakistan	British Embassy (PO Box 1122) Diplomatic Enclave Ramna 5 Islamabad Pakistan	35 Lowndes Square London SW1X 071 235 2044
Panama	British Embassy (Apartado 889) Torre Banco Sur 4th & 5th Floor Calle 53 Este Marbella Panama 1 Panama	119 Crawford Street London W1H 071 487 5633
Papua New Guinea	British High Commission (PO Box 4778) Kiroki Street Waigani Boroko Papua New Guinea	14 Waterloo Place London SW1Y 071 930 0922
Paraguay	British Embassy (Casilla 404) Calle Presidente Franco 706 Asunción Paraguay	Braemar Lodge Cornwall Gardens London SW7 071 937 1253

Embassies

Country	Local British Embassy	London Embassy
Peru	British Embassy (Casilla 854) Edificio El Pacífico Washington (Piso 12) Plaza Washington Avenida Arequipa Lima 100 Peru	52 Sloane Street London SW1X 071 235 6867
Philippines	British Embassy 15th-17th Floors LV Locsin Building 6752 Ayala Avenue Corner Makati Avenue Makati Metro Manila Philippines	9A Palace Green London W8 071 937 5699
Poland	British Embassy Aleje Róz 1 00-556 Warsaw Poland	47 Portland Place London W1N 071 580 4324
Portugal	British Embassy Rua de S Domingos à Lapa 35-37 1296 Lisbon Codex Portugal	11 Belgrave Square London SW1X 071 235 5331
Qatar	British Embassy (PO Box 3) Doha Qatar	115 Queen's Gate London SW7 071 581 4292
Romania	British Embassy 70154 Bucharest Strada Jules Michelet 24 Romania	4 Palace Green London W8 071 937 9666
Russia	British Embassy Moscow 72 Naberzhnaya Morisa Toreza 14 USSR	10 Kensington Palace Gardens London W8 071 727 6888
Rwanda	British Consulate avenue Paul VI Kigali Rwanda	None

Country	Local British Embassy	London Embassy
St Kitts & Nevis	British High Commission in Antigua (PO Box 483) 38 St Mary's Street St John's Antigua	High Commission for Eastern Carribean States 10 Kensington Court London W8 071 937 9522 ·
St Lucia	British High Commission (PO Box 227) Columbus Square Castries St Lucia	Same as for St Kitts
St Vincent & The Grenadines	British High Commission (PO Box 132) Granby Street Kingstown St Vincent	Same as for St Kitts
Saudi Arabia	British Embassy (PO Box 94351) Riyadh 11693 Saudi Arabia	30 Belgrave Square London SW1X 071 235 0303
Senegal	British Embassy 20 rue du Docteur Guillet Dakar Senegal	11 Phillimore Gardens London W8 071 937 0925
Seychelles	British High Commission (PO Box 161) 3rd Floor Victoria House Victoria Mahé Seychelles	Eros House 2nd Floor 111 Baker Street London W1M 071 224 1670
Sierra Leone	British High Commission Standard Chartered Bank Building Lightfoot-Boston Street Freetown Sierra Leone	33 Portland Place London W1 071 636 6483
Singapore	British High Commission Tanglin Road Singapore 1024	9 Wilton Crescent London SW1 071 235 8315

Embassies

Country	Local British Embassy	London Embassy
Solomon Islands	British High Commission (PO Box 676) Soltel House Mendana Avenue Honiara Solomon Islands	None
Somalia	British Embassy (PO Box 1036) Mogadishu Somalia	60 Portland Place London W1N 071 580 7148
South Africa	British Embassy 255 Hill Street Arcadia Pretoria 0002 South Africa	South Africa House Trafalgar Square London WC2 071 930 4488
Spain	British Embassy Fernando el Santo 16 28010 Madrid Spain	24 Belgrave Square London SW1X 071 235 5555
Sri Lanka	British Embassy (PO Box 1433) 190 Galle Road Kollupitiya Colombo 3 Sri Lanka	13 Hyde Park Gardens London W2 071 262 1841
Sudan	British Embassy (PO Box 801) New Aboulela Building Off Sharia Al Baladiya Khartoum East Sudan	3 Cleveland Row London SW1A 071 839 8080
Surinam	British Consulate (PO Box 1300) c/o VSH Buildings Van't Hoger-Huysstraat Paramaribo Surinam	None
Swaziland	British High Commission Allister Miller Street Mbabane Swaziland	Pont Street London SW1 071 581 4976

Country	Local British Embassy	London Embassy
Sweden	British Embassy Skarpögt 6-8 115 27 Stockholm Sweden	11 Montagu Place London W1 071 724 2101
Switzerland	British Embassy Thunstrasse 50 3005 Bern Switzerland	16/18 Montague Place London W1 071 723 0701
Syrian Arab Republic	British Interests Section Australian Embassy c/o Immeuble Kotob 11 rue Muhammad Kurd Ali Damascus Syria	Syrian Interests Section 8 Belgrave Square London SW1 071 245 9012
Tanzania	British High Commission (PO Box 9200) Hifadhi House Samora Machel Avenue Dar es Salaam Tanzania	43 Hertford Street London W1 071 499 8951
Thailand	British Embassy Wireless Road Bangkok 10330 Thailand	30 Queen's Gate London SW7 071 589 2857
Togo	British Consulate Agence Maritime Atlantique du Togo, SARL 1 rue l'Hotel Miramar Ablogame 2 Lomé Togo	30 Sloane Street London SW1 071 235 0147
Tonga	British High Commission (PO Box 56) Vuna Road Nuku'alofa Tonga	New Zealand House Haymarket London SW1 071 839 3287
Trinidad & Tobago	British High Commission (PO Box 778) Furness House 3rd & 4th floors 90 Independence Square Port of Spain Trinidad	42 Belgrave Square London SW1 071 245 9351

Embassies

Country	Local British Embassy	London Embassy
Tunisia	British Embassy 5 place de la Victoire Tunis Tunisia	29 Princes Gate London SW7 071 584 8117
Turkey	British Embassy Sehit Ersan Caddesi 46/A Çankaya Ankara Turkey	43 Belgrave Square London SW1 071 235 5252
Tuvalu	British Embassy Victoria House 47 Gladstone Road Suva Fiji	None
Uganda	British High Commission (PO Box 7070) 10-12 Parliament Avenue Kampala Uganda	Uganda House Trafalgar Square London WC2 071 839 5783
United Arab Emirates	British Embassy (PO Box 248) Abu Dhabi UAE	30 Princes Gate London SW7 071 581 1281
United States of America	British Embassy 3100 Massachusetts Avenue NW Washington DC 20008 USA	24 Grosvenor Square London W1 071 499 9000
Uruguay	British Embassy Marco Bruto 1073 Montevideo Uruguay	48 Lennox Gardens London SW1 071 589 8735
Vanuatu	British High Commission (PO Box 567) Melitco House rue Pasteur Port Vila Vanuatu	None
Vatican City	British Embassy Via Condotti 91 00187 Rome Italy	54 Parkside Wimbledon London SW19 081 946 1410

Country	Local British Embassy	London Embassy
Venezuela	British Embassy Apartado 1246 Edificio Torre Las Mercedes Avenida la Estancia Chuao Caracas 1060 Venezuela	1 Cromwell Road London SW7 071 584 4206
Vietnam	British Embassy 16 Pho Ly Thuong Kiet Hanoi Vietnam	12 Victoria Road London W8 071 937 1912
Republic of Yemen	British Embassy (PO Box 1287) 129 Haddah Road Sana'a Republic of Yemen	57 Cromwell Road London SW7 071 584 6607
Yugoslavia	British Embassy 11000 Belgrade Generala Zdanova 46 Yugoslavia	5/7 Lexham Gardens London W8 071 370 6105
Zaire	British Embassy 191 avenue de l'Equateur 5ème étage BP 8049 Kinshasa Zaire	26 Chesham Place London SW1X 071 235 6137
Zambia	British High Commission (PO Box 50050) Independence Avenue Lusaka Zambia	2 Palace Gate London W8 071 589 6655
Zimbabwe	British High Commission (PO Box 4490) Stanley House Stanley Avenue Harare Zimbabwe	Zimbabwe House 429 Strand London WC2R 0SA 071 836 7755

World languages

The main languages spoken in each country

Country	Languages
Country	*Languages*
Afghanistan	Persian, French
Albania	Albanian, Greek
Algeria	Arabic, French
Andorra	Catalan, Spanish, French
Angola	Portuguese
Anguilla	English
Antigua & Barbuda	English
Argentina	Spanish
Aruba	Dutch
Australia	English
Austria	German
Bahamas	English
Bahrain	Arabic, English
Bangladesh	Bengali (Bangla), English, Urdu
Barbados	English, Bajan Creole
Belgium	Flemish, French
Belize	English, Spanish
Benin	French, English, Fon/Yoruba
Bermuda	English, Bermudian Patois
Bhutan	Dzongkha, Sharchop Kha, Nepalese, English
Bolivia	Spanish, Aymara, Quechua, English
Bonaire	Dutch, Papiamento
Botswana	English, Setswana
Brazil	Portuguese, French, German, Italian, English
Brunei	Malay, English, Chinese
Bulgaria	Bulgarian, Russian, German, French
Burkina Faso	French
Burma	Burmese, English
Burundi	French, Kirundi, Kiswahili
Cambodia	Khmer
Cameroon	French, English
Canada	English, French
Cape Verde	Portuguese, Crioulo, English, French
Cayman Islands	English
Central African Republic	French

Country	Languages
Chad	French
Chile	Spanish, English
China (People's Republic of)	Modern Standard Chinese, Cantonese, Wu, Fukienexe, Xiamen, Hsiang, Kam and Hakka
Colombia	Spanish
Comoro Islands	French, Arabic
Congo	French
Cook Islands	Maori, English
Costa Rica	Spanish, English
Côte d'Ivoire	French, Dioula, Baoule
Cuba	Spanish, English, French
Curaçao	Dutch, Papiamento, English, Spanish
Cyprus	Greek, Turkish
Czechoslovakia	Czech, Slovak
Denmark	Danish, English, German, French
Djibouti	French, Arabic
Dominica (Commonwealth of)	English, Creole French
Dominican Republic	Spanish, English
Ecuador	Spanish, English
Egypt	Arabic, English, French
El Salvador	Spanish, English
Equatorial Guinea	Spanish
Ethiopa	Amharic, Galla, English, Italian, French
Falklands Islands	English
Fiji	English, Fijian, Hindi, Cantonese
Finland	Finnish, Swedish, Lapp
France	French
French Guiana	French, English
Gabon	French
The Gambia	English
Federal Republic of Germany	German
Ghana	English
Gibraltar	English, Spanish
Greece	Greek
Greenland	Danish, Greenlandic
Grenada	English
Guadeloupe	French
Guatemala	Spanish
Guernsey	English
Guinea Republic	French
Guinea-Bissau	Portuguese, Guinean Creole
Guyana	English
Haiti	French
Honduras	Spanish
Hong Kong	Cantonese, English
Hungary	Hungarian, German

World languages

Country	Languages
Iceland	Icelandic, English, Danish
India	Hindi, Urdu, English
Indonesia	Bahasa Indonesian
Iran	Persian, Arabic, Turkish
Iraq	Arabic, Kurdish
Ireland (Republic of)	English, Gaelic
Israel	Hebrew, Arabic
Italy	Italian
Jamaica	English
Japan	Japanese, English
Jersey	French, English
Jordan	Arabic, English, French
Kenya	Kiswahili, English
Kirabati	I-Kiribati, English
Korea, DPR (North)	Korean
Republic of Korea (South)	Korean, English
Kuwait	Arabic, English
Laos	Laotian, French, English
Lebanon	Arabic, French, English
Lesotho	Sesotho, English
Liberia	English
Libya	Arabic
Liechtenstein	German, English
Luxembourg	French, German, Luxembourgeois
Macau	Portuguese, Cantonese
Madagascar	Malagasy, French
Malawi	English, Chichewa
Malaysia	Bahasa Malaysia, English
Maldives Republic	Dhivehi, English
Mali	French
Malta	Maltese, Italian, German, French
Martinique	French, Creole Patois
Mauritania	Arabic, French
Mauritius	English
Mexico	Spanish, English
Monaco	French, Monégasque, Italian
Mongolia	Khalkha, Mongolian
Montserrat	English
Morocco	Arabic, Berber, French, Spanish, English
Mozambique	Portuguese
Namibia	Afrikaans, English
Nauru	Nauruan, English
Nepal	Nepalese, English
Netherlands	Dutch, English, French, German
New Caledonia	French, Polynesian, Melanesian
New Zealand	English, Maori
Nicaragua	Spanish

Country	Languages
Niger	French
Nigeria	English
Norway	Norwegian, English
Oman	Arabic, English
Pacific Islands of Micronesia	English, Japanese and nine local languages
Pakistan	Urdu, English
Panama	Spanish, English
Papua New Guinea	English
Paraguay	Spanish, Guaraní
Peru	Spanish, Quechua, English
Philippines	Filipino, English
Poland	Polish, German, Russian, English, French
Polynesia (French)	French
Portugal	Portuguese
Puerto Rico	Spanish, English
Qatar	Arabic, English
Reunion	French, Creole Patois
Romania	Romanian, Hungarian, German
Russia	Russian, English, French
Rwanda	Kinyarwanda, French
Saba	English, Dutch
St Eustatius	English, Dutch, Papiamento, French, Spanish
St Kitts & Nevis	English
St Lucia	English, French Patois
St Maarten	English, Dutch, Papiamento
St Vincent & The Grenadines	English
San Marino	Italian
Sao Tomé e Principe	Portuguese, French, English
Saudi Arabia	Arabic
Senegal	French
Seychelles	Creole, English, French
Sierra Leone	English, Krio
Singapore	Chinese (Mandarin), English, Malay, Tamil
Solomon Islands	English
Somalia	Somali, Arabic, Swahili
South Africa	Afrikaans, English
Spain	Spanish (Castilian), Catalan, Galician, Basque
Sri Lanka	Sinhala, Tamil, English
Sudan	Arabic, English
Suriname	Dutch
Swaziland	English, Siswati
Sweden	Swedish, Finnish, English, German, Lapp
Switzerland	Swiss-German, French, Italian, Romansch, English
Syrian Arab Republic	Arabic, French, English
Taiwan (Republic of China)	Chinese (Mandarin/amoy dialects), English, Japanese

World languages

Country	Languages
Tanzania	Kiswahili, English
Thailand	Thai, English, Tachew
Togo	French
Tonga	Tongan, English
Trinidad & Tobago	English
Tunisia	Arabic, French
Turkey	Turkish, French, English
Turks & Caicos	English, Creole
Tuvalu	Tuvuluan, English
Uganda	English, Luganda, Kiswahili
United Arab Emirates	Arabic, English
United Kingdom	English, Welsh, Gaelic
United States of America	English, Spanish
Uruguay	Spanish
Vanuatu	Bislama (Pidgin English)
Vatican City	Italian
Venezuela	Spanish, English, French, German, Portuguese
Vietnam	Vietnamese
Virgin Islands, British	English
Western Samoa	Samoan, English
Republic of Yemen	Arabic, English
Yugoslavia	Serbo-croatian (Serbian), Croato-serbian (Croatian), Macedonian and Slovene
Zaire	French, Lingala, Swahili, Tshiluba, Kikongo
Zambia	English
Zimbabwe	English, Shona, Ndebele

International direct dialling codes

Country	Country Code
Albania	355
Algeria	213
Andorra	33 628
Anguilla	1 809 497
Antigua & Barbuda	1 809 46
Argentina	54
Aruba	297 8
Australia	61
Austria	43
Bahamas	1 809
Bahrain	973
Bangladesh	880
Barbados	1 809
Belgium	32
Belize	501
Benin	229
Bermuda	1 809 29 or 1 809 23
Bolivia	591
Bonaire	599-7
Botswana	267
Brazil	55
Brunei	673
Bulgaria	359
Burkina Faso	226
Burma	095
Burundi	257
Cameroon	237
Canada	1
Cayman Islands	1 809
Central African Republic	236
Chad	235
Chile	56
China (People's Republic of)	86
Colombia	57
Congo	242
Cook Islands	682
Costa Rica	506
Côte d'Ivoire	225

International direct dialling codes

Country	Country Code
Cuba	53
Curaçao	599 9
Cyprus	357
Czechoslovakia	42
Denmark	45
Djibouti	253
Dominica (Commonwealth of)	1 809
Dominican Republic	1 809
Ecuador	593
Egypt	20
El Salvador	503
Ethiopia	251
Fiji	679
Finland	358
France	33
French Guiana	594
Gabon	241
The Gambia	220
Federal Republic of Germany	49
Ghana	233
Gibraltar	350
Greece	30
Greenland	299
Grenada	1 809 44
Guadeloupe	590
Guatemala	502
Guernsey	0481
Guinea Republic	224
Guyana	592
Haiti	509
Honduras	504
Hong Kong	852
Hungary	36
Iceland	354
India	91
Indonesia	62
Iran	98
Iraq	964
Ireland (Republic of)	0001 (for 6-digit numbers)
	353-1 (for 7- digit numbers)
Israel	972
Italy	39
Jamaica	1 809
Japan	81
Jersey	0534 (from UK), 534 (from elsewhere)
Jordan	962
Kenya	254

Country	Country Code
Republic of Korea (South)	82
Kuwait	965
Lebanon	961
Lesotho	266
Liberia	231
Libya	218
Liechtenstein	41 75
Luxembourg	352
Macau	853
Madagascar	261
Malawi	265
Malaysia	60
Maldives Republic	960
Malta	356
Martinique	596
Mauritius	230
Mexico	52
Monaco	33 93
Montserrat	1 809
Morocco	212
Mozambique	258
Namibia	264
Nauru	674
Nepal	977
Netherlands	31
New Caledonia	687
New Zealand	64
Nicaragua	505
Niger	227
Nigeria	234
Norway	47
Oman	968
Pacific Islands of Micronesia:	
Belau	680
Marshall Islands	692
Micronesia	691
Pakistan	92
Panama	507
Papua New Guinea	675
Paraguay	595
Peru	51
Philippines	63
Poland	48
Polynesia (French)	689
Portugal	351
Puerto Rico	1 809
Qatar	974

International direct dialling codes

Country	Country Code
Reunion	262
Romania	40
Russia	7
Saba	599 4
St Eustatius	599 3
St Kitts & Nevis :	
St Kitts	809 465
Nevis	809 469
St Lucia	809
St Maarten	599 5
St Vincent & The Grenadines	1 809
San Marino	39 549
Sao Tomé E Principe	23 912
Saudi Arabia	966
Senegal	221
Seychelles	248
Sierra Leone	232
Singapore	65
Solomon Islands	677
Somalia	252
South Africa	27
Spain	34
Sri Lanka	94
Sudan	249
Surinam	597
Swaziland	268
Sweden	46
Switzerland	41
Syrian Arab Republic	963
Taiwan (Republic of China)	886
Tanzania	255
Thailand	66
Togo	228
Tonga	676
Trinidad & Tobago	809
Tunisia	216
Turkey	90
Turks & Caicos	809
Uganda	256
United Arab Emirates	971
United Kingdom	44
United States of America	1
Uruguay	598
Vanuatu	678
Vatican City	39 66982
Venezuela	58
Vietnam	84

Country	Country Code
Virgin Islands, British	1 809 49
Western Samoa	685
Republic of Yemen	969
Yugoslavia	38
Zaire	243
Zambia	260
Zimbabwe	263

Time differences

World time differences from the UK

Country	Time difference (ignoring summer time)
Afghanistan	+4.5
Albania	+1
Algeria	+1
Andorra	+1
Angola	+1
Anguilla	-4
Antigua & Barbuda	-4
Argentina	-3
Aruba	-4
Australia	
East	+10
Central	+9.5
West	+8
Austria	+1
Bahamas	-5
Bahrain	+3
Bangladesh	+6
Barbados	-4
Belgium	+1
Belize	-6
Benin	+1
Bermuda	-4
Bhutan	+6
Bolivia	-4
Bonaire	-4
Botswana	+2
Brazil	-3
Brunei	+8
Bulgaria	+2
Burkina Faso	GMT
Burma	+6.5
Burundi	+2
Cambodia	+7
Cameroon	+1
Canada:	
Pacific	-8
Mountain	-7
Central	-6
Eastern	-5

Atlantic	-4
Newfoundland	-3
	(+1 hour in summer
	except in Saskatchewan)
Cape Verde	-1
Cayman Islands	-5
Central African Republic	+1
Chad	+1
Chile	-3
China (People's Republic of)	+8
Colombia	-5
Comoro Islands	+3
Congo	+1
Cook Islands	-10
Costa Rica	-6
Côte d'Ivoire	GMT
Cuba	-1
Curacao	-4
Cyprus	+2
Czechoslovakia	+1
Denmark	+1
Djibouti	+3
Dominica	
(Commonwealth of)	-4
Dominican Republic	-4
Ecuador	-5
Egypt	+2
El Salvador	-6
Equatorial Guinea	+1
Ethiopia	+3
Falkland Islands	-4
Fiji	+12
Finland	+2
France	+1
French Guiana	-3
Gabon	+1
The Gambia	GMT
Federal Republic	
of Germany	+1
Ghana	GMT
Gibraltar	+1
Greece	+2
Greenland	
East Greenland	GMT
Scoresby Sound	-1
Ammassalik and west coast	-3
Thule area	-4
Grenada	-4
Guadeloupe	-4
Guatemala	-6
Guernsey	+1
Guinea Republic	GMT
Guinea-Bissau	GMT
Guyana	-3

Time differences

Haiti	-5
Honduras	-6
Hong Kong	+8
Hungary	+1
Iceland	GMT
India	+5.30
Indonesia :	
Banga, Billiton, Java, West and Middle Kalimantan, Madura and Sumatra	+7
Bali, Flores, South and East Kalimantan, Lombok, Sulawesi, Sumba, Sumbawa and Timor	+8
Aru, Irian Jaya, Kai, Moluccas and Tanimbar	+9
Iran	+3.5
Iraq	+3
Ireland (Republic of)	GMT
Israel	+2
Italy	+1
Jamaica	-5
Japan	+9
Jersey	GMT
Jordan	+2
Kenya	+3
Kirabati	+12
Korea, DPR (North)	+9
Republic of Korea (South)	+9
Kuwait	+2
Laos	+7
Lebanon	+2
Lesotho	+2
Liberia	GMT
Libya	+1
Liechtenstein	+1
Luxembourg	+1
Macau	+8
Madagascar	+3
Malawi	+2
Malaysia	+8
Maldives Republic	+5
Mali	GMT
Malta	+1
Martinique	-4
Mauritania	GMT
Mauritius	+4
Mexico	-7
Monaco	+1
Mongolia	+8
Montserrat	-4
Morocco	GMT
Mozambique	+2

Namibia	+2
Nauru	+12
Nepal	+5 hrs 45 minutes
Netherlands	+1
New Caledonia	+11
New Zealand	+12
Nicaragua	-6
Niger	+1
Nigeria	+1
Norway	+1
Oman	+4
Pacific Islands of Micronesia:	
Republic of Belau	+11
Marshall Islands	+12
Federated States of Micronesia:	
Yap	-10
Pohnpei and Chuuk	
(formerly Truk)	+11
Pakistan	+5
Panama	-5
Papua New Guinea	+10
Paraguay	-3
Peru	-5
Philippines	+8
Poland	+1
Polynesia (French)	-10
Portugal	GMT
Puerto Rico	-4
Qatar	+3
Reunion	+4
Romania	+2
Rwanda	+2
Saba	-4
St Eustatius	-4
St Kitts & Nevis	-4
St Lucia	-4
St Maarten	-4
St Vincent & The Grenedines	-4
San Marino	+1
Sao Tomé e Principe	GMT
Saudi Arabia	+3
Senegal	GMT
Seychelles	+4
Sierra Leone	GMT
Singapore	+8
Solomon Islands	+11
Somalia	+3
South Africa	+2
Spain:	
Mainland Spain/Balearics	+1
The Canaries	GMT
Sri Lanka	+5.5
Sudan	+2
Surinam	-3.5

Time differences

Swaziland	+2
Sweden	+1
Switzerland	+1
Syrian Arab Republic	+2
Taiwan (Republic of China)	+8
Tanzania	+3
Thailand	+7
Togo	GMT
Tonga	+13
Trinidad & Tobago	-4
Tunisia	+1
Turkey	+2
Turks & Caicos	-5
Tuvalu	+12
Uganda	+3
Union of Soviet Socialist Republics:	
Amderma, Arkhanagelsk, Kiev, Leningrad, Moscow, Odessa	+3
Baku, Tbilsi, Volgograd	+4
Ashkabad, Novvy Port, Sverdlovsk	+5
Alma-Ata, Omsk, Tashkent	+6
Krasnoyarsk, Novosibirsk	+7
Irkutsk	+8
Tiksi, Yakutsk	+9
Khabarovsk, Okhotsk, Vladivostok	+10
Magadan, Sakhalin Island	+11
Anadyr, Petropaviosk	+12
Eulen	+13
United Arab Emirates	+4
United States of America:	
Eastern Standard Time	-5
Central Standard Time	-6
Mountain Standard Time	-7
Pacific Standard Time	-8
Alaska	-9
Hawaii	-10
Uruguay	-3 (-2 from December to February)
Vanuatu	+12
Vatican City	+1
Venezuela	-4
Vietnam	+7
Virgin Islands, British	-4
Western Samoa	-11
Republic of Yemen	+3
Yugoslavia	+1 (+2 in summer)
Zaire:	
Kinshasa and Mbandaka	+1
Haut-Zaire, Kasai, Kivu, Shaba	+2

| Zambia | +2 |
| Zimbabwe | +2 |

Index

Index

Tolley
Order Line

081-686 0115

The above Order Line number is a direct line to our Customer Liaison staff and can be used for a faster, more convenient service when ordering any Tolley publication.

(Outside office hours an answering machine is in operation)

Tolley Publishing Co. Ltd.,
Tolley House, 2 Addiscombe Road, Croydon, Surrey, CR9 5AF.